THE MASS COMMUNICATION PROCESS

A Behavioral and Social Perspective

Keith R. Stamm
John E. Bowes

University of Washington
School of Communications

KENDALL/HUNT PUBLISHING COMPANY
2460 Kerper Boulevard P.O. Box 539 Dubuque, Iowa 52004-0539

Cover art by Obadinah Heavner

Copyright © 1990 by Kendall/Hunt Publishing Company

Library of Congress Catalog Card Number: 90-62082

ISBN 0-8403-6045-2

Printed in the United States of America
10 9 8 7 6 5 4 3 2 1

Contents

CHAPTER 6: **Advertising and Public Information**, 125

CHAPTER 7: **Mass Communication and Political Campaigns**, 151

Preface

We have taught introductory courses to students of mass communication for many years. Finding a text to fit our needs has been an annual problem, not because there is a lack of generally good texts available, but because few focus exclusively or efficiently on the contributions of social and behavioral sciences toward our understanding of mass communication processes. We hope our does.

This is not a book which concerns mass media history, except as that history illuminates some present-day questions of media effects or long-standing policy questions which spring from them. As well, we don't do much to describe the state of mass media in the United States—current laws, the number of television stations or the personalities found in particular programs or media executive suites. The research we discuss, however, has frequently much to do with the sort of regulations enacted, programs aired and management choices made. Issues raised by new communications technologies, targeting of children in television advertisements and the possible harm of violent program content are among the many important questions we discuss. We leave day-to-day activities of mass media management to other texts to describe. Rather than tell you about how to bill customers for television spot advertisements, for example, our concern is with the audience effects—intended and unintended—that such a commercial message may have.

In writing this work, we wish to acknowledge the many contributions from the literature of speech-communication, sociology, psychology, political science, marketing and social psychology—as well as the growing literature from the mass communication field itself. We draw heavily on research from our present colleagues here at the University of Washington and former associates at other institutions who have tried to consider basic, if troublesome, questions about mass communication.

We start with a history of research in mass communication and an account of research methods commonly used. Our second chapter concerns the psychology of perception and information processing, since observation and its interpretation is basic to the news reporting process. We also examine many topics typically taught in courses in interpersonal communication—but do so in a mass communication context. How do group communication principles help us understand, for example, the making of editorial decisions in the newsroom or the response of reporters to rumor?

The balance of the book is almost exclusively concerned with the traditional mass media and the extensive research on their effects. Research ranging from effects of advertising to violent behavior as a consequence of television content is examined. Certain groups, such as children, are discussed separately, reflecting the special concerns of many nations over unanticipated (and undesirable) influences suspected from the mass media.

We also consider new media which promise to challenge some of the traditional research assumptions and findings we have grown accustomed to over the past 30 years of intensive research. Our approach shifts somewhat to reflect a more intensive interest in policy and regulation which always seem a strong concern when very little is known.

We spend our final chapter with a criticism of the research in our field— not unsympathetically, since our own research often reflects the biases and omissions of our peers.

For some students, without some prior experience in the social sciences, parts of this text may be difficult. But with particular attention given to the first two chapters, our expectation is that most will encounter very few major problems thereafter.

Over-zealous or inappropriate application of some research findings has troubled past decision-making by the mass media. As both print and electronic media turn to increasingly sophisticated research as a way of improving the competitiveness of their products, it is vital to recognize its limitations. We know that the findings of many studies are uncertain, or only apply under limited and carefully qualified conditions. Research which is misused creates practical and, occasionally, ethical problems. The studies we discuss and the conclusions we reach are valuable tools, but like any tool, they have to be used carefully and with respect. Consequently, we spend considerable time talking about problems in doing and applying mass communication research.

This book is our first edition, based on a preliminary book that has been "battle tested" during three years of student use at the University of Washington and several other major schools. Based on these experiences, much of the content has been revised, rewritten and better illustrated. We hope these efforts help you understand and appreciate major trends in mass communication research.

Keith R. Stamm
John E. Bowes

1   Introduction

Why Study Communication?

Our personal communication skills, whether as users of the mass media, casual writers or simply individuals who wish to converse clearly and effectively with friends, are vital in many ways to careers, education and social relationships. And some of what we discuss in this book may help you improve or better understand these. But our central interest is with mass communication, the collective, institutionalized activity of message creation for audiences. Many who read this book will go on to jobs in public relations, print or broadcast journalism, advertising, film production, corporate communications or media management. For them, the growing body of research we discuss is vital both for their professional skills and their sense of ethics and responsibility. But all of us are consumers of mass communication, and as such we should know more of how it functions in our day-to-day thinking and in the society of which we are part.

Much of what we will discuss are long-standing problems clearly identified by headlines, lobbyists and angry citizens. Media portrayal of violence, political campaigning by TV, uncontrolled rumor and deceptive advertising—are but a sampling of these. But some influences are subtle, and really may not be fully appreciated until historians and social critics look back on our society and compare it to times before and since. Consider, for example, the influence on American language and culture of network television. Regional differences in values, style, and way of life can be blended and standardized by media content, bringing slow but inexorable change which cannot be seen clearly for many years. That's one of our problems in writing a book of this kind. Some communication influences cannot be easily observed because we don't ''see'' them or feel threatened by what we may observe. It may take major changes of research interest or decades of persistent study to focus on subtle but important phenomena. At the end of this book we'll consider some of these quiet issues. But realize that these will be simply our opinion, constrained by our own prejudices, training and interests.

At other times, we're prone to "reinvent" an issue. Take for example current debate over violence and sex in media content. A half dozen or more of national organizations—from parent teacher associations to religious groups—monitor U.S. television content for violence and other "unsuitable" themes. The U.S. Congress has expressed strong concern over alleged themes of sex, violence and satanism in popular music records—some of which had to be played at double speed or backwards to "really hear" the "secret" messages. History shows us that concerns arose over many once new media forms—silent movies, juke boxes, radio soap operas, comic books and dime novels (Wartella & Reeves, 1985). Media are intrusive and influential, and governments, parents, religious leaders and "old" media are at once interested in and cautious about these new influences on society. From time-to-time, we'll try to give you some historical perspective so you can appreciate the lifespan of some of the issues we consider.

As mentioned earlier, we emphasize mass communication in this book, recognizing that there is a tremendously rich and useful literature focusing on interpersonal, group and organizational communication, the origins of language and non-verbal communication. We'll use some of this material to provide a context for examining mass communication, but at the same time we want to encourage you, the reader, to seek out other books and courses which emphasize the topics we only skim. Hopefully, we'll give you enough information on these so you'll be motivated to continue on your own or through other courses in communication. Reference notes at the end of each chapter will give you starting points for further reading.

We can organize interest in mass communication under several headings:

Questions about the social impact of the mass media: Probably the tap root of this interest hearkens back to early research in propaganda and advertising which grew with the rise of modern mass media at the turn of the century. Until recently, the prime focus of communication study—mass and interpersonal—was persuasion. Persuasion encompasses a range of interests from the innocence of basic education and learning skills to the most cynical of political propaganda and exploitative advertising to children. The implication in both cases is that we as an audience are being encouraged to do or think things which we would not otherwise do. The media, then, are seen as intrusive, politically and socially active agents with (perhaps) poorly understood influences. Violent content, pornography, subliminal advertising, exploitative children's TV programs, political "spot" advertising, corruption of cultural heritage, financially and politically powerful TV evangelists, "pseudo events" concocted by politicians to grab media attention, media-spawned rumor—to name a sampling—are "social impact" questions which trouble citizens, media organizations and government alike. Whether to regulate media content, censor it completely, or export it to other countries are key questions which depend on mass communication research for answers.

Questions about media effectiveness: These ask whether media are really effective when we want them to be. Media owners and particularly advertisers want to know the influence of the media because their incomes depend on it. All who use media to convey messages should know the most effective ways of reaching a target audience. Much research, for example, is used to simply place advertising before an audience most likely to buy a given product. Ever wonder why toothpaste for false teeth is advertised during evening news on television? Why toys are advertised on Saturday morning TV programs? Why food sections appear in newspapers on Wednesdays, or entertainment sections on Fridays? Clearly, editors and advertisers have research that suggests where and when certain key audiences are available.

But beyond such questions of content timing and placement are more subtle questions of technique—how to write clearly, persuasively, or how to blend illustration with text or merge sight and sound into effective combinations to give a total effect which is more than just the sum of constituent elements. Art and science meet here, because the complexity of media are so great. Producers, editors, copywriters, graphic artists and so on learn effective ways of using media which cannot be easily captured in the controlled research we discuss throughout this book. Indeed, this is sometimes very frustrating.

Think a moment about creating suspense and excitement. Alfred Hitchcock in his unforgettable horror movie, ''Psycho,'' constructed a now famous scene of a woman stabbed to death while taking a shower. In less able hands, this could have been simply a gruesome depiction. But with just the suggestion of vulnerability, menace from the story and the naked defenselessness of someone surprised by an attacker in the shower, a scene of high suspense and horror is created. The bloody effects of the attacker were hinted at, never shown completely. The viewer's imagination filled in the gaps, creating involvement in the emotion of the film.

To research this scientifically, the many cinemagraphic techniques could have been isolated and tried one-at-a-time on test audiences to see the contribution of each to emotional involvement. The strong effects here, however, come from complex combinations of techniques, not their use in isolation. So the simplification imposed by the careful scientist can often make the situation studied unrealistic. Yet we might still have learned something about which techniques were effective by themselves, a useful legacy for future producers of not just horror films but of films generally where certain emotions and viewer involvement is desired.

The point of this digression is that much valuable knowledge comes from the creative, artistic side of mass communication where there is an intuitive, not scientific grasp of what works well. Techniques, both simple and complex, have evolved over years of trial-and-error experimenting. The ability of the researcher to adequately explain why techniques have a certain influence can be limited and frustrating when you want clearcut, work-all-the-time answers. Mass communication is a complex activity. We mostly have partial explanations for what happens, if any at all. So don't expect the research we discuss to cover all points or contain all the answers. It won't. It may even raise more questions than you had at the outset.

However, partial answers can be of great importance. Media management routinely depends on findings which offer only incomplete explanations of why something works. The answers of communication research often provide an invaluable confirmation of the artistic hunch or guess. On many occasions, they provide the basic lead itself which artists and others follow. The themes or story lines of television commercials increasingly are based on research which shows the sorts of situations where people need a particular product. American Express, for example, knows from their research how people lose money while traveling. Their television advertising is constructed around showing these instances. Why? The cost and difficulty of producing consumer motivation through media effects is simply too great to be left solely to guesswork or artistic experimentation.

Mass Communication and the needs of society: A democratic society depends on its informed citizens to participate in government. Media, largely, provide us with this essential information. Do they do an adequate job? Consider the evening television news with some 20 minutes of news time after commercial announcements are removed. The content read is barely enough to cover two-thirds of the average newspaper page, yet television is the news medium of choice for the most, and the source most believed. Few stories are granted more than 2 minutes of coverage. Special news features and documentary productions help, but they usually attract a much smaller audience than regular newscasts. The hope of those concerned about the quality of information citizens have rests on the assumption that newspapers and newsmagazines will fill-in the details the broadcast media miss. But reader interest for political and "hard" news pales against advertisements, sports news, comics and personal advice columns. Often just headlines are skimmed. Few news stories are read beyond the page on which they start.

The dilemma, of course, is that privately owned media can't be expected to educate an unwilling public. It simply doesn't make sense in terms of attracting maximum audiences for profits. Countries with state-run media may try to do this. But in either case what can compel an unwilling or disinterested audience to watch or read certain content? In our last chapter, we discuss some new media; ones which depend less on large, massive audiences. These cater more to specialized needs and user requests as with computerized electronic publishing. Still, with these, there is no guarantee that the public will be served better by or be more attentive to important information they need.

The research discussed throughout this book may give you enough information to decide for yourself about the adequacy of media-provided information. In doing so, however, we will tell you much about the audience or marketplace for information and its complexity. One cannot blame or praise the media exclusively for the level of public participation in a democracy. The audience is inseparable from it, and the ultimate arbiter, as consumers, for what the media accomplish. We often get just what we demand!

Origins of the Communication Discipline

Communication is new as a scholarly field. Some 40 years ago, there were no university communication programs as such. Practical training in speech and journalism was available to would-be teachers and reporters. In the U.S., scholarly interest in communication was fragmented among a half-dozen or more disciplines as diverse as psychology, library science, English and agricultural extension. Elsewhere, primarily Europe, interest arose in such fields as literature, philosophy and political science. Indeed, you may be majoring in one of these programs yourself, taking a course in communication simply for "background."

Over a century ago, a number of influences gradually converged, causing growth of the mass media and interest in communication techniques generally:

1. *The industrial revolution*: Machines replaced brute human force in many manufacturing processes. Organizational and engineering advances such as interchangeable parts and mass production greatly improved productivity in the work place. The length of the typical workday decreased while salaries rose. A growing middle class had the leisure time and disposable income providing both the time and the means for mass communication consumption. Of course, the inventions of the time included high speed printing presses, semi-automated typesetting, photography, recorded sound, telegraphy and telephone, and the beginnings of radio transmission and computing machines. These inventions are fundamental to the mass media of today.

2. *The spread of literacy*: "Universal" public education which diffused rapidly in the latter part of the 19th century gave the basis of literacy necessary for mass consumption of print media. With leisure time available, print media became prime sources of diversion and self-education. They also were seen as tools for participation in government and civic concern.

3. *Increasing national and international interdependence*: The world economy and its politics increasingly were internationalized. The media, aided by newswires and correspondents, extended the reach of business and government across continents. Far-away wars and bank failures could affect local factories and agriculture. Local newspapers could bring these distant events home.

4. *Frontier needs and scientific agriculture*: During the 1860s, over half of the U.S. workforce occupied itself with agriculture, mostly at a subsistence level. Homestead laws and other land grants promoted the settlement of frontier lands. The Morrell Act (1868) established colleges for training in agriculture and established a large network of field agents to spread information on new agricultural practices to farmers. The Cooperative Extension Service through the U.S. Department of Agriculture, has encouraged communication research on the transfer of tech-

nologies—new agricultural practices, for example. In some cases, academic programs grew from this work.

5. *Mass merchandising*: Advertising became a powerful marketing force, providing the high and steady levels of consumption needed by mass production industry. The support of most media changed from a reliance on political party sponsorship and subscriptions to advertising fees. High speed printing and efficient transportation brought "modern" merchandising to the frontier through mail-order.

6. *"Big" government, social "engineering" and wartime needs*: With the increasing complexity of life, government became a major communicator. Programs ranging from war time propaganda to industrial safety and conservation campaigns required professional communicators and knowledge of effective communication techniques.

7. *Special interest groups*: With the growth of large business and increasing appeals to voters to resolve major issues, efforts to persuade the public using new mass communication tools intensified. The political needs of business spawned public relations and institutional advertising at the beginning of this century. Research by these new professionals was a logical extension of communicating effectively.

8. *Universal education*: The latter half of the 19th century saw the rise of free schooling in many developed nations. Often simple literacy and computation skills were the focus, but cheap printing of books, and later films and audio recordings provided important new tools. Today, the mass media have made their way into most classrooms to provide experience and skills unobtainable locally. How best to use media has been a recurrent research question in situations ranging from intellectually gifted children to third world farmers.

9. *Expanding transportation and communications*: The steamship, railways and, later, motor cars created a high speed and complex network which could only be regulated through evolving communications technologies. The telegraph, for example, was instrumental to the safe, efficient functioning of railways. Radio became an essential of steamship and aircraft safety.

10. *Growth of cities*: Many of the influences just described led to the formation of the modern city. Specialized, skilled people were necessary to industries making increasingly sophisticated products. Transportation and telecommunications were essential to their coordination (think of the materials and specialized parts in an automobile and the scheduling and transport needed to bring them all to the assembly point on time and in proper sequence). Mass mediated communication became essential to diffusing even the most rudimentary message throughout a city of millions. Simple posters, church orators or street criers, which sufficed in villages and cities prior to industrialization, could not deal with a truly mass population.

Those living during the latter half of the 19th century saw the small agricultural community replaced by the modern metropolis. The ''progressive'' movement, popular with social critics of that era (and still today), sought to use some of the very basis of this change—science, industry and government—to rebuild a sense of community as it once existed in village life.

John Dewey was a philosophical pivot of this societal view (Delia, 1988). Key in Dewey's thinking was an individual's empathic ability—his or her ability to understand the circumstances of others, to have a sort of ''social foresight.'' Empathy expanded one's participation in the community through an ability to share with others an understanding of what was important symbolically. Mass communication, through a free press, was seen as a central agent of this sharing, informing us of others in the community, their needs and ideas, and helping to build consensus for solving problems.

Dewey's views remain firmly rooted in the advice of early 20th century social science and progressive institutions; that there is a ''best way'' for society to manage the forces shaping modern life. Scientific research, often employing a host of sophisticated statistical methods, were expected to light the way. Few disagreed in a flood of useful research activity that provided advertisers with marketing tools, government with data on effective propaganda and the media with suggestions on building larger audiences. Indeed, there were many practical problems and issues awaiting communication solutions.

One of the earliest problems to receive research attention was political communication. During the First World War, major governments involved used the media to keep morale and shape public opinion. Lippmann (1922), for example complained of modern media and their ability to create ''stereotypes,'' appealing not to reason but to categorical thinking based in myths and wishful thinking. By the late 1920s, ''attitudes'' were extracted as things to be created or changed and certainly to be measured by increasingly sophisticated techniques of psychology and sociology. In 1937, the academic journal, *Public Opinion Quarterly*, was founded to serve as a scholarly forum for this new field.

Since that time, the effect of media on attitudes has been a recurrent theme in research. In the 1930s, ''scientific'' public opinion measurement began to play a large role in elections and in media content. Election reporting could become as engaging as the racetrack since a number could be placed on how much one candidate led another. Public relations practitioners built their careers on an ability to ''read'' public opinion, alter it, or change their clients' policies to conform. Advertisers saw these same techniques as important marketing tools, since attitudes toward, say, protection of the environment could suggest the sort of appeals and products to push.

After the turn of the century, the press grew not only in size but in stature as a social institutionNo longer could its running be entrusted solely to apprentice-trained writers and editors. Those with college education were increasingly sought to help the press fulfill its lofty social goals. Schools of journalism arose at a number of universities: Columbia, Northwestern, Wisconsin, Minnesota and Washington, to name a few. While their mission was (and largely remains) vocational training of journalists, after World War II interest in journalism research expanded greatly. During much of this period, the journal, *Journalism Quarterly* (as it still does today) served to diffuse this research.

Questions were asked ranging from ideal page layout to readership studies to find out the sort of stories readers wanted. The ratings industry became established in the 1930s to provide a crude form of this information to radio (and later, television) broadcasters. William Paley, the owner of the Columbia Broadcasting System, was so convinced of the value of research that he named Dr. Frank Stanton, an Ohio State University psychology professor, as president of this powerful radio network. Among other innovations of the time, Stanton (with his colleague, Lazarsfeld) wired up controls for use by test audiences as applause indicators and were thus able to measure moment-to-moment reactions to various actors, changes in plot and commercials. Similar systems are used today to pretest new television series and commercials before they are finally aired.

Not all research of this inter-war era was so commercially focused. The University of Chicago's sociology department developed as a center of research in urban society and life. As with Dewey (who was also at Chicago), Robert Park concerned himself with the social and political functions of news. How did the immigrant press help newcomers mesh in with the life of their new city? How did news involve citizens in the political life of the community? How, indeed, did the press contribute to a sense of community? The "Chicago School" represented a major, early thrust in sociological scholarship generally, and of research into the social role of the mass media in particular.

Social psychological research on communication begun after WWI reached high levels during the 1930s. The Payne Fund studies conducted under the auspices of the Motion Picture Research Council, attempted objective research on the influence of movies on children. How did age, parents and playmates work in conjunction with movies on children's' activities—school work, sleep patterns and delinquency, to mention just a few.

The Second World War provided another opportunity for this tradition to make rapid gains in understanding communication processes. By this time, it was well known that warfare was as much based on success with the emotion and determination of a nation as it was on material strength. The rise of fascism in Europe, leveraged largely by skillful propaganda, was intensely studied.

Wartime propaganda in the United States centered about attitude change research pioneered at Yale University's psychology department under Carl Hoveland and Irving Janis. The "Yale School" provided research with practical outcomes for wartime needs: the *Why We Fight* motivational films shown in movie houses and to military recruits were intensively examined for their influence (we discuss them later in this book), techniques to change the behavior of U.S. families (to get them to change eating habits to conserve food supplies) were tried, and, of course, tools for wartime propaganda were developed for the enemy (how can you psychologically "reach" people with opposed beliefs).

Following the Second World War, during the late 1940s, considerable change took place in the study of communication. Efforts begun at Yale under Hoveland and at Columbia University during the war continued, aimed at:

1. Defining agreed-on key terms and models of a communication process; that is a linked, interdependent set of activities.

2. Further researching effects of the mass media using the established techniques and ideas of sociology and psychology which had worked so well for wartime research.

3. Developing theoretical structures for communication in an effort to find general principles explaining many communication situations.

Wilbur Schramm at Stanford University stressed the urgency of understanding persuasive effects of media so that they could be harnessed for maximizing the public good. Others, such as Lasswell, saw communication research critical to the problems of democratic life. Media, ideally, facilitate rational judgments of citizens. Through the use of "objective" scientific methods, a "value-free" basis for evaluating communication policy could be obtained. Gradually, however, the use of communication research to find practical tools for reforming society yielded to increasing pressure to develop a more purified communication science aimed not so much at practical needs, but at basic theory-building.

A number of key, integrative books and events set the foundations of this activity. At a conference convened by the Rockefeller Foundation in 1948, it became clear that Lasswell's now well known summary of communication research, "If who says what through what channels of communication, to whom, what will be the results . . . ," was a call to organize research about "communicators, communications institutions and their control, contents, channels and effects." (Delia, op. it, p. 61). In 1949, Wilbur Schramm first published an edited reader of key mass communication research, *Mass Communications*, in a pioneering effort to forge organization on the new field. Other works followed in this tradition. Shannon & Weaver's (1949) work on *The Mathematical Theory of Communication*, provided a model for engineering problems in long distance telephone, but metaphorically, provided a convenient organizing framework for those interested in modeling human communication. This linear flow, "telephone" model of communication became enshrined over the next 10 years as the basic, accepted description of human communication. Berlo's (1960) book, *Process of Communication*, Schramm's *Process and Effects of Communication* (1954) and Joseph Klapper's *The Ef-*

fects of Mass Communication (1960) were influential texts of this period, each reinforcing this Lasswellian, Shannon-Weaver view of communication.

There were some other directions followed as well. Opinion leadership and the "two step flow" of messages from media through "opinion leaders" to the public emphasized the vital role of personal influence in mitigating direct media effects (Westly & McLean, 1955). The role of "gatekeepers" in news organizations (White, 1950)—editors and others who selected certain stories over others—examined social networks as did Everett Rogers (1962) in his early work on the diffusion of innovations. But the basis of this scholarship and instruction was treated more as elaboration on the basic Lasswell formulation. The National Society for the Study of Communication was founded (in the late 1950s, later renamed the International Communication Association) to foster scholarly exchange.

Traditions established in European and U.S. university departments outside the now traditional reach of communication programs followed different paths. This largely historical and cultural research eschewed the "scientific" approach favored in mainstream American communication study. The political commentary, the assertions that culture could bias and dictate the kind of questions asked even with scientifically-based psychology and sociology, and the often easy mixing of humanities with social science kept this work on the fringes. Linguistics, semiotics, media history and culture, comparative literature, legal studies, and film studies all prospered, but typically remained in splendid isolation from American communication-as-social science scholarship. To provide a scholarly forum for these interests, the International Association for Mass Communication Research was established.

During the 1960s, mainstream communication scholarship flourished, much of it sustained by an America eager to engineer its "Great Society" though social reform. Mass Communication work increasingly concentrated in former schools of journalism or radio-TV studies, which by now had expanded their purview as schools of communication or mass communication. Little work now came from the elite universities in the East. Depressingly, little joint work existed between schools of speech-communication and mass communication, the phenomena under study at each somehow considered inappropriate at the other. Thus, while the study of mass communication achieved a consolidation of sorts, much was being left aside. The effects of media were being increasingly revealed, but within a range set by the social science traditions established over the previous 40 years.

The late 1960s and early 1970s was a time of challenge to traditional institutions and assumptions. Studies, for example, which evaluated communication of Western technology to third world farmers, had once concluded that those slow to change their traditional ways were "fatalistic," "superstitious" or just plain "laggards" (see Rogers, 1962, for example). When this research was re-examined, critics suggested that the third world farmers had developed practices which were practical, appropriate to their technical skills and which preserved desirable features of their culture. Media messages about an alien technology didn't work because both messages and technologies were inappropriate. The world was a complex, multicultural environment which didn't always conform to research conducted on Americans living under the influence of American institutions. A consolidation of American work in mass communication had on one hand established a field and had served to organize scholarship. But, on the other hand, it constrained vision and sidelined other important, less orthodox work.

In the 1970s, academic journals, reflecting consolidation of American communication interest, grew in both circulation and number. The *Journal of Communication* evolved under the auspices of the International Communication Association. *Communication Research* developed as a publication focused on communication theory and research methodology. The *Journal of Broadcasting*, sponsored by the Broadcast Education Association, was established as a scholarly forum for study of the electronic media. *Speech Monographs* had existed for many years as a journal devoted to research in interpersonal communication. *Human Communication Behavior* was established to help bridge interests across the interpersonal/mass communication divide. Communication research had a variety of platforms, now independent of the older, more established fields of psychology and sociology from which it evolved.

The late 1970s and early 1980s are too close in time to the present to allow considered historical reflection, but it has been clear that during this period much reassessment of our field has taken place. Second and third generations of scholars have replaced those who established the early traditions of this field during the 1940s. These scholars are situated in university departments of mass or interpersonal communication having as a central focus human communication behavior and the institutions supporting it. As well, they have dealt with early "telephone" style models of the communication process enough to appreciate their limitations. Indeed many new formulations have been advanced to better understand human communication. Few today would suggest that any one of them should hold sway over all others. Further there is increased appreciation of European scholarly traditions and those from related fields found in many U.S. universities.

History, popular culture, critical social studies and semiotics are a sampling of once peripheral fields now blending and contributing to—or competing with—a social science based understanding of communication. As one issue of *The Journal of Communication* (Spring, 1984) suggested by its title, communication is "a field in ferment," actively growing and assimilating once again. Our hope, as authors, is to bring you both the traditional knowledge of our field, but to suggest as well where new growth and controversy exists within it.

How Is Communication Defined?

There are of course dictionary definitions, but most fail to recognize the usage and research traditions which give this term scholarly meaning. For many years, communication, communications, telecommunications, mass communication and human communication were used often interchangeably. Over the past several decades the terms have taken on distinctions, some subtle, others obvious.

"Communications" (with an "s") refers to the technologies of communication—transmitters, telephone networks, microwave links and so on. Telecommunications refers to the same things, though it occasionally is claimed for exclusive use by those in telephony or television broadcast. Frequently "telecomms" is seen as a contraction of this term. The corporation responsible for telephonic communication in the United Kingdom, for example, is called British Telecomms. In short "communications" and "Telecommunications" are engineering terms used by those who work with technologies.

"Communication" (without an "s") refers to communication behavior, usually human. For many years, this term had implications of persuasion, reflective of the practical research traditions of propaganda, advertising and political campaigns. For purposes of this book, we take communication to imply the building and maintenance of shared meaning. This definition, we feel, is most sensitive to problems of communication, be they pragmatic, semantic or of transmission. Our interest, as well, is restricted to human communication, though we acknowledge much useful and interesting work done in the field of animal communication.

"Mass Communication" (again, no final "s") refers to behavior and social questions which result from traditional media institutions as well as other, smaller-scale efforts to communicate with large numbers using technology. It also covers questions of policy and regulation aimed at social issues (permissible levels of violence in television programming, for example).

"Mass Communications" (with a final "s") speaks, again, to technology of mass communicating directly (say, adequacy of transmitter power to cover a geographic region). For some, this might seem academic hair-splitting. And these terms still are often used interchangeably. Nevertheless, we can only encourage the foregoing distinctions to make our discussion of communication—mass or otherwise—better shared by you the reader.

Research Methods in Communication

Given the diverse origins of communication as a field of study, it should come as no surprise that its methods of research are diverse as well. Furthermore, the major methods of inquiry are not unique to this field, but are commonly employed in several other social science disciplines. A comprehensive discussion of communication research methods would have to include content analysis, experimentation, surveys, qualitative methods, statistics, historical methods, and legal research. However, for purposes of this book we will confine our attention to the three methods most widely employed in studies of communication behavior.

Content Analysis

Content analysis is a tool for the objective, systematic study of message content (Berelson, 1952). What does this mean? Suppose someone raises the following question: does network television news have a liberal bias? One way to answer this question would be to ask the opinions of persons who view network news. If we did so, we would probably find little agreement. The perception of a liberal bias in network news would depend as much on who you ask as it does on the actual content. The content analyst would proceed by getting transcripts of the broadcasts and devising an objective, systematic procedure for identifying and counting instances of liberal bias.

The first thing that is required is an "objective" definition of liberal bias—i.e., a definition that conforms to a generally accepted meaning of "liberal," and can be clearly linked to instances of liberal bias in the transcripts. For example, the following definition would be clear, but unacceptable:

Liberal bias: favorable statements made about people I don't like or policies that I disagree with. (This definition is personal and subjective.)

The following definition would be less personal, and more objective:

Liberal bias: a function of the ratio of statements supporting liberal politicians and causes to statements supporting conservative politicians and causes. A liberal bias exists if the former outweighs the latter.

A clear and objective definition of the content characteristic to be analyzed is just the first step. Next, we need an objective and systematic procedure for applying the definition to the transcripts. This will require considerable refinement of the definition in which we state explicitly what is meant by "supportive statement," "liberal politicians," "liberal causes," "conservative politicians," and "conservative causes." This cannot be done arbitrarily. It must be based on a meaningful distinction between liberal and conservative—not simply the researcher's opinion as to which politicians are liberal and which are conservative.

The net result of following such a step-by-step procedure is verifiability. Other investigators, regardless of their own political persuasion, should be able to follow these procedures and get the same results. For example, numerous studies of political endorsements by newspapers consistently show that endorsements favor conservative candidates. Without an objective, systematic approach, you can see what would happen in studies of network news bias. We would get one set of studies by conservative investigators that would show a liberal bias, and a second set of studies by liberal investigators showing a conservative bias.

In fact, something very much like this happened. One of the first studies of network news bias was done by a conservative investigator, and found the "liberal bias" that was expected (Efron, 1971). Unfortunately, Efron's study did not adequately document the definitions and procedures that were employed, so it was impossible to determine whether the study's findings reflected the investigator's own bias, or a bias of the networks. The question was cleared up by a later study designed to detect *either* a liberal or conservative bias (if either were present). This study did not find evidence of either kind of bias (Stevenson, 1973).

To give you a better idea how content analysis is done, let's examine in more detail a recent study of anti-social acts on prime-time television (Potter & Ware, 1987). Studies of anti-social acts (sometimes called "violence") on television have been numerous given the Surgeon General's concern with the possible effects of such content. Of course, content analysis cannot document effects, but it can describe the occurrence of such acts in the media. (If other studies have documented effects, then there is all the more reason to monitor the presence of anti-social content.)

The authors began by defining *anti-social acts*: any attempt by one character to harm another. The definition included both physical acts (destruction of property, larceny, burglary, robbery, assault, rape, killing) and symbolic acts (deceit, insults, threats). However, these authors were not interested only in the incidence of anti-social acts. They were interested in the *context* in which they were presented. Here is why. The implication of an anti-social act to the viewer may depend on the consequences that it has for the television character. It's one thing to portray anti-social acts in the context of a "morality play" in which characters suffer the consequences of anti-social behavior. It's quite another thing to portray television characters as benefiting from this kind of behavior.

To pursue this difference in context, Potter & Ware decided to determine whether anti-social acts were portrayed as rewarded and/or justified. They defined each of these:

Reward—a situation in which the perpetrator receives a benefit as a direct consequence of an anti-social act, either something tangible (e.g., money) or an experience of satisfaction (e.g., success, pleasure, or social approval).

Justification—the character indicates that he or she felt warranted in committing the act, rather than feeling remorse or saying that he or she did not feel right about committing the act.

Potter and Ware applied these definitions to the following example. Suppose a teen-age boy is shown robbing a convenience store. He might be portrayed as unjustified, if he acknowledges that he is breaking the law. Or, he might be portrayed as justified, if society has made him poor and he is just trying to get what is due him. The act might be portrayed as rewarded—he is shown spending money and receiving praise from his peers.

With these definitions in hand, the next step was to obtain a representative sample of dramatic programs selected from prime-time during winter and spring of 1985. A total sample of 88 hours of prime-time programming was analyzed. Two undergraduate students were trained to use the coding definitions to identify each instance of an anti-social act and to determine whether or not each act was rewarded or justified. A cross-check (called a "reliability test") was made between the two coders, showing that they agreed over 80 percent of the time on whether an act was rewarded or justified. A further cross-check was made using four non-student coders (both male and female, of different ages). These coders agreed with the student coders about 80 percent of the time.

The point of all this is not to suggest that these procedures insure the infallibility of the study's results. The chances of obtaining erroneous results are minimized, but never completely eliminated. The point is that by using such procedures, and documenting them carefully, other investigators will be free to challenge the results (if they seem suspect).

In this case, a surprising discovery was made. Over 88 percent of all anti-social acts were portrayed as rewarded, and over 93 percent were portrayed as justified. Contrary to the concept of television as a "morality play," it appears that television presents a social environment with values unlike those of the society in which we live.

Survey Research

The implication of the content analysis of television drama is that television teaches viewers that anti-social behavior is justified and effective. Therefore, it would seem to follow that watching such programs would influence viewers to engage in anti-social acts. Perhaps. Actually, this is only conjecture. The results of a content analysis may suggest what the effects of certain messages could be, but by itself content analysis does not provide any evidence of effects. To obtain such evidence, researchers turn to other methods—either surveys or experiments.

With a survey we might do the following. We might interview a sample of television viewers to determine their exposure to programs which portray anti-social acts as rewarded and justified. (Our "hunch" is that persons who watch these programs often will be more likely to use anti-social solutions to problems.) In addition, we might ask another set of questions in which a variety of hypothetical situations is presented. Each respondent would be asked what he would do in each of these situations. Now we might have some evidence of effects. What if the persons who watch this kind of

15

programming are more likely (than non-viewers) to provide anti-social solutions to the hypothetical situations?

We seem to have evidence now that two things are related—i.e., that television viewing makes a difference in what people *say they would do*. This is a common application of survey research nowadays, to collect evidence that can be used to test hypotheses about communication effects. (Often this evidence is not conclusive, as we shall see later.) But his is not what survey research was originally used for, nor its only use at present.

In the communication field, one of the earliest uses of survey research was to predict the outcome of an election based on the expressed voting intentions of a *sample* of voters. In 1936 *Literary Digest* magazine polled over two million voters by mail and predicted that Landon would defeat Roosevelt by nearly 15 percentage points (Babbie, 1973). This prediction proved to be wrong, largely because the Digest had drawn its sample from telephone directories and automobile registration lists, which underrepresented the record numbers of poor people who voted in that election.

Subsequently, election polling methods were improved by George Gallup, who developed *quota sampling*, a method which insured that voters of all types would be adequately represented. But even this method failed in 1948 when Gallup predicted Dewey would defeat Truman. Since that time pollsters have relied on *random sampling*, a method which insures that each member of a population has an equal chance of being included in the survey sample. The success of sample surveys in predicting election outcomes has led to its wide use by the media and candidates alike. However, there are still cases where poll predictions fail. For example, in many primary elections substantial numbers of voters have still not made up their minds when polls are taken; thus, their votes cannot be easily predicted. In other cases the samples used by the media are not large enough to make accurate predictions. It must be remembered that samples are only *estimates* of the characteristics of a population, and the accuracy of the estimate can be influenced by many factors—e.g., size of the sample, timing of the poll, the phrasing of questions, and so on. Another of the early applications of survey research was the study of mass media audiences. In 1938 a nationwide survey was conducted to measure the effects of a now famous radio broadcast—Orson Welle's "War of the Worlds" (Cantril, 1940). Two years later a major study of American voters was conducted to determine the effect of mass media campaigns on voting behavior (Lazarsfeld, Berelson & Gaudet, 1948).

In the years that have followed, survey research has become a permanent partner of mass communication:

(1) Surveys, in the form of public opinion polls and election forecasts, have become a common news-gathering tool.

(2) Surveys have become the predominant means by which mass media describe their audiences.

(3) Surveys are a major tool of academic researchers for studying audience behavior and mass media effects.

In our previous discussion of the content analysis method, we stressed that content analysis cannot document communication effects. However, content analysis used in conjunction with surveys has become a common approach to searching for communication effects. One of the best known examples is the series of studies designed to test the "agenda-setting hypothesis" (see Chapt. 2).

The agenda-setting studies began with a study of undecided voters in the 1968 presidential campaign (McCombs & Shaw, 1972). Personal interviews were conducted with a randomly selected sample of 100 undecided voters. They were asked, "Regardless of what the politicians are saying, what do you think are the three main issues facing the country today." Answers to this question were coded into categories representing the major issues.

At the same time, researchers conducted a content analysis of the five newspapers, two news magazines and two evening news broadcasts serving these voters. The news content of these media was sorted into the same categories of major issues. In order to test the agenda-setting hypothesis, the rank ordering of these issues needed to be established for both voters and the media. The "voter agenda" was based on the number of times an issue was ranked first by voters. The "media agenda" was based on the amount of coverage that an issue received. Then the two agendas were compared. This comparison revealed a remarkably close agreement between the two agendas.

Despite the apparent strength of this finding, additional surveys were needed to confirm it. Subsequent studies with samples from different populations and different media configurations yielded similar results. The survey results seemed to firmly establish a relationship between what is emphasized in the media and what members of the audience perceive as important. But there was still a contribution to be made by experimental research.

Experimentation

Although survey research can often provide useful evidence of communication effects, it is seldom conclusive. For example, take the findings of the Chapel Hill agenda-setting study. Does it show that media emphasis influences what the audience views as important? Or, does it show that what the public thinks is important influences what the media decide to emphasize? Using the Chapel Hill survey, it is impossible to decide which interpretation is correct. Thus, the study can only be regarded as tentative support of the agenda-setting hypothesis.

This question about the actual direction of influence could be more readily answered by designing an experiment to test for the agenda setting effect. With an experiment we might be able to demonstrate that public perceptions of what is important can be *changed* as a result of exposure to media content.

At this point you should be asking, "Why didn't they do an experiment in the first place?" Or, "If surveys don't provide conclusive evidence, why apply them to this kind of question?" There is no simple answer to these questions, but it is important to recognize that the findings of surveys and experiments complement one another. Both methods have strengths and weaknesses. While experiments can clear up questions about the direction of effect, they are often criticized for utilizing unrealistic (laboratory) settings that do not generalize to the "real world."

This question about *"external validity"* came up very early in the application of experimental method to questions about communication effects. The first systematic program to experimentally study effects of communication had been launched at Yale with impressive results. Numerous experiments had been conducted showing that subtle differences in the construction of messages made significant differences in the effects of the messages on opinions, attitudes and beliefs (Hovland, Janis & Kelly, 1953). It appeared that the results of these experiments provided the basis for powerful new theories of persuasion.

However, efforts outside the laboratory to manipulate attitudes and opinions did not meet with the same results. Attitude change was frequently observed in laboratory studies, but infrequently observed in field studies. Hovland (1959) pointed out that there were a number of differences between the laboratory and the field setting that accounted for this. For example, in the laboratory one could control who would be exposed to a persuasive message, while in the field the message might reach mainly those persons who already agreed with it. More recently, the television industry challenged the validity of dozens of experimental studies which demonstrated the ability of filmed violence to cause aggressive behavior. The argument went something like this: in the laboratory subjects are given the opportunity to behave aggressively without fear of retaliation, but this doesn't mean they would do so in a more realistic situation where retaliation is likely.

There are two ways to answer such a criticism. One can build the possibility of retaliation into the experiments and do them over again. And one can seek corroborating evidence from field surveys.

Returning to the agenda-setting hypothesis, let's see how an experimental approach was used to clear up the question posed at the beginning of this section. Three Yale researchers designed an experiment to test the hypothesis that the issues played up in network newscasts would cause changes in viewers' rankings of the importance of those issues (Iyengar, Peters, and Kinder, 1982) (see Figure 1.1).

Pretest	Treatment	Posttest
Subjects asked to rate importance of several current issues.	Exp. group—views newscasts with heavy coverage of defense issue. Control—views newscasts with no defense stories.	Subjects asked to rate importance of issues again.

Figure 1.1. Design of an Agenda-setting Experiment.

The experiment began with a "pretest" in which all subjects were asked to rate the importance of several current issues, including the issue of weakness in U.S. defense capability. The pretest provided a baseline from which the hypothesized effect of the newscasts could be measured. Next the subjects were divided into two groups, an *experimental group* that saw newscasts that had been modified by inserting additional stories dealing with defense weakness, and a *control group* that saw the same newscasts without the defense stories. The control group was needed to rule out the possibility that changes in the experimental group could be due to causes other than the newscasts. The expectation was that the defense issue would increase in importance in the experimental group, but remain the same in the control group.

In this particular experiment the researchers did their best to simulate a "natural" viewing situation. They used videotapes of actual television newscasts, and led subjects to believe that they were viewing the regular newscasts of the day. Although subjects were brought to Yale University for the study, they were shown to an informal lounge with a television set and asked to view as if they were at home.

What did the study find? The importance of the defense issue increased significantly in the experimental group, providing the first experimental evidence that manipulation of the media agenda does cause changes in the audience agenda. This complemented the previous findings from survey studies, and placed the agenda-setting hypothesis on more solid ground.

Concepts, Models, and Theories

It is not only the use of objective, systematic research methods that distinguishes communication as a scientific study of human behavior. The study of communication is also guided by the search for general statements about behavior in the form of concepts, models and theories.

To the communication researchers, these are invaluable tools. They provide the initial framework for research, serving to justify the importance of the research problem and to state it in terms that are clearly understood. Once the research is conducted, they provide the framework for interpreting findings and for locating the findings within a cumulative body of knowledge. You might say that concepts, models and theories are the "road maps" of the scientist.

For the student of the communication literature, these general statements have a different use. One is confronted with a vast body of studies and an incomplete body of knowledge that is constantly changing. It makes little sense to try to become familiar with the individual studies. There are too many, and more being added every day. And you need to see the relationships between studies that have pursued a common question. In short, the student also needs a "road map." Concepts, models and theories are like signposts. They help you to find your way around the literature, and to remain conversant with what's going on after dozens of new studies have been added. Beyond their value as a learning tool, concepts, models and theories have a practical value to the student as well. Some students are looking forward to careers in mass communications. It used to be sufficient to learn a skill such as writing or reporting, but getting into mass communication professions has become more difficult. In addition to traditional skills, communicators of the future need to be more aware of how communication works, and more aware of its social significance (McCombs & Becker, 1979). A major reason is that the demands which society places on mass communication keep changing. New ways of communicating and new communication services are being invented all the time. Those who have a strong grounding in *communication* (not just message production) are often at the forefront of new developments.

Other students do not see their careers in mass communications, but will find careers in organizations that may depend on mass communication (e.g., through advertising or public relations), and are affected by news coverage of their activities. On the one hand, as consumers of mass communication services, it is important to have an informed perspective on what can (and cannot) realistically be accomplished by such mass communication services. On the other hand, it's important to be able to see 'unwanted publicity" from a broader perspective than the interests of a single organization. All of us in one way or another become "consumers" of mass communication. Consumers, not just in the sense that we buy newspapers and magazines, and barter our time (to watch ads) in exchange for radio and television programs. We are also consumers in the sense that we depend on mass communication to meet some of our individual needs, and the needs of the democratic society in which we are citizens. In many ways, our ability to meet our individual responsibilities as citizens depends on the effectiveness of our system of mass communication. As consumers, we may also suffer the side effects of the many efforts to sell us, persuade us, entertain us, and so on. Thus, we need to be aware of the potentially harmful effects of mass communication, as well as the ways in which it is essential to the functioning of a complex society.

We assume that most students want to share in some of the insights provided by communication research, and whenever possible apply these insights to their own experience. To share these insights, the student must to some extent begin to think like a scientist. This means grasping communication problems in the general terms used by the scientist, since this is one means to understanding what scientists thought was important and why. Ultimately, it also means learning to think conceptually yourself so that you can begin to develop your own ideas in dealing with the communication situations in your own experience.

Concepts

This book will introduce you to many new concepts that describe communication phenomena. Some of these concepts may strike you as rather strange "scientific jargon," and leave the impression that concepts are esoteric scientific tools that have little to do with everyday life. This would be a mistaken impression on two counts. First, scientific concepts do help to focus our attention on what is significant in everyday experience. Second, certain concepts may at first be unfamiliar, but the practice of using concepts is certainly not limited to science.

But before we can talk about how concepts are used, we'd best explain what is meant by a concept. Are concepts just words? No, although words are often used to label concepts and to provide a definition. More to the point, concepts reflect a way of thinking—a way of thinking *abstractly* in which we are able to point to the common features of several objects or events. By thinking in this way, we can often see connections between events that had previously seemed unrelated.

For example, at an early age most of us begin to think of other individuals in abstract terms. We recognize certain kinds of people with characteristics in common. Someone might say, ". . . the Smiths', they're 'real people.' " The concept here (real people) is undefined, but clearly the expression refers to an abstract category which the speaker uses to describe a characteristic the Smiths' have in common with some other people. The formation and use of such concepts provide a powerful way to simplify our social environment.

Similar kinds of concepts are used by communication practitioners to simplify and make sense of the large audience with which they are trying to communicate. Take the case of the advertising agency presented with the problem of developing the first advertising campaign for the BMW automobile. The advertising strategist commonly employs the concept of an audience segment—a group of consumers with certain characteristics in common which make them likely purchasers. In this case, the *segment* was called "baby boomers." Baby boomers were people born shortly after World War II who shared certain values and now had reached the stage in life where they had their own families and had achieved some success in their occupation. (In scientific jargon, this method of grouping would be called a *cohort*). They seemed to be the kind of people who would buy a solid, conservative and expensive car like the BMW. Fortunately for

Figure 1.2. Primitive Cave Model. From the *Journal of Communication,* 1987, 37(1) p. 180 © 1987 *Journal of Communication.* Used with permission.

the agency, the concept worked well. The agency owners went on to build a multi-million dollar organization based on communicating with baby boomers.

The point of this story is not simply that concepts can be profitable (if you are astute enough to see their applications). The point is that concepts are as indispensable to thinking about practical communication questions as they are to scientific analysis. And often concepts of use to scientific thinking are equally useful for thinking about practical questions.

Models

Often two or more concepts can be combined to present a more comprehensive picture of some communication phenomenon. These pictures are called models. They are not models in the usual sense of a small-scale reproduction, rather in the sense of a map of relationships between major elements of a communication process.

The most familiar communication models are those that attempt to present an overall picture of "the communication process" (see Figure 1.3). Of course, these models are not to be taken literally. They are not "the communication process," but merely an attempt to represent some of the most salient features of communication. For example,

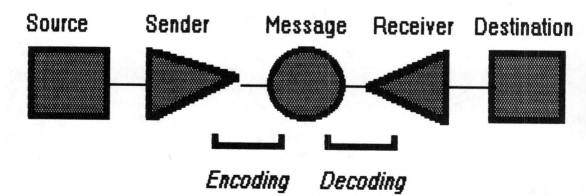

Figure 1.3. A Generalized Model of a Communication System.

in the model below the major elements required for communication (i.e., an information source, transmitter, receiver, and destination) are arranged to show the transmission of a message in a single direction. The major application of such models has been to the engineering problems of mechanical systems (e.g., the telephone), since such a model does not attempt to account for the behavior of a speaker and a listener (Osgood, 1954). Many other models are designed to depict a particular communication phenomenon, or a particular part of a communication process. To explain, let's return to the problem of finding useful ways to describe mass communication audiences. Above we saw how the concept of "baby boomer" was a useful way for certain advertisers to think about the audience they wanted to reach. This was a way to identifying a single audience segment. But for other purposes it might be useful to distinguish among several different audience groups.

This was the approach taken by researchers who tackled the question of why there should be a huge difference in the rate of newspaper subscribing between those under 30 years of age and those over 30. Most observers in the newspaper industry speculated that the difference was due to heavier reliance on television by persons in the younger age groups. But contrary to this idea were studies showing that those who watch television news generally read a newspaper as well (Bagdikian, 1971). Researchers at the University of Washington suspected that the difference was due to a major change (or "transition") in the life patterns of individuals around age 30 (Jackson & Stamm, 1979). Subsequently, a group of concepts (called a "typology") was developed that described the newspaper audience in terms of four types of individuals:

1. *Drifters*—individuals who have yet to think about establishing any kind of long term attachment to a local community.
2. *Settlers*—individuals who are just beginning to form long term attachments.
3. *Settled*—individuals who have formed long term community attachments.
4. *Relocators*—individuals who have formed long term attachments, but are thinking about breaking them.

We do not yet have a model. As stated above, a model depicts the relationships among a group of concepts. To produce a model from the above concepts, it was necessary to "reconceptualize"—i.e., change their meaning. Instead of thinking in terms of types of persons, the investigators began to think in terms of stages in a process of relating to a local community. Thus, "drifter" became "drifting" and "settler" became "settling," and so forth. The investigators conceived of individuals as passing through each of these stages at different times (Stamm, 1985). This led to the development of the model shown in Figure 1.4.

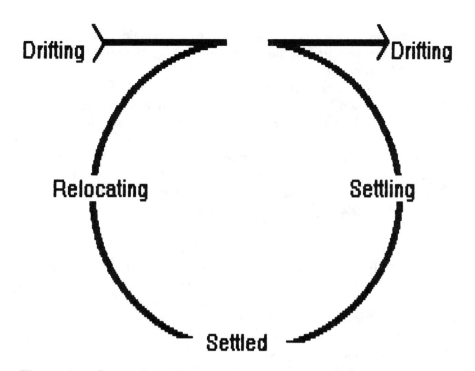

Figure 1.4. Stages in a Process of Community Attachment.

This particular model did prove to be useful for studying certain questions about newspaper circulation and readership. For example, one study found that the highest percentage of new and recent subscribers occurred during the settling stage of the model (Stamm & Weis, 1982). Surprisingly, the average age of persons in the stage was nearly 40. This suggested a reason why newspaper subscribing is so infrequent among those under 30—most people don't begin to develop a permanent community attachment until after they reach 30 years of age.

The settling model also suggested new questions for research on newspaper audiences—a major function of models. For example, it leads one to ask whether people have very different ways of settling into communities, and if so, how would these differences affect relationships with newspapers? What does it take to move a person from the drifting to the settling stage? Does the information provided by newspapers play any role in moving a person from one stage to the next? All of these questions generated by the model can lead to new research that has practical implications for how newspapers can relate to readers (current and potential). Of course, what we are illustrating here for this particular communication model applies just a well to the other models to be discussed in this book.

Theories

This book will discuss several "theories" about mass communication, but it's sometimes difficult to distinguish a theory from a model. This is not made any easier by the widespread practice of blurring the distinction and referring to models as theories, and of simply using the terms interchangeably. Models and theories do after all have some things in common. Both are usually based on concepts and relationships between them. Even so, there is to our minds a major difference. The major purpose of models is to provide a useful *description* of some phenomenon. The purpose of a theory is to provide an *explanation*

In a model the relationships between concepts are simply drawn to indicate passage of time or some kind of spatial relationship. In a theory, however, the relationship between concepts requires some kind of explanatory mechanism. This mechanism explains how or why the concepts are believed to be related as described by the theory.

All of this should become clearer if we discuss an example of a communication theory. Later in the book we will discuss the phenomenon of "selective exposure" and a theory which attempts to explain its occurrence. The "theory of cognitive dissonance" explained that selective exposure is a consequence of the individual's efforts to maintain consistency among related beliefs and attitudes (Festinger, 1957). There are several pieces to this theory:

(1) An account of how various beliefs and attitudes (called "cognitive elements") can be either consistent or inconsistent.

(2) The postulate that the occurrence of cognitive inconsistency produces an unpleasant drive state called "dissonance."

(3) Identification of the various behaviors (e.g., avoidance and rationalization) by which an individual can reduce dissonance.

The attractiveness of dissonance theory (and of most theories) stems from its wide applicability. It seems capable of explaining a wide variety of behavior, and of leading to nonobvious predictions that provide new insights. More on this in the next chapter. But before leaving the topic of theory, there are some misconceptions that need to be confronted.

Sometimes people equate theory with some kind of final truth. But any theory represents only what we believe to be a useful explanation at one point in time. The "truth" of any theory is not final, but rather hangs by a thread. The "thread" is nothing more than the body of evidence that supports the theory. Inevitably, as more and more tests of a theory are conducted, discoveries will be made that the theory cannot explain. Then the theory will need to be revised, or a new theory devised.

Another misconception of theory is that it is simply wild speculation that is of little or no practical value. Actually, there are two misconceptions here. First, theory is not just any wild speculation that might explain a given phenomenon. The theory we will be discussing in this book is carefully formulated, and subjected to tests.

There are a number of ways in which theory can have practical value. In many cases theories are constructed because of a practical problem that demands explanation. If an explanation can be found, then the problem can be better understood. Take the problem of the uninformed voter. If we had an adequate theory of how voters arrive at choices we should be able to do a better job (through mass communication) of providing voters with the right information at the right time.

Theory also leads to new ways of doing things that contribute to the improvement of communication. For example, theories of communication effects are widely applied to devising new and more effective ways of conducting information campaigns (Chapt. 6). For example, if mass communication is to be effectively used in promoting the concept of preventive medicine, then communicators need to understand how communication works to obtain the desired effects—e.g., changes in knowledge, beliefs and behavior concerning diet, exercise, addictive drugs, etc. Often theory brings awareness of unforeseen barriers, and leads to improvements in campaign strategy.

It is not the purpose of this book to present a compendium of mass communication theories. Our purpose is to examine the phenomena of mass communication from the perspective of human behavior. In so doing we will only call upon those theories that are useful to our purpose. In this way we hope to provide our readers with a solid base from which to begin study of a communication profession, or to gain a greater understanding and appreciation of the process and effects of mass communication.

Key Terms

AAPOR
Chicago School
communication
communications
concept
content analysis
control group
empathic ability (also "social foresight")
experiment
experimental group
external validity
industrial revolution
linear flow models (also "telephone" models)
mass communication
mass communications
model

Payne Fund Studies
quota sampling
random sampling
scientific agriculture
scientific public opinion
social engineering
survey
theory
universal education
value-free evaluation
Yale School

Summary

Questions about the influence of mass media can range from its social impacts and intrusiveness, to its level of effectiveness for advertisers and for fulfilling critical social needs such as a politically well-informed public.

There were multiple causes promoting the growth of the mass media in the 19th century. These included such important developments as the media technologies themselves, public education and literacy to expand the consumer base for information, the rise of "big" government and the spread and growth of population, particularly in rapidly growing cities.

Schools of Journalism were established at major universities, predominately the large "land grant" universities of the Midwest.

The First World War (WWI) caused considerable interest in mass communication techniques. Media were used for propaganda, building civilian morale and raising money.

In the 1930s, public opinion research developed swiftly, spurred by the advertising industry. Audience ratings for radio and consumer studies for marketing products used these techniques.

Dewey, Park and others attempted to analyze the role of mass media, especially newspapers in the life of the American city. This research anchored a tradition of seeing the media as positive forces for community growth.

There was intensive communication research during WWII for many of the same reasons which motivated the efforts during WWI. The major difference here, was more effort to find models and theories which helped to explain how and why people changed attitudes, accepted propaganda, could be lead, willingly, by dictators and the like. There was, as well development of specialized terminology for the field.

In the years immediately following WWII, there was intense scholarly activity in communication. The use of "value-free" social science methods were becoming the dominant method of analysis and theory construction.

By the 1960s, traditional social science thinking in communication research was paramount, and was engaged to solve many problems ranging from negative effects of TV programming in the U.S. to development needs of the third world.

The 1970s witnessed challenges to much of conventional thinking. Communication researchers say instances where techniques and theories which seemed to fit conditions in the U.S., encountered problems when applied in other cultures.

In the 1980s, there has been considerable reassessment of scholarship in communication. The contributions of anthropology, history, cultural studies, popular culture, political science and other scholarly directions are receiving better attention alongside the social sciences.

Questions about the process and effects of mass communication can be studied by a variety of research methods, the most common of which are content analysis, surveys, and experimentation.

Content analysis is an excellent technique for describing the manifest content of mass communication, but a poor technique for assessing effects.

The most critical problem in content analysis is arriving at objective procedures for coding content that will yield the same results with different observers.

Surveys are commonly used to estimate characteristics of a population by using the procedure of random sampling. Surveys are commonly used to provide evidence of communication effects, but have the shortcoming of not being able to separate cause from effect.

Experiments allow for the study of communication processes under controlled conditions which separate cause from effect, but often lack "external validity" (i.e., ability to generalize findings to real-world settings).

In addition to research methods, the primary tools of the communication researcher are concepts, models and theories.

Concepts are a tool for introducing important distinctions between phenomena, as well as for recognizing similarities between events that had previously seemed to have nothing in common.

Models are a tool for mapping out connections between events that had previously seemed unrelated.

Theories serve to explain why connections should be expected between events covered by the theory.

References

Babbie, E. R. (1973). *Survey Research Methods*. Belmont, Ca.: Wadsworth.

Bagdikian, B. H. (1971). *The Information Machines*. New York: Harper & Row.

Berelson, B. (1952). *Content Analysis in Communication Research*. New York: The Free Press.

Berlo, D. K. (1960). *The Process of Communication*. New York: Holt.

Cantril, H. (1940). *The Invasion from Mars: A Study of the Psychology of Panic*. Princeton, N.J.: Princeton University Press.

Delia, J. G. (1988). "History of Communication" in Berger, C. R. and Chaffee, S. H. (Eds.). *Handbook of Communication*. Beverly Hills, Ca.: Sage, pp. 20–98.

Efron, E. (1971). *The News Twisters*. Los Angeles: Nash.

Festinger, L. (1957). *A Theory of Cognitive Dissonance*. New York: Row, Peterson.

Hovland, C., Janis, I. and Kelly, H. (1953). *Communication and Persuasion*. New Haven: Yale U. Press.

Hovland, C. (1959). Reconciling conflicting results from experimental and survey studies of attitude change. *American Psychologist*, 14, 8–17.

Iyengar, S. M.D. Peters and D. R. Kinder (1982). Experimental demonstrations of the "not-so-minimal" consequences of television news. *American Political Science Review*, 76, 848–858.

Jackson, K. and K. Stamm (179). Locating and identifying stable subscribers. *ANPA Newspaper Research Report*, No. 21.

Katz, E. and P. Lazarsfeld (1956). *Personal Influence*. Glencoe, Il.: Free Press.

Klapper, J. T. (1960) *The Effects of Mass Communication*. New York: Free Press.

Lazarsfeld, P. F., B. Berelson and H. Gaudet (1948). *The People's Choice*. New York: Columbia U. Press.

_____ and F. Stanton (1940) *Radio Research*. New York:

Lippmann, W. (1922). *Public Opinion*. New York: Harcourt, Brace, Jovanovich.

McCombs, M. E. and D. L. Shaw (1972). The agenda-setting function of mass media. *Public Opinion Quarterly*, 36, 176–187.

_____, and L. B. Becker (1979). *Using Mass Communication Theory*. Englewood Cliffs, N.J.: Prentice-Hall.

Osgood, C. E. (1954). Psycholinquistics: a survey of theory and research problems. *Journal of Abnormal and Social Psychology*, 49, suppl.

Potter, W. J. and W. Ware (1987). An analysis of the contexts of antisocial acts on prime-time television. *Communication Research*, 14, 664–687.

Rogers, E. M. (1962). *The Diffusion of Innovations*. New York: Free Press.

Schramm, W. (Ed.) (1954). *The Process and Effects of Mass Communication*. Urbana, Il.: U. Illinois Press.

_____ (Ed.). (1949). *Mass Communications*. Urbana: U. Illinois Press.

Shannon, C. and W. Weaver (1949). *The Mathematical Theory of Communication*. Urbana, Il.: U. Illinois Press.

Stamm, K. and R. Weis (1982). Toward a dynamic theory of newspaper subscribing. *Journalism Quarterly*, 59, 382–389.

_____ (1985). Newspaper Use and Community Ties: Toward a Dynamic Theory. Norwood, N.J.: Ablex.

Stevenson, R. L., R. A. Eisinger, B. M. Feinberg and A. B. Kotok (1973). Untwisting "The News Twisters": A replication of Efron's study. *Journalism Quarterly*, 50, 211–219.

Westley, B. and M. McLean (1955). A conceptual model for communication research. *Audio-Visual Communication Review*, 3, 3–12.

White, D. M. (1950). The "gate-keeper": A case study in the selection of news. *Journalism Quarterly, 27*, 383–390.

2   Information Processing

Introduction

To better understand communication, which we have described in Chapter 1 as an exchange of meanings between persons, it is helpful to begin by focusing on some processes within persons. By focusing on "information processing" we hope to shed some light on the encoding and decoding terms included in the Chapter 1 models. From the standpoint of information processing, both encoding and decoding involve similar processes of exposure, attention, cognition (i.e., thinking), and memory. These processes shed light on how meaning is constructed and shared.

The importance of information processing can be demonstrated in a number of ways. For example, if we assume that communication involves a simple transfer of a message from a sender to a receiver, then we should expect that someone who watches the evening news telecast will be able to tell us what all the news items were. However, research shows that on the average less than 10% of the items sent will be remembered a short time afterward (i.e., less than one hour). Take another case, in which the results of two studies of message effects don't agree. One investigator finds that opinion change is greatest if the strongest argument is presented first. Another investigator finds greater opinion change when the strongest argument is presented last. In reviewing the findings of several such contradictory studies, Hovland (1954) concluded that the lack of agreement could not be explained by differences in the messages. One must understand, he said, how individuals absorb and integrate the bits of information provided by the message.

Perhaps an anecdotal example will illustrate this point more clearly. The story is told of a female reporter for the NY Post who covered some of the early feminist demonstrations at the Miss America Pageant in Atlantic City in 1968. This journalist later wrote a story reporting that the demonstrators had burned their bras. These same demonstrations were later carefully studied by scholars of the women's movement, and no evidence was ever uncovered to indicate that bra-burning had actually occurred. The reporter may have recalled that she had observed bra-burning, but as Fabun (1968) has stressed, when we write about something we are describing processes that happened inside of us—not just what happened in the external environment.

What could have happened "inside" this reporter that would explain the (apparently) erroneous report? During the same time period a number of Viet Nam war protests also took place and were widely reported. During these protests the burning of draft cards did actually take place. It's possible that the reporter associated the two different demonstrations in her mind, and thereby attributed "burning things" with both of them. It is a well-known memory phenomena that we store only the general or more salient features of any event, and that specific features are often inferred from the general framework.

The purpose of this chapter is to probe a little more deeply into such processes, to see how they work and what their implications are for understanding why communication through mass media is often difficult and presents surprising outcomes.

Information

Of course, is we're going to talk about information processing, how we talk about it depends in large part on how we define information. The concept of information has been widely employed both inside and outside the field of communication, and is used in many different ways. Before we discuss any particular definition of information it will therefore be helpful to sort out some of these differences in usage.

Messages and Things

One of the most common usages is to equate information with a message. Either a message is itself information, or it contains information. This is not necessarily an incorrect understanding of information, but it is incomplete. It overlooks the fact that messages are informative because they refer to something. So perhaps the "real" information is whatever it is that the message refers to. Just so that we can keep these two different usages separate, we'll refer to:

(1) *First-hand information*—information that is derived from direct observation of an object or event;

(2) *Second-hand information*—information that is derived from a message describing someone else's observation of an object or event.

Second-hand Information

An important point to recognize about second-hand information is that it cannot be equated with the experience to which it refers. It provides a means of describing experiences so that two or more persons can relate to the same experience, but it is not a replica of the experience itself. Certainly this is obvious in the use of language, where the words employed do not in any way resemble their referents (e.g., the word "dog" does not look, sound, smell, feel or taste like a dog).

The point is not so obvious when it comes to visual messages; perhaps here is where it is most important to bear it in mind. A drawing or a picture of a dog does look like a dog. There can be an advantage to this. You could show a picture of a dog to persons using different languages and they could probably figure out what you're talking about without knowing the word "dog." This is why such stylized visual symbols are widely employed in airports, on highway signs, etc. Despite this, any drawing or photograph of a dog does not represent an exact replica. The artist's rendition only captures her particular experience of the dog and is constrained by her artistic ability, the medium employed, and so on. The photographer's picture reflects his choice of camera angle, quality of the lens and film material, and so on.

As another example, we might consider the second-hand information available in a televised debate between two political candidates. As we view the debate, we have the definite sense of being there—of receiving first-hand information. We remain largely unaware of the extent to which the televised debate differs from the debate observed by those actually present.

A well-known study of television's portrayal of the McArthur Day parade (Lang & Lang, 1960), shows, however, that this is far from the case. This study revealed that television coverage of an event (second-hand information) differs from the actual event in some important respects. First, the televised version is usually more interesting and/or exciting because the television camera is kept focused on the action. Second, the television version is incomplete because by focusing on certain things the television camera must necessarily miss other aspects of an event (Figure 2.1). For example, if the camera focuses on the candidate who is speaking, you do not get to watch the reactions of the other candidate, although you might well choose to do that if you were in the audience.

This difference between first- and second-hand information will have very important implications when we consider effects of mass media. The reason is that in many cases we do not have access to first-hand referent information. For example, our only access to information about events in other parts of the world is through second-hand information provided by foreign correspondents. If we never visit these countries ourselves, then we end up forming impressions based largely on media coverage which dwells primarily on coverage of "coups and earthquakes" (Giffard, 198_). In this way mass media are sometimes said to create a "socially perceived reality" based entirely on

Figure 2.1. From the *Journal of Communication,* 1980, 30(4) p. 139
© 1980 *Journal of Communication.* Used with permission.

second-hand information, and in many ways different from social conditions as they actually exist.

First-hand information

Let us return now to the idea of first-hand information. We have said that second-hand information is available in the form of messages about the external environment. First-hand information is based on our ability to use our senses to "pick up" information directly from the external environment. Even this process, of producing first-hand information, is not as direct as it might appear to be.

According to Gibson, the information that we receive from the external environment is not an exact replica of objects as they exist. For example, if we are talking about visual information, information in this case is derived from the light reflected from objects in the environment. The light that is reflected from any object has a distinctive pattern that corresponds to such things as edges and surface texture of the object. Gibson refers to these distinctive patterns of reflected light as an "optic array." What we "see" is dependent upon the correspondence between the optic array and shape and texture of the object. In other words, when we talk about first-hand (visual) information, we really mean an optic array. Or, as Fabun has put it, "What we see is not the thing itself, but a happening—the emission or reflection of light. (Extending this same definition to auditory information, tactile information, etc., we could speak of an "auditory array," "tactile array," etc.)

In discussing human communication, it is important to understand this point about the nature of first-hand information. If we understand that (even) first-hand information is not absolute, then we can comprehend why there would often be problems in sharing first-hand information. Two persons viewing the same object will not experience the same optic array because no two persons can be in exactly the same spot at the same time. Often we forget this, assuming that observers of the same event receive identical information, when in fact they don't.

Information is always relative to a particular observer. So how is it that we often try to distinguish between information that is "objective" and information that is "subjective." Given the above statement, how could "objective" information (or "objective reporting," etc.) ever be possible? Is such an idea totally misleading? Well, yes and no. Certainly no one can claim to be a completely detached observer who receives information totally unaffected by the act of observing. Probably few people are so naive as to make such a claim. However, we often assume when we read direct quotes in the media that we are reading exactly what was said. In some cases that may be true, but we must remember that what was said (and thereby available to be quoted) was in many ways influenced by the presence of a particular listener.

What it comes down to is that there is no hard and fast distinction between "objective" and "subjective" information. Information is more or less objective only to the extent that we try to be objective and use procedures which minimize the intrusiveness of the observer. Even the objectivity of scientific information cannot be assumed; it rests on careful description of the methods for observing. Some methods are more objective than others, but none is objective in any absolute sense.

The important point in assessing the objectivity of information is to know something about how the information was obtained. Thus, for example, a mass media report is supposed to identify the source of the information. The common practice by many news media of using "veiled sources" makes it more difficult for the reader to assess the objectivity of the information attributed to the (veiled) source (Culbertson, 1975). Stories that are attributed to "high government officials" or "sources close to the Palestine Liberation Organization," don't offer us names, qualifications or, often, exact organizational affiliation. These conditions make it difficult for critical readers to determine the quality of the observations they are invited to share.

Meaning

One of the most popular views of information processing emphasizes the concept of a sensory image. It suggests that considerable cognitive processing acts upon the raw sensory data we receive (Keeler, 1981). For example, in the case of visual information processing, it appeared to some scholars that the visual sense alone was inadequate to account for such phenomena as depth perception. How can we see depth when sensations are only two-dimensional? The retina of the eye, where vision is stimulated, is a two-dimensional surface. Many things we see, such as photographs, convey a sense of three dimensions from two-dimensional planes. The "sensory image" explanation proposes that (somehow) mental processes create information which go far beyond the raw data supplied in a sensory image.

This seems to leave open the question of the relationship between first- and second-hand information. Some have gone so far as to deny the importance of first-hand information. According to Muller, ...

"all we ever see directly are our retinal images." (see Diamond, 1974)

In other words, the only relevant definition of information is concerned with "meanings" constructed by the individual. Thus, it is sometimes argued "meanings are found in people, not in words," which denies the relevance of second-hand information as well. Thus we have moved from an earlier idea that information is largely contained in a message itself to one where much of the information is contained in meaning constructed by an individual or audience to interpret messages.

In relation to mass communication, this notion of information may be used to explain the well-known phenomenon that the same message (e.g., word or picture) often has different implications at different times, or to different persons.

The key assumption of this cognitive approach to information is that information is not a result of a literal decoding of messages; it is assumed to be (in part) created through cognitive processes such as inference and interpretation. Such a view of information seems to be required to explain cases in which the same event, or the same message, mean different things to different people.

Until fairly recently linguistics studies assumed, to the contrary, that the decoding of language was literal—i.e., determined by the information in the message. Hundreds of experiments were done in which individuals were asked to remember nonsense words or phrases. It is not surprising that such experiments seem to demonstrate literal recall of messages, since nonsense words have no meaning (i.e., previously learned associations). More recent work, however, has taken a different turn. Bransford and Frank (1971) reported that individuals seem to listen to the 'meaning' of a sentence, not merely to its surface wording. For instance, you hear the separate sentences: "The ants ate the jelly," and, "The ants were in the kitchen." You might well recall later that you had heard, "The ants in the kitchen ate the jelly." To Bransford and Franks this suggests that you are inferring meaning rather than remembering the literal content.

A similar view has sometimes been taken of what occurs when voters are exposed to televised political debates. A distinction can be drawn between:

(1) *First-hand information*—the candidate's behavior as observed by someone present at the debate;

(2) *Second-hand information*—the candidate's behavior as it appears on the television screen; and

(3) *Meaning*—the voter's image of the candidate.

Some researchers assume that voters simply "learn" the message portrayed via television. Thus, if the debate coverage focuses on candidate personalities, viewers simply learn a personality image for the candidates. But consistent with the third definition, cognitively-oriented researchers have found that voters use debates to try to infer what kind of person the candidate is or how the candidate might perform in office (Lang & Lang, 1964). According to Stamm, et al. (1986), the voter's interpretation of political messages yields information that goes well beyond the content of the message.

This cognitive approach to information has gained tremendous momentum in recent communication research. According to one authoritative account, cognitive studies of mass media effects is one of the most active research areas to emerge in recent years (Roloff & Berger, 1982). Increasingly, research accords cognitive behavior a pivotal role in describing information processing. On one hand, the processing of messages is seen as being controlled by cognitive processes that determine what is relevant and what "meaning" the message is to have in the context of ongoing behavior. On the other, the effects of mass communicated messages are generally seen as having some effect on what the voter "thinks". Earlier studies were less interested in how political messages affected thinking, such as how candidates were evaluated and chosen, and more concerned with some kind of visible outcome such as a vote in favor of a particular candidate. This earlier approach served the need of finding message techniques that produced certain outcomes, but offered little to explain how that outcome happened.

One of the central problems that stood in the way of a cognitive treatment of information was the lack of accepted tools for measuring information (as meaning). Osgood, Suci and Tannenbaum's (1975) development of a tool for actually measuring "meaning" helped to dispel the argument that meaning was an inaccessible mental event. Osgood (1963) conceived of meaning as the location of any object (e.g. word, person, etc.) in semantic space. He conceived of semantic space as having multiple-dimensions, with its center representing total meaninglessness. As an audience positioned objects away from center, meanings of various sorts were given to them. The distance between any two objects in semantic space defined the difference in their meanings (called a "semantic differential").

Given this definition of meaning, Osgood & Tannenbaum sought a measurement tool that would measure the distance between any two objects in a three-dimensional *semantic space*. The tool that they developed to measure meaning has come to be called the "semantic differential." It consists of: (1) a series of bipolar or adjective-opposite scales on which objects can be treated (see Figure 2.2), and (2) a statistical technique (called "factor analysis") which identifies the dimensions of "semantic space" from these ratings and allows the distances between objects to be calculated.

In a common example, political consultants use this technique to describe political candidates. Contenders such as Michael Dukakis and George Bush in the 1988 U.S. presidential election are rated by a sample of voters on a large set of scales (often 40 or more) tapping personal characteristics like "good-bad," "safe-unsafe," "fast-slow,"

Compassionate	—	—	—	—	—	—	—	Noncompassionate
Experienced	—	—	—	—	—	—	—	Inexperienced
Trustworthy	—	—	—	—	—	—	—	Untrustworthy
Weak	—	—	—	—	—	—	—	Powerful
Professional	—	—	—	—	—	—	—	Unprofessional
Intelligent	—	—	—	—	—	—	—	Unintelligent
Honest	—	—	—	—	—	—	—	Dishonest
Sensitive	—	—	—	—	—	—	—	Insensitive

Figure 2.2. A Semantic Differential Scale Used in the Measurement of Candidate Image.

etc. When analyzed by computer, scales which work the same way for a candidate are clustered together by a technique called factor analysis. Mr. Bush might have been rated highly on characteristics of kindness, personal warmth, being relaxed, but might also have been rated as low in "potency," "activity" and "speed." The factor analysis would suggest two strong Bush characteristics: friendly, but (alas), weak, perhaps naive. As we observed from later stages of this campaign, Bush's speeches emphasized his toughness and experience together with his promise of a "kinder, gentler" government under his leadership. With this tool, the effects of a televised debate on perceptions of candidates can be assessed by comparing semantic space structures from before and after the telecast. Products, such as frozen versus fresh vegetables, or Mercedes autos versus Cadillacs, can be compared for their meaning to consumer panels. Probably more than any other research tool, the semantic differential has served to objectify research into the cognitive effects of mass communication.

Information Processing In Four Steps

Discussion of the concept "information" has given us some glimpses of what is believed to be involved in information processing. This prepares us to examine in more detail how people process information. The notion of a "process" suggests that there is more than one step involved—that information processing consists of a series of interrelated steps, (Figure 2.3). We will discuss information processing in terms of the following four steps:

(1) Exposure,

(2) Attention

(3) Cognition

(4) Memory.

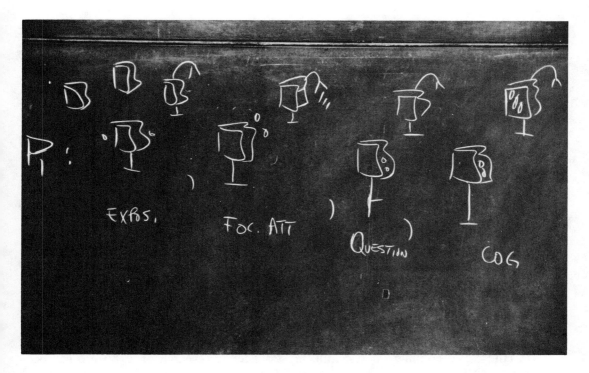

Figure 2.3. A Blackboard Model of Information Processing. The above model divides information processing into four behavioral steps—exposure, focused attention, questioning, and cognition. The top row of figures represents objects in a person's (P1) field of observation. The second row represents the behavior of P1 in relation to those objects. (Model by Richard F. Carter, U. of Washington School of Communication.)

Research on information processing generally consists of identifying a particular step in the process and observing what happens within that step. For example, studies concerned with the first step have asked why individuals selectively expose themselves to certain messages while (apparently) avoiding others.

The Exposure Step

In the world of commercial mass media, a multi-million dollar industry is maintained largely for the purpose measuring levels of exposure. For example, print media such as newspapers and magazines do "readership" studies to determine the percentage of subscribers who are exposed to each article appearing in a given issue. Television and broadcast ratings represent the percentage of households within a media market who listen to a particular station, or watch a particular program.

A major reason for investing so much in obtaining exposure measures is that advertisers base decisions about when and where to advertise on such information. Advertising rates are also based to a large extent on size of the audience.

It may seem like a simple matter to obtain information on media exposure levels, but in practice there are difficulties. And given that advertisers tend to use this information as an estimate of the relative effectiveness of various channels, there are also questions about whether exposure measures are adequate. For many years the standard techniques for measuring television exposure consisted of "diaries" and an electronic device called an "audimeter." Diaries were needed to supplement the audimeter, since the device could only record (automatically) when the set was turned on and what channel it was tuned to. The diary was needed to keep track of who was watching (if anyone).

Obviously, the accuracy of such a method depended on how reliably the diaries were kept by television viewers. Doubts about their reliability has led to development of a different electronic device called a "people meter." These meters assign a push button to each member of the household. Whenever the button is pushed the viewer is automatically identified. Some meters even provide viewers with several buttons, which allows them to express opinions about programs while they watch.

In contrast to commercial research, most academic research on exposure has been concerned with explaining either the effects of exposure (called "effects research," see Chapt. 5–8) or the underlying reasons for exposure. One of the earliest inquiries into information-processing by mass communication scholars was concerned with a phenomenon known as "selective exposure." Some of the earliest studies of the effectiveness of mass media information campaigns noted that large numbers of people were not exposed to heavily publicized messages. To some observers it appeared that certain messages were deliberately ignored or avoided. This led to raising the first widely studied question about information-processing—why would members of a mass media audience be selectively exposed to readily available messages?

What is the underlying basis for selectivity—does the individual select which messages to attend to and which to ignore? These questions are important for researchers and communication practitioners alike.

For several years communication researchers tested the idea that there was a psychological basis for selecting one message in preference to other competing messages. The "selective exposure" hypothesis holds that individuals expose themselves to messages that agree with existing attitudes and beliefs, and avoid messages that contradict them (Chaffee et al., 1969). One theory, the "theory of cognitive dissonance" (Festinger, 1956), even postulated the existence of a "drive" to reduce dissonance (a tension-producing psychological state) by seeking out supportive information (i.e., messages) and avoiding non-supportive information.

The notions of "supportive" and "non-supportive" information can be explained with reference to a mass media election campaign. Suppose that John Q. Voter was a strong supporter of George Bush during the 1988 presidential campaign, and opposed to the election of Michael Dukakis. Imagine further that numerous political ads appeared dealing with the strengths and weaknesses of each candidate:

    a. strengths and weaknesses of Bush;

    b. strengths and weaknesses of Dukakis.

According to dissonance theory, "supportive information" would be any message that is consistent with John Q. Voter's decision to support Bush:

    a. supportive information—strengths of Bush
                                    —weaknesses of Dukakis

"Non-supportive information" would therefore be any information inconsistent with John Q. Voter's decision to support Bush:

    b. non-supportive information—weaknesses of Bush
                                        —strengths of Dukakis

To test your understanding of this selective exposure hypothesis, imagine that John Q. Voter has changed his mind to being a Dukakis supporter. Now which information is supportive and which is non-supportive?

The phenomenon of selective information processing was amply documented, but it proved difficult to demonstrate that it could be adequately explained through theories such as cognitive dissonance. Several studies bearing on this question were reviewed by Freedman and Sears (1960), who concluded that the evidence was doubtful. Of the studies reviewed, several (but not all) demonstrated a preference for supportive information, while few showed avoidance of non-supportive information.

Freedman and Sears (1960) suggested that there was abundant evidence that selective exposure exists; several studies document that people tend to be exposed to messages with which they agree. But, they warned, there could be many explanations for such selectivity. For example, it's likely that people more often come in contact with supportive information as a result of general social choices. This does not prove that they prefer information that agrees with their existing attitudes and beliefs, nor that they avoid information which does not. In fact, some studies have yielded contradictory findings. For example, in one study smokers preferred to see an article going against their belief that smoking does not cause cancer. Why?

The answer, according to subsequent studies, may lie in the "relevance" of the message. Guerrero (1969) observed that the "supportive information" in most studies tended to also be relevant (to future behavior). He demonstrated that supportive information is preferred only when it is also relevant, and that non-supportive information is avoided only when it lacks relevance. For example, new car owners will not prefer supportive information unless it pertains to a car they actually considered buying, nor will they avoid non-supportive information so long as it pertains to a considered brand.

Many text books still treat the selective exposure hypothesis as a 'scientific truth' despite evidence to the contrary. They assume that the basis for selectivity is a kind of built-in defense mechanism that serves to protect existing beliefs and attitudes from information that threatens the status quo (an assumption perfectly agreeable with cognitive dissonance theory). Apparently this is not entirely the case. There is evidence that people attend to information that could be considered aversive or threatening. Thus, it seems that "selective exposure" is not so much a defense mechanism as it is a relevance test. This is a critical point because, as we shall see in Chapter 5, a dominant theory of mass communication claims that effects are limited by a "selective filter" which serves to screen out information with which the receiver disagrees.

Attending Principles

Have you ever found yourself in this situation? A friend has called you on the telephone and you're trying to talk, but someone else also wants to be in on the conversation. He/she wants to know who you're talking to and what the call is about. If you succeed in shutting out this person, you have a chance of tracking with the friend on the phone. But as soon as you turn any of your attention to the interloper, you quickly lose track of the person on the phone. According to Deutsch & Deutsch (1969) there is a limit to the number of things to which we can attend at one time; we have great difficulty, for example, in simultaneously processing information from two different sources. Situations such as this come up frequently in "real-life" communication and help to illustrate an important principle—the *principle of singularity*. According to this principle, in the processing of information we can attend to one thing at a time (Carter, 1973). The basis for this principle lies in how we process information. To "pay attention" to something requires that the sense organs be pointed in a certain direction (e.g., because we only have eyes on one side of our head) (Figure 2.4). It also seems to require "focusing"—i.e., screening out competing information.

The critical reader will very likely come up with apparent exceptions to the principle of singularity. Perhaps you yourself are fond of reading while you watch television. Does this refute the principle? Probably not. What's really going on here is that you are shifting your attention back and forth between the written message and the television program. This is not that hard for a couple reasons. The written message does not vanish while you're attending to the television screen, and the televised message is so repetitive and follows such a familiar format that you usually fill in what you miss while reading.

Figure 2.4. From the *Journal of Communication,* 1985, 35(3) p. 146 © 1985 *Journal of Communication.* Used with permission.

If you were trying to watch two television programs at once, or carry on a conversation while watching television, the applicability of the singularity principle would probably be more apparent. A more convincing demonstration can be found in an early study by Broadbent (1954) who presented strings of numbers simultaneously to both ears. Subjects were best able to report the digits accurately if they reported separately on what they heard first in one ear and then the other. This suggests that attention was not simultaneous but divided—divided by switching attention from one ear to the other. In another experiment Mowbray (1964) reported that when subjects were specifically asked to recall single target words presented to one ear, they were unable to repeat words presented to the other ear at the same time as the target words.

What is the explanation for this limit on attention? Is it a limit on our ability to identify and analyze incoming messages? Or is it a limit on our ability to organize and store information in long-term memory? Broadbent's well-known information processing model (1958) was the first to propose a limit on attention. He proposed that information coming in through the senses is placed in short-term storage (a "buffer"), and then selectively filtered before being processed any further. According to Broadbent, attention is directed only toward that information that passes through the filter. This insures that limited attention capacity is directed only toward relevant sensory data.

Broadbent's explanation has been supported in experimental work. Treisman and Geffen (1969) say that their experiments overwhelmingly favor a perceptual limit with a filter selecting before the messages are fully analyzed. This may explain why we only seem to remember what we deliberately focus our attention on. How often have you been introduced to a new person and found that you couldn't remember the name a few minutes later? You remember being told the name, but at the time your attention was focused on the person's appearance, or perhaps the topic of conversation.

There are innumerable practical applications of the singularity principle, far more than we could mention here. They range from such homely advice as "Don't try to tell someone what to say to another person while he's talking to her on the phone" to message design techniques which strive for a clear and consistent focus of attention. It is always painfully obvious when others violate our need for singularity of attention, but skill in communication requires that we be just as aware of the information processing limits of those we communicate with. For example, recent research indicates that multi-channel media (e.g., television) demand more attention capacity than single-channel media, a difference that producers of audio-visual media need to be constantly aware of (Thorson, et al., 1985).

Such practical questions were raised in a recent study of the optimum amount of redundancy between auditory and visual channels (Drew, et al., 1987). Because television newscasts, for example, present information over two channels simultaneously, the singularity principle dictates that viewers must divide their attention between audio and visual channels. This suggests that there must be an optimum level of redundancy between the two channels. Otherwise, the attending capacity of the viewer will be exceeded and parts of the message will be missed. If there is redundancy (e.g., overlap) between channels, viewers should be able to most effectively divide their attention. The Drew, et al. study found that when individuals watched redundant stories they focused most of their attention on the audio portion while switching between the two channels. When redundancy was low, viewers simply attended to the channel that was easiest to follow.

Another principle, called the *stopping principle*—follows readily from the principle of singularity. If attention is to one thing at a time, then switching of attention is obviously necessary. To switch your attention, you must first stop attending to the present object of your attention. This may seem terribly obvious and elementary, but the occurrence of "stops" can tell us a great deal about information processing. In particular, it can tell us about communication behavior *within* a message (Carter, et al., 1973). This is important because messages are not processed in one large unit; they are processed a "piece" at a time with frequent stops in between the smaller units.

The location of stops tells us the size of these message units, and can also aid in describing the individual's behavior with respect to each part of the message. For example, stops might indicate that receivers are having difficulty processing a particular part of a message. Consistent with this idea, research by Jacoubovitch (1972) shows that readers stop more often within parts of a message that contain ambiguous information. Locating the exact source of difficulty allows the communicator to redesign (only) the part of the message that is causing trouble.

The significance of stopping, then, is that is represents a communication act that pertains to the "how" of information processing. Messages are not processed whole, but in discrete units. The receiver must "stop" between units to switch attention from the present unit to the next one.

Research on reading shows that the reader's eyes move along a line of type in a series of discrete jumps (called "saccades"), and that comprehension of the content takes place during the brief pauses between saccades.

The principle of stopping has been applied to trying to understand how people attend to information from the media. Ultimately, such studies help us to understand why, in most cases, only part of the message gets through. One theory of media attention argues that receivers divide messages into "frames" or "chunks" (Newtson, 1973). Stops within a message may indicate where one frame ends and another begins.

The stops, or "breakpoints" tend to come around significant transition points in the message (e.g., at the end of an action sequence), and people tend recall the most detail from those parts of the message near the breakpoints. Another way of putting this is that attention within a message is very uneven; attention is greatest at those points where the person stops. Furthermore, researchers believe that details recalled from in between breakpoints are not actually remembered; rather they are filled in or inferred to be consistent with information at the breakpoints (where attention is high). In this way people can "remember" (i.e., reconstruct) details from a message without paying continuous attention.

Cognition

Earlier in this chapter we observed that receivers do not decode a "literal meaning" from any message. The interpretation of messages seems to be both somewhat less and somewhat more than the literal content. It would appear that the fact that interpretations leave things out could be explained by selective attention, but to account for things being added as well we turn to the role of thinking (i.e., cognition).

Our understanding of cognition's role in information processing needs to allow plenty of room for selective interpretation. The inherent ambiguity of messages tends to be resolved in favor of interpretations consistent with the receiver's habits of thinking. In effect we're saying that the cognitive interpretation of any message involves a slight "bending" or "slanting" by the receiver.

The most basic reason for this is that all messages are to some extent incomplete and ambiguous. What's being said and what's being talked about are two different things. The receiver has to make a connection between the two. (That connection is what we sometimes refer to as meaning.) A favorite demonstration of this phenomenon is to show a group of people a picture of an accident scene. After brief exposure to the picture, each person is asked to give an account of what happened. It becomes very clear that accounts of the accident go well beyond what's in the picture, and may even misrepresent "facts" in the picture. For example, most persons will assign blame to a "seedy-looking character" shown in the picture as a mere bystander.

One account of cognition's role in information-processing explains that what the receiver actually "sees" is influenced by what she expected to see. Sometimes what is seen is so strongly conditioned by what was expected that the resultant interpretation is termed an "illusion."

A well-known demonstration of this cognitive phenomenon is called the "monocular distorted room" (Ames, 1951). The room is constructed so that it will appear to be an ordinary rectangular room to an observer looking through a small hole at the front the room. But in fact the rear wall of the room is not rectangular, but rather trapezoidal, with the vertical edge on the left longer than that on the right (see Figure 2.5). What do you suppose you would see if two persons of equal height stood in the rear corners of the room? You would not see two persons of equal height, because you perceive a normal, rectangular room in which the walls and ceiling are parallel. To compensate for this "perceptual distortion," you see the person on the right as closer to the ceiling (and therefore taller). (If the (shorter) person on the left changes places with the person on the right, you will then see that person as being taller.)

The influence of expectations on information processing can also be illustrated through the phenomenon of *perceptual sets*. For example, Bruner and Postman (1949) lead their subjects to expect normal playing cards, but instead showed them cards in which the suits (hearts, spades, etc.) and colors did not agree. Many subjects reported seeing the cards as they would normally appear (i.e., red hearts and diamonds, black clubs and spades). Some even reported compromise perceptions—e.g., brown or purple hearts. According to Bruner (1957), this results because an object is perceived only after it is (cognitively) categorized. The perceptual set provides the category before the act of attention; therefore, one attends to that part of the sensory field that fits the category.

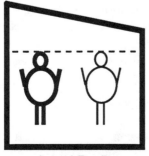

Actual Room   Perceived Room

Figure 2.5. The Monocular Distorted Room.

There are many opportunities for such perceptual sets to influence the processing of mass communication messages. A newspaper headline may result in selective interpretation of the story which it is intended to describe. This happens if the headline is misleading and cues readers to see the story differently than it is actually described. A cutline may influence perception of a picture by directing attention to a certain part of the picture or by describing it inaccurately. The voice-over narrative will influence the interpretation of motion pictures in the same manner, but perhaps to an even greater degree.

Theories about the role of cognition in information processing can be traced back to early origins in language studies and psychology. Edward Sapir's studies of language suggested that culturally accepted pre-conceptions are built into language that strongly condition the way in which we process first-hand information. Bartlett's studies of the serial transmission of messages (second-hand information) suggested that pre-conceptions (called "schema") influence the interpretation and retelling of messages.

According to the Sapir-Whorf hypothesis, words describe things as we *conceive* them, not as we *see* them. In other words, we see what we expect to see, and language tells us what to expect. Clearly, this complicates "information-processing." This idea suggests that (first-hand) information is not simply picked up, but is strongly influenced by the cognitive pre-conceptions incorporated into the language:

> . . . No two languages are ever sufficiently similar to be considered as representing the same social reality. The worlds in which different societies live are distinct worlds, not merely the same worlds with different labels attached. (Sapir, 1929).

This hypothesis has been extensively investigated in relation to the perception of color by peoples of different cultures (and languages). The hypothesis leads to the prediction that people from different cultures will actually perceive colors differently. For example, if a language does not contain a label for a certain range in the color spectrum, then will members of that culture tend to lump that range into a category containing the nearest "codable" color in the spectrum? Does this imply that colors that have not been named will be difficult to recognize?

We could contrast this hypothesis with an alternative view, that color is picked up from reflected (ambient) light and depends upon surface properties of the object. Regardless of langauge, we should all be capable of picking up the same information from ambient light. We may talk about this information differently, but the same information is available to all regardless of language differences.

One of the earliest studies designed to test the Sapir-Whorf hypothesis provided only partial support (Brown & Lenneberg, 1954). Subjects were briefly exposed to a small set of colors, some of which were readily named ("codable") and some not readily named ("not codable"). Next they were shown several hues and asked which of these they had seen before (in the previous set). The codable colors were remembered somewhat better than the not codable ones.

We might argue that this study was not a proper test of the Sapir-Whorf hypothesis. The observation that "not codable" colors were poorly recalled does not mean that they were not recognized.

However, it was not until nearly two decades later that a more conclusive test was made (Rosch, 1970). In this study Rosch included both a *naming* task and a *recognition* task. The study was done with the Dani, a Stone Age tribe that has a limited color vocabulary—"mola" for bright, warm colors and "mili" for dark, cold ones. Rosch showed the Dani forty color chips ranging in hue and brightness. On the naming task, a cultural effect was found; the Dani were able to name colors at the far end of the spectrum as "mola" or "mili" and had difficulty naming chips from the middle of the spectrum. However, the results of the recognition task were contrary to Sapir-Whorf (and consistent with our contrasting hypothesis). In this task the Dani were first shown a test chip, asked to wait 30 seconds in the dark, then asked to pick (from the array of 40) the one previously seen. On this task the Dani performed no differently than American subjects; recognition proved to be equally keen for adjacent hues whether or not they lay on different sides of a language boundary.

We have learned from these studies that the Sapir-Whorf hypothesis does not apply to color perception. On the other hand, that does not mean the hypothesis has no application to communication. As Rosch found, color vocabularies do present difficulties when it comes to naming colors that do not fit the prototype (e.g., an "off" green) of a category. The implication of this is that langauge can constrain our ability to communicate about ranges of the color spectrum that have not been named. Presumably we could extend this reasoning to other domains; for example, the science reporter trying to explain the discovery of some new phenomenon when the only words that refer to it explicitly are "scientific jargon" unfamiliar to most people. In such cases we may be forced to resort to analogy and metaphor—i.e., by describing phenomena that are similar to those we are trying to explain.

One of the earliest notions about this kind of cognitive distortion of meaning was that the individual incorporates information into memory in the form of abstract *schema*. These schema supposedly reflect the way in which certain kinds of information have been organized cognitively. If one assumes the existence of such schema, then it follows that processing of new information would involve interpreting and organizing it along the lines of an existing schema. (Presumably, truly novel information could force development of an entirely new schema.)

In a similar vein, cognitive pre-conceptions—called "schema"—have been invoked to explain why interpretations of second-hand information often deviate so far from the original content of the message. This notion of "schema" was introduced by Bartlett (1932) to explain certain anomalies in the "serial transmission" (i.e., repeated reading and retelling) of messages. For example, Bartlett studied serial transmission of an Indian folk tale which seems to have many gaps and strange causal sequences that would not normally be found in a standard western story. Bartlett observed that none of his subjects retold the tale as it was told to them. They dropped certain parts of the story and revised other parts.

The story that people retold ended up with a story line and plot resembling that of a standard western story. This apparently prompted Bartlett to speculate that his subjects possessed a *cognitive structure* ("schema") based on other stories they had heard, which they used as a basis for reconstructing the Indian folk tale.

After many years of neglect, Bartlett's notion of schema has been "rediscovered," and is being applied to studies of how people process information from the mass media. For example, Garramone (1983) has suggested that what people extract from a message depends in part on what kind of schema is activated for the processing of the message. What is learned from a political message should differ between persons using "personality schemas" and those employing, say, "issue schemas." (We shall find out in a later chapter whether this is the case.)

Recent schema inspired work on information processing has probed the behavior of both reporters and the mass media audience. Stocking and Gross (1989) have given several examples of how journalist's pre-conceptions can influence the gathering of news. Several investigators have begun to describe the role of schemas in the processing of mass media content.

According to Stocking and Gross, journalists construct hypotheses and theories about people and events that may bias their search for and selection of information. For example, a series of events in New York City were linked together in journalists' minds as constituting a "crime wave" against the elderly. A week-and-a-half after coverage started, the police wire was supplying fresh incidents daily.

However, one reporter examined overall police statistics and found that total crimes against the elderly had actually decreased. Still the crime wave theme remained in place, as journalists decided to ignore "unreliable and incomplete" statistics that contradicted their pre-conceptions.

Another example is given of Wall Street Journal coverage of Ivan Boesky, an individual who had pleaded guilty to "insider" trading on the New York Stock Exchange. Newspaper stories characterized Boesky as "a greedy crook," and even likened him to Jack-the-Ripper. When a report surfaced that Boesky had been looking for volunteer work to make amends, the newspaper explained that "a lot of white-collar crooks do it to impress sentencing judges."

The import of such examples is that the processing of information by media people is no less reliant on culturally accepted schemata than our own. Reeves, et. al. (1982) point out that films and television programs are built on stereotypes and familiar scripts, and that presentations which run counter to such widely accepted pre-conceptions are unlikely to survive in the competitive world of mass communication, where so much depends on the size of the audience one can attract.

Returning to the role of schemas in audience research, the general principle is that receiver "schemas" make a difference in attention to the message and in the meaning derived. Loftus and Mackworth (1978) have shown that the "informative areas" of a picture tend to be areas of physical discontinuity, or objects whose presence is surprising. For example, these investigators showed subjects two versions of a farm scene; in one version a tractor had been replaced with an octopus. The octopus represented what we would define as "schema-inconsistent" information (i.e., it doesn't fit the observer's pre-conception of what belongs in a farm scene). Results of this study showed that subjects directed much greater attention to the octopus than to the tractor, a finding that demonstrates the interrelationship of cognition and attention.

In light of these findings, it is surprising that in some cases individuals will still misidentify schema-inconsistent objects in a picture. For example, if we present a picture with a mail box on a kitchen counter, the mail box is often misidentified as a loaf of bread. The briefer the exposure, the more likely this is to happen (since there is less opportunity for added attention).

Mass media news coverage tends to focus on the surprising and the unexpected. In cognitive terms, an apt definition of "news" would be "news is schema-inconsistent information." In the case of television news, this may be an effective way to attract the viewer's attention, but at the same time the viewer may require extra time to correctly interpret the informative, schema-inconsistent areas of a news video.

According to Collins (1979), the development of plot and story schemas are essential to comprehension of television and film presentations. A pre-conception of the plot or storyline is helpful in several ways:

(1) separating essential information from extraneous detail;
(2) apprehending the relationships among scenes;
(3) making inferences to fill in what is not explicitly shown.

What happens when viewers do not possess organizing schema? Collins research shows that second-grade children don't comprehend a chronologically ordered program any better than a program whose scenes have been randomly scrambled. Older children comprehend much better when scenes are ordered. Considering the utility of predictable story structure, Schickel (1989) has recently complained that "Hollywood seems to have lost or abandoned the art of narrative." That is, it is impossible to make sense of many recent films for lack of a predictable plot or storyline.

So far we have discussed the role of cognition in terms of the "schema" concept. A somewhat different way of understanding cognition—the concept of "cognitive strategy"—emerged from Bruner's studies of human problem-solving (1956). Bruner gave his subjects problems such as figuring out which of a set of cards, each with a different geometric form, belongs to a particular category. Bruner found that individuals often solved such problems through a series of inter-related steps, which was what he termed a "strategy."

To illustrate this in another context, suppose that you are making a long trip across country and have the recurrent problem of finding suitable places to eat three times a day. Rather than solving this problem in a different way each time that it comes up, you might simplify things considerably by constructing a strategy. You might, for example, try *hypothesis testing*; you adopt the hypothesis that truck drivers wouldn't eat at a place that wasn't good. If your hypothesis fails the test, you might create a new one, but you would still be using the same strategy.

One thing that you might notice from this example is that the selection of a strategy seems to narrow the range of relevant information. These particular travelers only need to know whether or not the restaurant is patronized by truck drivers. They may be paying no attention at all to the advertising on the restaurant billboards, instead scanning the parking lots in search of trucks. In other words, persons using this strategy would be extremely selective in their attention to information.

Up until recently the effects of such strategies on information processing were seldom tested. More often assumptions were made about strategy. For example, consumers and voters have often been assumed to be engaged in (the strategy of) decision-making. Decision-making is a certain idealized strategy for making choices; a person making choices in this way must consider all the alternatives and compare them in terms of all the relevant information.

If we assume that a consumer is engaged in decision-making, we can come to a number of conclusions about his/her information processing. The "decision-maker" should be open to information on all the alternatives, and should apply it to making several comparisons among them until an optimal choice can be reached. This strategy demands a great deal of a certain kind of information—information that's good for comparative discriminations, and requires exhaustive, step-by-step application. Referring back to our earlier example of hypothesis testing, it's clear that hypothesis testing requires far less information than decision-making. For this reason it may be a far more convenient and efficient strategy in many situations. And clearly the communication practitioner who assumes that consumers are "decision-making" will be providing far more information than is required by those who are "hypothesis testing."

These are just some reasons why strategy is important to information processing. As an individual, you need to select strategies appropriate to the amount of effort you can invest in information processing, and consistent with the relative availability of certain kinds of information. For example, why employ a complex, information intensive strategy (such as decision-making) to reach a low cost, low risk choice?

51

The ideas and research of Bruner, et al. broke new ground by showing that people have many ways to solve problems, more than one way to make choices. This is a current focus for communication research, to identify the strategies that individuals use for making consumer choices, voting choices, and so on, and finding out what difference this makes in how they use information. The results of some of these studies will be taken up later when we consider the effects of advertising and of political campaigns.

Memory

One implication of the schema concept is the notion that the processing of information is determined by the way that information is organized in the process of storing it in long term memory. Apparently, we do not store information in the same form it comes to us. We must simplify it and store it in a prototypical form. One of the reasons for this is the limited capacity of short-term memory. According to a familiar information-processing rule—Miller's "magic number seven"—we may attend to several pieces of information, but we can only hold (about) seven in short term memory at any one time. Miller described the concept in a 1956 article:

> "There seems to be some limitation built into us either by learning or by the design of our nervous systems, a limit that keeps our channel capacities in this general range."

Miller's principle undoubtedly has application to the design of individual messages. What about, for example, those mail order ads you see on late night television. There's usually a toll number to remember that's over 10 digits long. What would be more effective, to repeat the number several times, or tell the viewer beforehand to have pencil and paper ready? Miller's concept might be applied to other design questions. How many points should be included in a 60-second commercial? How fast should a radio newscaster read?

Schemas are important to short-term memory because them allow us to make more efficient us of this limited capacity. For example, a schema might be a pattern that allows you to group or "chunk" a message that would otherwise exceed the storage capacity. Have you ever noticed how telephone numbers such as 333–1212 are easier to remember than 354–0172? Now you know why. With the first number we store the pattern, not all seven numbers.

Information in long-term memory (i.e., anything beyond a few seconds) is thought to be organized in the form of schemas. The storing of new information in long-term memory is not random; new information is "attached" to an appropriate existing schema. unfamiliar information can be hard to remember because there is no place to "file" it. Generally, schema-consistent information is remembered better than information that is schema-inconsistent.

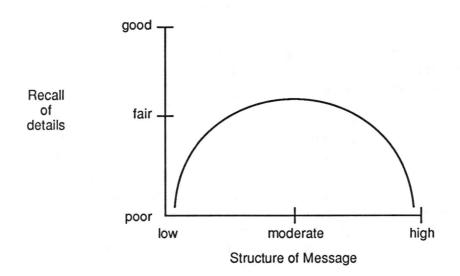

Figure 2.6. U-Shaped Relationship between Recall and Amount of Message Structure.

At the beginning of this chapter we pointed out that recall of information from mass communicated messages is often very poor. This is an important communication problem for the designers of advertising messages, who have developed tactics for working with these limitations. They design brief, highly redundant messages, and strive for repeated exposure.

Many other items, such as news and weather forecasts, are not treated in this way and don't fare so well in viewers' memories. In a study conducted for the National Association of Broadcasters, Stern (in Barrett, 1973) reported that more than half the listeners could not recall a single news story one hour after the broadcast. Specific content is forgotten, and only a general notion of the message is retained. For example, viewers of TV weather reports retain a general notion of the next day's weather, but do not recall temperatures, wind velocities, or barometric pressure.

According to Kellerman (1985) memory for mass media content can be described as an inverted U-shaped function between recall and ''orderedness' of the message (Figure 2.6). The message may be highly ordered, as in heavily stereotypical TV action-adventure shows, where a crisis develops, the hero appears, a chase/fight occurs, and the crisis is resolved. In such cases, Kellerman says that recall of details will be poor; the program is remembered as just another instance of the same script.

At the other end of the U-shaped curve we have nonscripted messages with little apparent structure. These messages place greater demands on short term memory, and are not readily organized into long term memory. According to Wagenaar (1978), weather and traffic reports are good examples of nonscripted messages—they present the listener with a list of facts which does not follow standard grammar or a chronological sequence. Wagenaar says it must be processed like "nonsense material" rather than structured prose. Consequently, it is not surprising that recall of such reports is so poor.

In the middle of the curve we have scripted messages which are not so over-scripted as to be highly redundant. In such cases possession of an appropriate schema aids recall. For example, individuals who had well formed "baseball game" schemas were better able to recall what happened during an inning of baseball (Chiesi, Spilich and Voss, 1979). Such individuals seemed better able to relate each action to an overall context.

We have already discussed some ways in which information processing behaviors can shape the effects of mass media messages through differences in attention and cognition. The same can be said of memory. A well-known example involves the *sleeper effect*, a phenomenon whereby the impact of a message increases with the passage of time. For a long time this phenomenon defied explanation, although it was suspected that memory was somehow involved. Recent research demonstrates that sleeper effects can be explained by the principle that memory operates on a last-in-first-out- basis—i.e., more recently processed information is more available. Therefore, if a message is initially presented and associated with a low credibility source, the availability in memory of a discounting cue (source credibility) weakens the effect of message. With the passage of time, however, other (more positive) cues may be associated with message. Since these cues would now be last-in they would be first-out, and the effect of the message would increase (Hannah & Sternthal, 1984).

That may seem a bit involved, so let's take an example. Suppose a newscast reported to you that *Pravda*, the major newspaper of the Russian Communist Party, claims that pollution from U.S. factories causes destructive "acid rain" in Canada. Now, your belief in this message might be low, due to your suspicions about the objectivity of the Russian newspaper. But as time passed, several things might happen. First, you might hear other news from "better" sources, which substantiate the Russian claim. Further, you might increasingly forget that it was a Russian newspaper that first alerted you to the acid rain problem. The net effect, as time passed, would be to raise the believability you held in the acid rain claim. This is not so much due to a sudden change in mind as it is to forgetting the original Russian source and remembering better subsequent, more credible sources on the same topic. Propagandists know this phenomenon well. Messages they plant that you might dismiss at the time made due to low source credibility may later have increasing persuasive impact due to a sleeper effect.

Hopefully this chapter has provided some new insights into information processing, even though we are far from being able to understand it fully. We have seen that there are many ways of defining "information," and that "processing" also refers to several different processes. Even this limited understanding of information processing can be useful to communication practitioners, who sometimes base their methods on faulty assumptions about the information processing behavior of individuals in the audience.

Later in the book, when we take up mass communication effects, it will also become more clear that assumptions about information processing are often the key to understanding how and why effects occur (or fail to occur).

Key Terms

Attention
Cognition (cognitive process)
Cognitive strategy
Exposure
First-hand information
Meaning
Memory
Perceptual set
Schema
Second-hand information
Selective exposure
Selective filter
Sensory image
Singularity principle
Sleeper effect
Stopping principle
Whorf-Sapir hypothesis

Summary

Only a fraction of the information presented in most mass communication messages is recalled a short time afterward.

We store only the general features of any event or message and infer the details from an abstract prototype (schema).

Media help to create a "socially perceived reality" by providing second-hand information about events for which audience members have no first-hand information.

First-hand information is never exactly the same for any two persons observing the same event.

Selective exposure is more the result of a test for relevance than a result of psychological defense mechanisms (e.g., "supportive" information is preferred when it is more relevant than "non-supportive" information).

Due to the necessity of focusing our attention, we can only attend to one thing at a time (principle of singularity).

Those parts of the message to which we selectively attend are the parts that pass through our "selective filters" into long-term memory.

Messages are processed a "piece" at a time with frequent stops between cognitively defined units of attention (stopping principle).

Receivers tend to recall the most information from those parts of a message nearest a "stop" or breakpoint.

All messages are to some extent incomplete and ambiguous because what is being said and what is being talked about can never correspond exactly.

Language is constructed with built-in pre-conceptions (e.g., categories) that influence recall and our ability to communicate about information that does not fit preconceived categories (Whorf-Sapir hypothesis).

The receiver's interpretation of a message is influenced by schema—i.e., cognitive structures which serve to organize information in long-term memory.

The development of recognizable plots and story lines are essential to the comprehension of TV and film presentations.

Information is not stored in memory in the same form in which we receive it—it is simplified and stored in a prototypical form (called a "schema").

The capacity of short-term memory is limited to about seven units of information at a time.

References

Ames, A., Jr. (1951). Visual perception and the rotating trapezoidal window. *Psychological Monographs*, 65, 7-Whole No. 324.

Apple, R. W. (1976). Voter poll finds debate aided Ford and cut Carter lead. *New York Times*, Sept. 1, p. 1.

Barrett, M. (1973). The politics of Broadcasting. New York: Thomas Cromwell.

Bartlett, F. C. (1932). *Remembering*. Cambridge: Cambridge University Press.

Bransford, J. D. and Franks, J. J. (1971). The abstraction of linguistic ideas. *Cognitive Psychology*, 2, 31–50.

Broadbent, D. E. (1954). The role of auditory localization in attention and memory span. *Journal of Experimental Psychology*, 47, 191–196.

Brown, R. and Lenneberg, E. H. (1954). A study in language and cognition. *Journal of Abnormal and Social Psychology*, 44, 454–462.

Bruner, J. and Postman, L. (1949). On the perception of incongruity: a paradigm. *Journal of Personality*. 18, 206–223.

Bruner, J., Goodnow, J., and Austin, G. (1956). *A Study of Thinking*. New York: John Wiley.

Bruner, J. S. (1957). Neural mechanisms in perception. *Psychological Review*, 64, 340–358.

Carter, R. F. (1973). Application of signalled stopping technique to communication research. In P. Clarke (ed.), *New Models for Communication Research*. Beverly Hills: Sage.

_____. (1985). A journalistic cybernetic. In K. Krippendorf (ed.), *Communication and Control in Society*. New York: Gordon & Breach.

Chaffee, S. H., Stamm, K. R., Guerrero, J. and Tipton, L. (1969). Experiments on communication and cognitive discrepancies. *Journalism Monographs*, 14.

Chiesi, H., G. Spilich and J. Voss (1979). Acquisition of domain-related information in relation to high and low domain knowledge. *J. of Verbal Learning and Verbal Behavior*, 18, pp. 257–273.

Collins, A. (1979). Children's comprehension of television programs. In E. Wartella (Ed.), *Children Communicating: Media and Development of Though, Speech, Understanding*. Beverly Hills: Sage.

Culbertson, H. (1975). Veiled news sources—who and what are they? *News Res. Bull.* of the ANPA, May, pp. 2–23.

Deutsch, J. A. and Deutsch, D. (1969). Attention: some theoretical considerations. In R. N. Haber (ed.), *Information-Processing Approaches to Visual perception*. New York: Holt, Rinehart & Winston.

Diamond, S., (1974). *The Roots of Psychology*. New York: Basic Books.

Drew, D. G. and Grimes, T. (1987). Audio-visual redundancy and TV news recall. *Communication Research*, 14, 452–461.

Fabun, Don (1968). *Communications: The Transfer of Meaning*. San Francisco: Intntl Society of General Semantics.

Festinger, L. (1957). *A Theory of Cognitive Dissonance*. Stanford, Calif.: Stanford University Press.

Freedman, J. L. and Sears, D. O. (1965). Selective exposure, pp. 57–97 in L. Berkowitz (ed.), *Advances in Experimental Social Psychology*. New York: Academic Press.

Gardner, H. (1987). *The Mind's New Science: A History of the Cognitive Revolution*. New York: Basic Books.

Garramone, G. (1983). Issue vs. image orientation and effects of political advertising. *Communication Research*, 10, 59–76.

Gibson, J. J. (1979). *The Ecological Approach to Visual perception*. Boston: Houghton-Mifflin.

Giffard, C. A. (1989). UNESCO and the Media. New York: Longman.

Hannah, D. and B. Sternthal (1984). Detecting and explaining the sleeper effect. *J. of Consumer Research*, 11, pp. 632–642.

Hefner, M. B. D(1971). Mediated communication and subjective measures of accuracy. Paper read at Association for Education in Journalism convention.

Hovland, C. (1954). Effects of the mass media of communication. In G. Lindzey (Ed.) *Handbook of Social Psychology*.

Jackson, K. (1987). Practical Public Communication. Unpublished manuscript. Seattle: U. of Washington.

Jacoubovitch, M. D. 91972). Communication Consequences of Signification. Master's thesis. Seattle: University of Washington.

Keeler, M. A. (1981). Current Philosophical and Psychological Foundations for the Study of Pictorial Communication. Master's thesis. Seattle: University of Washington.

Kellerman, K. (1985). Memory processes in media effects. *Communication Research*, 12(1), pp. 83–132.

Lang, K. and G. Lang (1960), The unique perspective of television and its effect: a pilot study. I. R. Bryson (ed.), The Communication of Ideas, New York: Instit. for Relig. & Social Studies.

Lang, K. and Lang, G. E. (1968). *Politics and Television*. Chicago: Quadrangle Books.

Loftus, G. and N. Mackworth (1978). Cognitive determinants of fixation location during picture viewing. *J. of Experimental Psychology: Human Perception and Performance*, 4(4), pp. 565–572.

Miller, G. A. (1956). The magical number seven, plus or minus two: some limits on our capacity for processing information. *Psychological Review*, 63, 81–97.

Mowbray, G. H. (1964). Perception and retention of verbal information presented during auditory shadowing. *Journal of the Accoustical Society of America*, 36, 1459–1464.

Newtson, D. (1973). Attribution and the unit of perception of ongoing behavior. *J. of Personality and Social Psychology*, 28, pp. 28–38.

Osgood, C. E., Suci, G. J. and Tannenbaum, P. (1975). *The Measurement of Meaning*. Urbana: University of Illinois Press.

Reeves, B., S. Chaffee and A. Tims (1982). Social cognition and mass communication research. In Roloff & Berger, *op. cit.*

Roloff, M. and C. Berger (1982) *Social Cognition and Communication*. Beverly Hills: Sage.

Rosch, E. (1973). Natural categories. *Cognitive Psychology*, 4, 328–350.

Sapir, E. (1929). The status of linguistics as a science. In *Selected Writing of Edward Sapir*. Berkeley: U. of California Press.

Schickel, R. (1989). The crisis in movie narrative. *Gannett Center Journal*, 3(3), pp. 1–16.

Severin, W. and Tankard, J. (1988). *Communication Theories: Origins, Methods, Uses*. New York: Longman.

Stamm, K., (1985). The effect of the Bush/Ferraro debate on candidate characterizations. Presented to Assoc. for Education in Journalism and Mass Communication, Memphis, TN.

Stocking, H. and P. Gross (1989). How Do Journalists Think? Bloomington, IN: Eric.

Thorson, E., B. Reeves and J. Schleuder (1985). Message complexity and attention to television. *Communication Research*, 12(4), pp. 427–456.

Treisman, A. and Geffen, G. (1969). Selective attention: perception or response? In R. Haber (ed.). *op. cit.*

Wagenaar, W. (1978). Recalling messages broadcast to the general public. In M. Gruneberg et al. (Eds.) *Practical Aspects of Memory*. New York: Academic.

From the *Journal of Communication*, 1988, 38(1) p. 13 © 1988 *Journal of Communication*. Used with permission.

3 Mass Communication in an Interpersonal Context

Introduction

In this chapter we want to begin examining communication behavior in a broader context. Up to now we've looked at communication largely as the information-processing behavior of an individual. This is basic to understanding communication at any other level of analysis. Now, however, we want to examine communication as a process between persons as a perspective from which to understand mass communication.

One way in which can do this is to see mass communication as an extension of interpersonal communication. That is, mass communication would have been invented (initially) to handle communication situations that could no longer be dealt with on a face-to-face basis.

For example, consider the first crude "newspapers" that were created in the American colonies to disseminate information that would otherwise be passed along by word-of-mouth. Robert Park (1937) has suggested that community newspapers replaced interpersonal channels of information and gossip that became inadequate. They became inadequate for two reasons. First, the communities became large and heterogeneous enough that the people who needed to exchange information could no longer meet daily on a face-to-face basis, and might not be able to understand one another if they did meet. Second, members of local communities could not depend on interpersonal channels for information about extra-local events that affected the community. The persons who developed these first "newspapers" were often postmasters, who were strategically situated to be privy to information from a variety of interpersonal sources.

If mass communication had been developed as a replacement for interpersonal communication channels, we might safely ignore interpersonal communication. However, it is more accurate to say that mass communication has been added onto interpersonal communication so that the two processes do not operate independently of one another.

Another case in point concerns the circulation of rumor, which we ordinarily think of as an interpersonal process. In fact most studies of rumor deal with interpersonal exchange of ambiguous and/or distorted information (Allport & Postman, 1947; Rosnow, 1980). Generally, once a rumor starts to circulate through interpersonal channels it is not checked or corrected, rather it tends to become more and more distorted. Sometimes such rumors come to the attention of mass media, which now face a dilemma. Should they ignore the rumor and hope it will die out? Or, should they run a story denying its validity? (Some newspaper editors feel that attempts to stop rumors are futile; printing anything only spreads it further and faster.)

A familiar example of such a rumor, known as "the mutilated boy," has surfaced repeatedly during the 1980s. This rumor is a modern version of a centuries-old rumor about the (alleged) mutilation of a young boy by older youths of another race (Brunvold, 1984). According to Shibutani (1978), mass communication can be a powerful antidote against the spread of rumor through interpersonal channels. He explains that rumors most often start in ambiguous, threatening situations (e.g., racial tension), and are perpetuated when peoples' efforts to check out the rumor are frustrated. According to Shibutani, if enough news is not available, people engage in interpersonal transactions in which improvised explanations are constructed.

There are a number of other ways in which we can relate interpersonal communication and mass communication, each of which sheds some additional light on the nature of mass communication. We shall take each of these in turn, working from the simplest to the most complex.

Interpersonal Communication as Building Block

In a very meaningful sense interpersonal communication can be considered as a "building block" of mass communication. It goes on inside mass communication; it is part of the "stuff" of mass communication. We can't imagine that mass communication could occur without interpersonal communication.

How is this so? There are a number of ways. First, the mass communication process can be viewed as a chain of events in which an important link is interpersonal communication between a reporter and a source. In other words, the messages that are delivered to mass audiences are outcomes of interpersonal exchanges. The quality of the communication between source and reporter can affect the extent to which the message delivered results in understanding between the source and members of the mass audience (Tichenor et al., 1970).

University of Minnesota researchers (Tichenor, Olien, Harrison and Donohue) sought to document the importance of source-reporter communication by asking readers of science news stories to summarize what the articles said. They then took the state-

Figure 3.1. Rumor Transmission. From THE WORLD OF QUINO by Joaquin S. Lavado. copyright © 1986 by Joaquin S. Lavado. Reprinted by permission of Henry Holt and Company, Inc.

ments made by readers back to the original sources (scientists), and asked them to judge their accuracy. Several aspects of source-reporter interaction were related to the accuracy of statements made by readers. Among these was the amount and kind of interpersonal contact between scientist and reporter. Articles based on the heaviest face-to-face contact without using the telephone, had the highest accuracy scores. Also, reporters who used such tactics as reading back notes and checking back certain facts with the source wrote stories with the highest accuracy scores.

A later study (Tankard & Ryan, 1974) attempted to find out how much inaccuracy could be traced directly to journalists' stories. (In the Tichenor et al. study, much of the inaccuracy might be attributable to the reader's misinterpretation of the story.) These researchers took science news stories back to the sources who were quoted in them, and found that some stories (7 of 190) were judged to have no errors, while some (10) had over 20 errors. The average number of errors was six. Consistent with the Minnesota study, this study again found that a key factor in reducing errors was checking the story back before publication.

Considering the number of communication skills required of both journalists and scientists, it is not surprising that inaccuracies can often be traced to the interview. According to Ramsey (1988) there are no less than eight domains of "communicative competence" that are important to the success of a journalist/scientist exchange. Among these are the ability to arrive at an understanding of the appropriate definitions, ideas, examples and anecdotes that will constitute a story. Because of the cognitive complexity involved, the scientist will need to provide redefinitions and clarifications in terms understandable to the journalist, perhaps translating scientific ideas into different symbol systems (e.g., figures of speech, or illustrations). The journalist has to know when to seek clarifications, and how to recognize scientific jargon.

Studies such as these indicate that interpersonal communication is potentially a weak link in the mass communication process, especially if reporters do not take suitable precautions. Tankard & Ryan went so far as to suggest that writers consider letting the sources of articles review them for accuracy prior to publication.

Characteristics of interpersonal communication can also be seem in the relationship between mass media communicators and members of the audience. Have you ever noticed the interpersonal tactics of a various radio and television personalities? They . . .

- speak in conversational tones, as if they were addressing you directly rather than a large audience;
- engage in clever monologues that appear to require your participation;
- interact casually with "sidekicks" or (today) with other members of "the team";
- face directly into the camera as if they were maintaining eye contact.

These kinds of communication tactics are designed to create the illusion of face-to-face communication with members of a mass audience—a form of communication termed *para-social interaction* (PSI) (Horton & Wohl, 1956). Recent research (Levy, 1977; Rubin et al., 1985; Stamm & U.W. Students, 1986) has provided evidence of PSI. Local television news viewers in several studies reported interacting with newscasters by:

- watching and listening as if newscasters were talking directly to them;
- acknowledging an opening greeting or signoff;
- regarding the newscasters as almost like personal friends.

To broadcasting executives the significance of such an interpersonal process lies in its potential for promoting loyal viewership. There is some evidence that viewers who report the highest levels of PSI tend to be more loyal viewers. Broadcasters attempt to capitalize on this relationship with promotional slogans such as, "Have breakfast with a friend" (meaning the radio).

The broader social significance of PSI seemed to lie in its potential to substitute for "real" face-to-face interaction. Psychiatrists Horton & Wohl reasoned that the lonely and socially isolated would substitute PSI with radio and television personalities for interpersonal interaction that would otherwise be missing in their daily lives. Research so far has failed to verify such a relationship, but it should be noted that these tests were made primarily with television news programming, which is not directed at such an audience. This hypothesis, if at all valid, is more likely to be supported for other kinds of programming (e.g., PSI between viewers and favorite characters in afternoon soap operas).

Next, we ask you to imagine that you are a writer for a national cooking magazine. How do you relate to your audience? Do you just sit down at your terminal and write things with nary a thought of your readers? Probably not. At least that's not what books on writing advise you to do. You're supposed to consider your readers. The question is how?

There are various ways to consider the reader, but a common way is to create another person. This can be a familiar person (e.g., someone like yourself), an "ideal" reader, or a composite of many readers. The point is that one way to relate to such a vast audience of readers is to reduce it to the equivalent of writing for another person. Mass communication is thereby reduced to interpersonal communication in the mind of the writer.

And what purpose does this serve for the writer? This person in the writer's mind becomes a "sounding board." The writer can anticipate how this imaginary person would react. Will she be interested in this recipe? Would he have this ingredient on hand? Will she understand what I mean by "folding in the egg whites"?

Supposedly this interpersonal device makes for more effective mass communication—e.g., more interesting and readable messages for the members of a large audience. But some communication researchers have begun to ask whether this is necessarily so. The crux of the question, they have said, is whether communicators do in fact accurately estimate the views of audience members. If they do not, then perhaps they end up communicating with an imaginary audience that does not exist. As a result, they might even antagonize the real audience.

Several such studies suggest that communicators tend to use interpersonal *projection*. They assume that members of the audience are like themselves, with similar interests, opinions, likes and dislikes, etc. In a study of Wisconsin newspaper editors (Martin, O'Keefe and Nayman, 1972), the editors were found to assume that readers would (like the editors) be opposed to any kind of anti-war demonstration, and not be sympathetic to persons who participated (such as students). By surveying the opinions of Wisconsin newspaper readers, the researchers found that readers were not in agreement with the editors on this issue. The editors had overestimated their readers' hostility to student anti-war demonstrators, and greatly overestimated their readers' sympathy with the government's basic position on the Viet Nam War.

Sometimes television communicators use an imaginary viewer who is assumed to be attracted to certain production formulas—i.e., giving the viewer what they imagine he wants. That usually turns out to be programming that has been successful in the past at attracting audiences. The "imagined viewer" is the kind of person they think is watching, complete with motives. This process can have unfortunate outcomes. Tannenbaum (1963) found that television producers tended to focus on the bizarre and sordid aspects of mental health, thinking that this was in keeping with the "average viewer's" understanding of mental illness. In fact the "average viewer" was often offended by such portrayals, and both producers and viewers had more sophisticated views of mental illness than those represented in the television portrayals.

Because of the risk of misperceptions such as these, many mass media have begun to invest in periodic audience studies from which they can piece together more accurate pictures of the typical reader (or readers). In this case, survey research relies on hundreds of interpersonal exchanges between interviewers and audience members to create an overall audience picture.

Interpersonal communication has also become part of mass communication in the gathering of news. The interpersonal interview is no doubt the most widely applied news gathering technique. In a very real sense the quality of the news that reaches us through the media is dependent upon the interpersonal communication skills of reporters and their sources. Yet research tells us that often interpersonal communication between reporters and sources is fraught with difficulties.

If the journalist's job was simply to get an "objective" account of what a source said, the difficulties would be minimal. Perhaps they could be largely resolved through the use of tape recorders. But reporting accurately what sources say is probably the least of the problem. The reporter acts as more than conduit between source and consumers of the mass media. The reporter's job is to find out what readers (listeners, viewers, etc.) want and need to know (which may include things a source does not wish to reveal). He must also be able to present that information in terms that are relevant and readable to the audience he serves. If that still does not sound difficult, let's consider the case of a science reporter who is doing a story about some new research on the AIDS virus. Let's say the research is directed at describing the molecular structure of the virus and that a "discovery" has been made which suggests how the virus reproduces itself.

Now the reporter knows that most of her readers have only minimal acquaintance with molecular biology, and her own knowledge of molecular biology is fairly superficial. But one thing she does know: there's a story here if this discovery can be connected to the search for a cure.

The scientist, however, is interested in how viruses reproduce. She sees that eventually this knowledge will be applied to controlling viral diseases, but that still seems a long way off.

So when the journalist begins by asking, "How close are you to a cure for AIDS" the scientist is scarcely prepared for the question. "I don't know," she might demur, "but I've found out some really important things about how this virus reproduces" The reporter wonders, "why should my readers care how a virus reproduces?" The interview turns into a very sticky affair in which the scientist tries to stay within the context of her research, and the reporter tries constantly to push the scientist to address questions of possible relevance to her readers.

And thus are most stories about science born. The stories that result, according to several studies, are often somewhat at odds with what the scientist would consider to be an accurate description. Researchers have gone so far as to clip news stories about science and take them back to the scientist-sources for scrutiny. Typically, the sources point out a number of inaccuracies: a minor remark has been taken out of context and given too much attention, important information has been left out of the story, the source is given credit for other scientist's discoveries, and so on.

One of the strangest things about communication between reporters and scientists is that they both profess the same standards for "good" science news stories. They agree that stories should be accurate, important, interesting to read, and easy to understand (Stamm, 1968). But they seem to be unaware of this agreement. Scientists think that the journalists "ideal story" is long on color and sensationalism. Journalists think the scientists' "ideal story" is short on interest and long on unnecessary details.

Clearly, some improvement in interpersonal communication is basic to improving the quality of science news coverage (and of other news coverage as well). Research organizations are keenly aware of this, and have long supported a variety of programs (e.g., workshops, seminars, reporting internships) to promote better understanding between scientists and those who write about them. Generally, these are thought to be very worthwhile, but if you'd ever attended such an exchange yourself you would have noticed the inability to compromise professional autonomy. Most scientists prefer not to be bothered by journalists (it's time-consuming and risky), and journalists do not want to give scientists any control over what they write. (Most refuse to make checkbacks for accuracy, despite evidence that they are very beneficial; Tichenor et al., 1970)

Peer Group Communication

Interpersonal communication also plays a role in mass communication through its influence within the institutions of mass communication—the media. The classic study of this interpersonal process is Breed's (1955) study of the way in which the covert policy of the "newsroom" is made known to staffers.

According to Breed, the policy of a newsroom is implemented through the *slanting* of news—i.e., omission, differential selection, and preferential treatment. For example, an anti-policy story might be slanted by burying it in the back section. Some anti-policy stories will simply not be covered.

The question that Breed pursued was how a new staffer would learn how to conform to policy that is seldom made explicit. He found that the answer lies in (sometimes subtle) interpersonal communication with editors and other staffers. A number of interpersonal mechanisms were identified:

1. The new staffer's copy is edited, giving clues to what is not acceptable.
2. The staffer is obliquely reprimanded.
3. The staffer hears gossip concerning the interests and affiliations of the executives.
4. The staffer observes that certain kinds of stories are assigned to "safe" reporters.
5. The staffer observes that his editor gives no encouragement to certain kinds of stories.

Taking this a step further, we can ask what is the impact of covert policy implemented in this way? It influences what gets covered as "news" and what doesn't. It determines the treatment of news stories—whether they are given front page play or something less. Breed has gone so far as to contend that conformity to newsroom policy results in reinforcement of the status quo by protecting the dominant values and interests of American society.

According to Breed, newsroom policy upholds the status quo by identifying taboo'd areas that are simply not covered. Breed (1958) gave several examples. But more recent examples (than Breed, 1958), have been described by Severin and Tankard (1988). They point out that the paucity of media coverage of the inequities of the draft during the Vietnam War represented a taboo'd topic. They also describe the treatment of two stories on the same day in a major daily newspaper. The first story was played full-page width across the front page, headlined, "Up to 100,000 Soviets Believed Exposed to Radiation Harms." The second story was carried on page 5 with a two-column headline reading, "Nuclear Experts List Similarity of Plants in Chernobyl, U.S."

Interpersonal Antecedents of Mass Communication

Among the receivers of mass communication it is common for interpersonal communication to precede use of the media in ways that shape the functions of media use. A key idea is the social utility of media content—"information" that has anticipated relevance to interpersonal exchanges. Chaffee (1982), for example, has referred to "social predictors" of media use, meaning that the nature of an individual's interpersonal relationships can be used to predict his/her media use.

In other words, information from the media is not just sought for the individual's private use, but also for the purpose of being able to pass it on to others. Content that is worth passing on has social utility. Many people seem to gather information from the media largely for this purpose.

The interpersonal utility of mass communication is nicely illustrated by a study of teen-agers' attention to popular music. Clarke (1973) found that seeking of information about popular music was related to the existence of persons with whom this type of music is discussed. Knowing about popular music performed a number of possible functions within the context of the teenager's interpersonal milieu:

1. It provided a way to gain peer approval.
2. Served as a basis for initiating contact with others—i.e., "small talk."
3. A means of helping others who want/need the information.

One of the most ambitious attempts to predict media use from interpersonal communication is a series of studies of *family communication patterns* (FCP) initiated by McLeod & Chaffee (1970) at Wisconsin. The central proposition behind these studies is that the predominant communication patterns within the family determine what kind of media use has social utility within a youth's primary social milieu—the family.

The basic framework for these studies lies in the definition of a set of distinctive "family communication patterns" (FCPs). The authors defined four basic patterns, deriving them from what they felt to be two important dimensions of interpersonal communication between parent and child. The two dimensions are:

1. CONCEPT ORIENTATION—the family's emphasis on freedom to express one's ideas and beliefs, and to challenge the ideas and beliefs of parents.
2. SOCIAL ORIENTATION—the family's emphasis on harmonious personal relationships with parents—i.e., agreeing and getting along.

According to McLeod and Chaffee one or both of these dimensions may be operative in family communication; therefore, there are four possible family communication patterns:

a. LAISSEZ-FAIRE—neither dimension is emphasized, i.e., neither open discussion of ideas or agreeing with parents is particularly encouraged.
b. PROTECTIVE—social orientation is emphasized but concept orientation is not. Emphasis is on getting along with parents, steering clear of controversy.
c. PLURALISTIC—concept orientation is emphasized over social orientation. Exploring new ideas and exposure to controversy is valued more highly than agreeing with parents.
d. CONSENSUAL—both orientations given about equal emphasis. Children are encouraged to express ideas and beliefs, but also expected to learn from parents and adopt their values.

These four communication patterns have implications for the kind of information that would have social utility within the context of the family. For example, it would seem that the child inside a protective family would have little use for information about controversial ideas or political issues. On the other hand, such information might have a great deal of utility within the context of a pluralistic family. The typology led researchers to look for differences in media use between youths socialized to different kinds of family communication patterns. What differences might be expected, for example, in relative exposure to entertainment and public affairs programming?

The Wisconsin researchers did find differences, adding support to the proposition that interpersonal communication and mass communication are inextricably linked. They found that children from protective families were heavy viewers of television entertainment programming, but light users of public affairs and "hard news" programs. The children of pluralistic families were heavy users of media for public affairs and "hard news."

Research by Lull (1980) has shown some striking relationships between family communication patterns and the ways in which television is employed in family interaction. Lull's research contrasted socio- and concept-oriented families on their social uses of television. He found that socio-oriented family members were heavy television users,

Figure 3.2. Protective FPC. From THE WORLD OF QUINO by Joaquin S. Lavado. Copyright © 1986 by Joaquin S. Lavado. Reprinted by permission of Henry Holt and Company, Inc.

and employed it for a variety of social purposes—e.g., to provide common ground, provide an agenda for talk, reduce conflict in the home, etc. Concept-oriented family members not only watched less—they used television differently, in most cases rejecting the social utility of television in family interaction.

According to Lull, socio-oriented family members treat television as an important part of the family communication process. In contrast, concept-oriented members appear to have extreme disregard of television as a contributor to family interaction. They exercise more control over the medium, interpret programs, and refrain from identifying with violent characters.

The reader will probably notice a tendency to make value judgments based on these kinds of findings. Everyone has ideas about what is the "best" type of family, and what is the "right" way for people to behave. For example, it might appear that the pluralistic pattern is the "best" because they do all the "right" things, such as being more politically active. However, we should be careful not to read too much into such findings. First, it has only been shown that a pluralistic pattern is associated with more rapid *political socialization*. The children of pluralistic families seem to be ready to participate in the political process at an earlier age. But this cannot necessarily be considered the only, or even the most important outcome of socialization within the family. Perhaps the children of protective families develop superior "people skills," such as tact and diplomacy.

It may also be the case that family communication patterns are not as fixed and rigid as the model implies. Family communication patterns may evolve as the child becomes an adolescent with possibly greater influence over the communication behavior of parents. Also, the type of communication pattern employed may depend on the situation. Thus, there is still much to be learned about the dynamics of family communication patterns, which should lead to further discoveries about the relationship between interpersonal communication and media use.

Another recent theory that attempts to systematically relate interpersonal communication to mass communication is the "spiral of silence," a theory that explains public opinion formation as an outcome of communication processes at the interpersonal level (Noelle-Neuman, 1974). According to Noelle-Neumann, a "dominant" public opinion arises as a result of an interaction between individual's perceptions of the majority opinion, and individual willingness to engage in conversations with others holding different views.

What this means is that if an individual scans the social environment (e.g., by referring to mass media reports on an issue) and concludes that the majority opinion is different from his/her own, then that individual will be less likely to express his/her (minority) opinion in social situations involving others (who are assumed to hold the majority view). Noelle-Neumann gives two basic reasons for expecting that those holding minority opinions will remain "silent." One is fear of isolation (since deviant opinions are often ignored). Another is fear of criticism (since deviant opinions are often attacked or criticized by the majority).

One important point of Noelle-Neumann's theory is that it is the opinion *perceived to be in the majority* that will benefit from a "spiral of silence." That is, it is very possible that individual perceptions of the majority opinion will be inaccurate. For example, a very vocal minority that attracts a great deal of media publicity may be able to create the impression that their opinion has more support than it actually has. In that case, individuals who are in the majority, but perceive themselves to be in the minority, will be less likely to speak out. A "spiral of silence" should then result (according to the theory) in which the minority opinion is more freely expressed in interpersonal exchanges and as a result becomes the majority opinion.

Noelle-Neumann illustrates the spiral of silence theory with an example from Tocqueville's "L'Ancien Regime et la Revolution." Tocqueville (1856) described how contempt of religion had become widespread in 18th century France, largely because of the "falling silent" of the French Church. "People still clinging to the old faith were afraid of being the only ones who did so, and as they were more frightened of isolation than of committing an error they joined the masses even though they did not agree with them. In this way, the opinion of only part of the population seemed to be the opinion of all and everybody, and exactly for this reason seemed irresistible to those who were responsible for this deceptive appearance."

This example, when placed in context, does not seem an appropriate exemplar for "spiral of silence." At the time of the French revolution, it must be remembered that political arrests were extremely common, and executions were not uncommon. Given the omnipresence of such threats, people were silent about everything, not just about their religious beliefs.

In the modern context, one of the significant features of the "spiral of silence" model is the role given to the mass media in constantly calling attention to one opinion, and thereby contributing to a spiral of silence in which that opinion becomes dominant. The evidence bearing on this proposition is (so far) not very convincing (Salmon & Kline, 1985). To begin with, this proposition requires that the mass media be homogeneous in their promotion of a single opinion, an assumption that is too simplistic for the diversity of American media.

Salmon & Kline have examined this assumption in reference to data reported by Noelle-Neumann herself (Noelle-Neumann, 1973; table 3). These data show that her (German) respondents were not at all clear which was the majority opinion, although they should have been if the media had been uniform in promoting the majority opinion. For example, 271 respondents who held the majority opinion actually thought they were in the minority, while 198 respondents who held the minority view actually thought they were in the majority. It seems the role of the media in creating a "climate of opinion" is not that important if people are that confused over what the majority opinion actually is.

Let's conclude this section by considering an argument by Thayer (1982) that the interpersonal use of media fare places limits on how the media can define "news." According to Thayer, "the news" has to be what people expect, because anything truly novel has unknown social utility. Thayer's premise is that the primary use of media is to provide something to talk about in ritual, non-vital encounters with other people.

> "The more society is mixed, the more a person needs to know what to expect of the unlike-seeming stranger. You need security for and against his behavior."

Having relevant things to talk about provides the means of such security, according to Thayer. A businessman talking to a local in a Dallas bar will need to know the current ball standings, the current front page news, the names of characters in the currently popular television shows.

The problem with Thayer's concept is that it treats anticipated social utility as a necessity in the definition of news. This would require infallibility on the part of journalists in identifying what will have social utility. It also seems to overlook the purely personal utility of some news—the things that you want to know for your own use, but not share with others. Certainly, the social utility of information is an important dimension in the definition of news. It is not necessary to overstate the case to make this point. Consider the business person who reads USA Today enroute to Dallas: can you see how this would help prepare her for the interpersonal exchanges that await her in Dallas?

Interpersonal Communication after Mass Communication

So far we have seen that interpersonal communication is involved in the production of mass media messages, and that the anticipated interpersonal utility of media content is a major factor in media use. We will now add to this picture by discussing the ways in which interpersonal communication comes after mass communication—the right hand side of the diagram below.

Interpersonal . . . . . Mass Cmu . . . . . Interpersonal

Communication   Communication

Up until about 1955 the diagram above would not have made sense to most communication scholars. Mass media were viewed as singular sources distributing messages to individual receivers. The interpersonal relationships among members of the mass communication audience were seldom considered.

Consideration of the interpersonal exchange of mass communicated messages was finally forced upon researchers in a now classic study of media influence on voting behavior (Lazarsfeld et al., 1948). The study was interpreted as showing the superiority of interpersonal over mass communication as a social influence, apparently because the investigators were expecting far more dramatic evidence of media impact than they found (Chaffee, 1982).

One outgrowth of this discovery is the so-called two-step flow hypothesis of media influence, which simply states that information from mass media reaches many people indirectly through interpersonal networks rather than reaching everyone directly. This implied that the effects of mass communication, or even the simple diffusion of a message, could not be adequately described without reference to interpersonal communication.

Specifically, there are two implications that needed to be considered:

1. Interpersonal communication as extending the reach and influence of mass communication;

2. Interpersonal communication as mediating the influence of mass communication.

Extending Mass Communication

One of the first studies of the spread of a news event—called "diffusion"—noted the rapidity with which news of President Roosevelt's death (in 1945) was spread through interpersonal channels (Miller, 1945). This study suggested a kind of "two-stage" flow in which some people first heard of the event through a mass medium (radio), but the majority learned through interpersonal sources.

However, the two-stage flow idea was not consistently supported by subsequent studies of news diffusion. In some cases interpersonal channels seemed to play an important role, but in other cases played a minor role. For example, diffusion studies conducted of the 1963 President Kennedy assassination found that more people learned of this event through word of mouth than through either radio or television (Hill & Bonjean, 1964). But studies of many other events showed the reverse. Deutschman and Danielson (1960) studied four news events of a less dramatic nature: Sputnik I, Presidents Eisenhower's light stroke, Explorer I satellite, and Alaska statehood. They concluded that the major source for these events were the electronic media with some help from word of mouth. Thus, word of mouth in these cases appeared to play a minor role compared to direct diffusion from the media.

This contradiction in diffusion studies was later partly cleared up by the suggestion that the role of interpersonal communication (word of mouth) depended on the significance of the news event. The greater the event's significance, the more important the role of interpersonal communication. Greenberg (1964) tested this explanation by comparing diffusion of the Kennedy assassination with diffusion of 17 more typical news events. For most of these events mass media were the most important source, but news of the assassination was not the only exception to this rule. Word of mouth was also the major source of diffusing some rather obscure news events that were not of wide interest. Greenberg concluded that word of mouth is a major channel for news diffusion only if the event is of very high or very low news value. For most events, which fall somewhere in between these extremes, news diffuses directly from mass media to the audience.

According to Chaffee, there are many variables which affect whether or not information from the media will be passed on through interpersonal channels, and also affect whether the information will be believed. Unexpected, dramatic, and important information is most likely to be relayed; for example, the deaths and assassinations of leaders. A great deal of media disseminated information is not sufficiently interesting or important to pass on—a major papal encyclical was heard of interpersonally by only two percent (Adams et al., 1969). Sometimes dramatic news is widely relayed, but not immediately believed. When President John F. Kennedy was shot, many first heard of it from another person (rather than the media), but only 24 percent of these believed what they heard (Banta, 1964). In contrast, of those who first heard from television, 44 percent believed Kennedy had been shot.

Mediating Mass Communication

According to Katz & Lazarsfeld's two-step flow hypothesis, information from the media first reaches "opinion leaders" who pass it on to others within their interpersonal network. As we have seen, this is often not the case in news diffusion, but is more often the case with advice about consumer decisions, fashions, relationships, etc. In these cases it would appear that through opinion leaders, specialized information reaches persons who otherwise would not be exposed, and makes them indirectly susceptible to media influence. In fact, it has become a widely accepted idea that secondary dissemination through interpersonal channels is more influential than direct exposure to media.

This interpretation of "interpersonal influence" has recently been questioned (Chaffee, 1982). He points out that in the two-step flow formulation the primary role of interpersonal communication is to pass on information from the mass media—a sort of "relay function." But there may be other reasons for interpersonal exchange of information received from the media. It could be that the media message is only tentatively accepted until its validity and/or applicability can be checked out with a trusted person. In this instance we can see that the influence of the media message is mediated by (i.e., depends upon) an interpersonal exchange. The person who received the message directly is not an "opinion leader," rather a seeker of interpersonal advice.

In a case such as this, you can see that the influence of a media message may depend as much upon the views of others in the interpersonal network as it depends on the views of the original receiver. Furthermore, it may depend as well upon the receiver's position within the interpersonal network.

The mediating impact of interpersonal networks was demonstrated in a well-known study of the diffusion of a new drug among physicians in four Midwest communities (Coleman, Katz and Menzel, 1966). The study found that information about the new drug was first exchanged among doctors who regarded each other as professional peers and, secondly, among doctors who were close friends. Consequently, doctors who were integrated into the interpersonal network (as peers or friends) were generally the first to adopt the drug.

The potential mediating impact of interpersonal communication is certainly something that needs to be considered when trying to predict or explain mass communication effects. For example, the "change agent" who would introduce new ideas into a community must not only choose a medium that will reach the largest number of persons. He must also consider what kind of message will generate the most interpersonal exchange of a favorable nature.

Interpersonal and Mass Communication Parallels

Having considered some of the ways that mass and interpersonal communication are intertwined, it is appropriate to conclude this chapter with some observations of similarities between the two. The gist of this perspective has been aptly stated by Gumpert and Cathcart (1982):

"... all human communication is, in the final analysis, interpersonal." (p. 22)

What these authors meant to suggest is that more complex acts of communications, such as writing a magazine article, are only variations on the basic process of interpersonal communication and not different in kind. Every effort is made to achieve as much similarity as possible to interpersonal communication. Furthermore, interpersonal concepts and models are commonly applied to evaluate the effectiveness of communication through mass media.

One of the most widely utilized models of mass communication (Westley & Maclean, 1957) is basically an extension of Newcomb's (1953) popular model for analyzing interpersonal communication. The Newcomb model introduced the concept of *coorientation*—i.e., the interdependence between two persons and their orientations to some object or event. The Westley-MacLean model describes "coordination" between news sources and receivers that is facilitated by reporters and editors within the mass media.

The concept of coorientation, which originated from study of interpersonal communication, has recently enjoyed wide application to questions about mass communication. The question generally addressed is the effectiveness of mass communication efforts. For example, how does one evaluate the effectiveness of an organization's effort to communicate with a given target audience using the mass media?

The answer to such a question depends upon the kind of standard that is used to judge effectiveness. One common standard is simply the number of persons reached. As you can see, this has little to do with whether the organization has achieved ''coorientation'' with members of the target audience. According to Grunig (1976), the standard that most organizations use is persuasion. They want to know whether their mass communication efforts have resulted in producing desired attitudes and behavior.

But this is not coorientation either. Coorientation embodies the idea that both parties to communication can change and that both parties can contribute something. It implies a two-way process, in contrast with the one-way process implied by persuasion. Grunig challenges organizations to define their mass communication objectives in coorientational terms. This would mean, for example, that the organization has no business expecting others to pay attention to what they say unless they are willing to listen as well. They should not expect members of the public to change their views unless they, too, are open to change. As a standard for effective communication, this is what coorientation entails.

A number of studies have been done applying a ''coorientational'' standard to evaluating the effectiveness of communication efforts through the media. Usually, these studies have defined coorientation in terms of the accuracy with which the parties to communication could estimate one another's views on some problem. For example, one study sought to determine accuracy of communication between local citizens and the Army Corps of Engineers on the problem of local flood control (Stamm & Bowes, 1972). Citizens were asked what they thought the Corps would recognize as advantages and disadvantages of a proposed flood control project (see figure 3.1). This was compared to advantages and disadvantages that had been recognized in the agency's own project documentation. Results of this comparison showed that citizens were only half-accurate in their coorientation with the agency. They were well aware of the advantages (i.e., ''benefits'') the Corps recognized, but had little idea of what the agency would regard as disadvantages, even though citizens themselves saw some serious disadvantages.

This kind of coorientation deficiency is fairly common because organizations typically use mass media to try to promote their own interests—what Grunig calls persuasion. The effort to achieve coorientation is too seldom made. In the case above of the local flood control problem, the Corps did not make enough of an effort to exchange

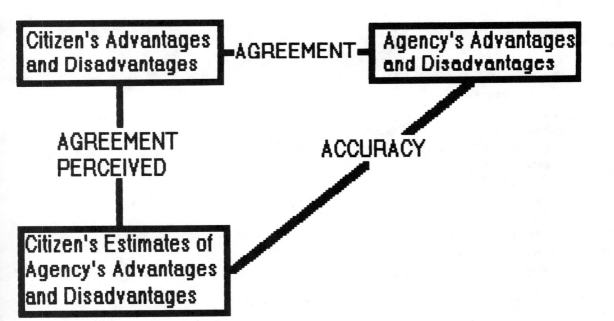

Figure 3.3. Coorientation Model Applies to Local Flood Control Communication Problem.

views on flood control with a cross-section of local citizens. Instead, they worked with a small group of local "leaders" who could be counted on to support the agency's proposals. When it came to communicating with other citizens, the expected benefits were stressed to the exclusion of drawbacks in order to better "sell" a proposed project. This resulted in the poor coorientation that was noted, and ultimately led to rejection of the project by local citizens who feared that significant disadvantages had been overlooked.

The potential value of interpersonal communication criteria in such contexts has been aptly stated by Hawver (1973):

"Many corporations . . . have developed their messages in soundproof towers and shouted them to publics which weren't listening or didn't believe. These publics have in turn been asking the corporations questions, but few have been listening, since most corporate communication machines are designed to transmit but not to receive."

You may be among the corporate executives of the future, and have the opportunity to do things differently. Or, you may become a public information officer, in which case it will be your responsibility to advise corporate executives on the importance of two-way communication.

Key Terms

Concept-orientation
Consensual
Coorientation
Diffusion
Family Communication Pattern (FCP)
Interpersonal projection
Laissez-faire
Opinion leader
Para-social interaction
Pluralistic
Political socialization
Protective
Rumor
Slanting
Social utility
Socio-orientation
Spiral of silence
Two-step flow hypothesis

Summary

Interpersonal and mass communication are closely inter-related, and interpersonal communication is in many ways an essential building block of mass communication.

Most rumors are circulated through interpersonal channels and are initiated by ambiguous and/or threatening situations.

The accuracy of most news stories is strongly conditioned by the quality of interpersonal communication between sources and reporters.

Mass communicators commonly employ communication tactics designed to promote a communication exchange resembling face-to-face interaction (called "para-social interaction").

Creating imaginary receivers gives mass communicators a way of anticipating audience reactions to a message.

Mass communicators often assume (sometimes erroneously) that the views of audience members are similar to their own (called "projection").

A news reporter's job is not only to accurately report what a source wants to say, but to find out what members of an audience want or need to know.

Improvement in interpersonal communication between sources and reporters offers an important key to improvements in understanding between various sources and publics (e.g., if reporters and scientists don't understand one another, it seems unlikely that reporter's stories will promote understanding between scientists and readers).

Newsroom policies are in large part conveyed and implemented through interpersonal channels.

Individual use of mass media can often be explained in terms of the social utility of news in interpersonal exchanges.

Adolescents' use of mass media can be explained (in part) by the communication patterns in their families, since these patterns influence the social utility of information within the family setting.

Family communication patterns play an important role in the development of adolescents' understanding of and participation in the political process (called "political socialization").

Interpersonal communication is thought to play an important role in public opinion formation by determining which opinions are spread and which ones kept quiet ("spiral of silence").

Having relevant things to talk (to "strangers") about may provide an important source of "social security."

Information from mass media sometimes reaches people partly (or largely) through interpersonal exchanges, rather than through direct exposure to the media (called "two-step flow").

The role of interpersonal communication in the diffusion of news often depends on the significance of the news event (i.e., the greater the significance of the event, the more diffusion by word-of-mouth).

The influence of the mass media sometimes depends upon the interpersonal influence of "opinion leaders."

As a standard for effective communication, coorientation requires a two-way process in which sources not only send messages but must also listen (to the audience); they must not only seek to influence others, but be prepared in turn to change their own views.

References

Adams, J. B., Mullen, J. J. and Wilson, H. M. (1969). Diffusion of a minor foreign news event. *Journalism Quarterly*, 46, 545–551.
Allport, G. and L. Postman (1947). The Psychology of Rumor (New York: Holt, Rinehart & Winston).

Banta, T. J. (1964). The Kennedy assassination: early thoughts and emotions. *Public Opinion Quarterly, 28,* 216–224.

Breed, W. (1955). Social control in the newsroom. *Social Forces,* May, 326–335.

_____ (1958). Mass communication and sociocultural integration. In Dexter & White (eds.), People, Society and Mass Communication. New York: Free Press.

Brunvold, J. (1984). The Choking Doberman and Other New Urban Legends (New York: W. W. Norton & Co.).

Chaffee, S. H. (1982). Mass media and interpersonal channels: competitive, convergent or complementary. In Gumpert & Cathcart (eds.), Inter/Media: Interpersonal Communication in a Media World. New York: Oxford U. Press.

Clarke, P. (1973). Teenager's coorientation and information-seeking about pop music. *American Behavioral Scientist, 16,* 551–566.

Coleman, J. S., E. Katz and H. Menzel (1966). Medical Innovation. Indianapolis: Bobbs-Merrill.

Gumpert, G. and Cathcart, R. (1982). Op. cit., Inter/Media.

Grunig, J. E. (1976). Organizations and publics: testing a communication theory. *Journalism Monog.,* March, No. 81.

Hawver, C (1973). President's address. *PR Reporter,* Dec., p. 3.

Horton, D. and Wohl, R. (1956). Mass communication and para-social interaction. *Psychiatry, 19,* 215–222.

Lazarsfeld, P., Berelson, B. and Gaudet, H. (1948). The People's Choice. New York: Columbia U. Press.

Lull, J. (1980). Family communication patterns and the social uses of television. *Communication Research, 7*(3), 319–334.

Levy, M. R. (1977). Experiencing television news. *Journal of Communication, 27,* 112–117.

Martin, R. K., G. O'Keefe, O. Nayman (1972). Opinion agreement and accuracy between editors and their readers. *Journalism Quarterly, 49,* 460–468.

McLeod, J. and Chaffee, S. (1970). Coorientation and the structure of family communication. Presented to International Communication Assoc., Minneapolis, MN.

Newcomb, T. M. (1953). An approach to the study of communicative acts. *Psychological Review, 60,* 393–404.

Noelle-Neumann, E. (1973). Return to the concept of powerful mass media, *Studies of Broadcasting, 9,* 68–105.

Noelle-Neumann, E. (1974). The spiral of silence: a theory of public opinion, *J. of Communication, 24,* 43–51.

Park, R. (1937). The natural history of the newspaper, in Mott & Casey (eds.), Interpretations of Journalism. New York: F. S. Crofts & Co.

Rosnow, R. (1980). Psychology of rumor reconsidered. Psych. Bulletin, 87(3), 575–586.

Salmon, C. & G. Kline (1985). The spiral of silence ten years later: an examination and evaluation, in Sander, Kaid & Nimmo (eds.) *Political Communication Yearbook 1984* (Carbondale: S. Illinois U. Press).

Severin, W. and Tankard, J. (1988). Communication Theories: Origins, Methods, Uses. New York: Longman.

Shibutani, T. (1978). Improvised News: A Sociological Study of Rumor (New York: Bobbs-Merrill Co.).

Stamm, K. M. (1968). Scientist's Views of Popularized Science. Master's thesis. Madison: U. of Wisconsin.

Stamm, K R. and Bowes, J. E. (1972). Communication during an environmental decision. *Journal of Environmental Education, 3,* 49–56.

_____ (1986). Characteristics of loyal and non-loyal television newscast viewers. Presented to Assoc. for Education in Journalism and Mass Communication, San Antonio, TX.

Tankard, J. W. and Ryan, M. (1974). News source perceptions of accuracy of science coverage. *Journalism Quarterly,* 51, 219–225.

Tannenbaum, P. H. (1963). Communication of science information. *Science,* 140, No. 3567, 579–583.

Thayer, L. (1982). On the mass media and mass communication: notes toward a theory. in Gumpert & Cathcart, op. cit.

Tichenor, P. J., Olien, C. N., Harrison, A. and Donohue, G. (1970). Mass communication systems and communication accuracy in science news reporting. *Journalism Quarterly,* 47, 673–683.

Westley, B. H. and MacLean, M. (1957). A conceptual model for communication research. *Journalism Quarterly,* 34, 32–35.

4

Communication and Mass Society

Introduction

This chapter considers the characteristics of mass communication apart from other forms of communication. What roles do its institutions have in modern society? How have social scientists examined them? And are there types of mass communication activity outside of the traditional mass media?

Figure 4.A. From THE WORLD OF QUINO by Joaquin S. Lavado. Copyright © 1986 by Joaquin S. Savado. Reprinted by permission of Henry Holt and company, Inc.

Mass Communication and Characteristics of Mass Media

The traditional mass media—radio, newspapers, television and magazines—have been the focus of most research and critical comment on the role of mass communications in society. Broadcast programs reach millions in a single evening and may become near-universal topics of conversation the next day: the interview with President Nixon a few months following his untimely resignation from office, the annual ritual of the Miss America beauty pageant and more common programs like Monday Night Football which routinely bring 20 percent or more of American households to their televisions. Many urban newspapers have circulations in the hundreds of thousands, while staple magazines such as *Reader's Digest* and *TV Guide* count their subscribers in millions.

Rarely do we consider much the complexity of this activity until we enroll in journalism courses, visit broadcast facilities or attempt such work ourselves. Nor do we often consider the recency of mass media until we examine the history of the past 100 years or so. If you enrolled in a university a century ago, the instruction available to you for mass media work would be very different indeed. Of course, no electronic, broadcast media were available. And the press served largely a literate, middle class. Great numbers, by virtue of distance from cities and a lack of literacy, free time and wealth, were essentially cut-off from the media. Courses in rhetoric and public address constituted the best preparation in mass communication skills available, in addition to basic liberal arts capabilities in written expression and familiarity with the scientific and philosophical conclusions of the day. Eventually, one either wrote for the press or spoke to large groups. Frequently, these were simple skills learned casually by apprenticeship rather than by university-level instruction.

Today it's important to learn of the special characteristics of modern mass communication. Those training for media work must appreciate special media characteristics as should those who want just to understand better the influence media institutions have in everyday life. The complexity mass communication presents to society has caused a large growth of university-level instruction and research over the past 30 years.

What sets mass communication apart from other communication activity? Part of the difference can be seen in the technologies commonly used, the institutions which support them and the skills needed to construct messages for the mass media. So let's first look at the media in contrast to the interpersonal and group communication we've been discussing to this point. (See Table 4.1 at the end of this chapter.)

Mass media depend on technologies. High-speed presses, computerized graphics and layout, satellite transmission of page facsimile and on-location television coverage, photography, broadcast transmission are but a sampling on the technologies used daily. We say, then, technology mediates a human sender and receiver of messages. While this is terribly obvious, think a moment about . . .

. . . the institutions—broadcast networks, news wire services, advertising and public relations agencies, newspaper syndicates, for example—who organize skilled employees to produce and diffuse content

. . . the professional skills involved—journalists, producers, camera operators, editors, technicians, advertising and public relations specialists.

. . . the technologies and related hardware—presses, cameras, computers, satellite transponders.

. . . the software—shows, articles, advertisements, news releases, photos—which are the visible products of the media.

. . . the policies, legal codes and ethical standards which arise to insure that media are used for the general social benefit. Agencies of the U.S. government—the FCC, the NTIA and the Department of Commerce—oversee media policy as does the Congress. Industry organizations, such as the National Association of Broadcasters, the Public Relations Society of America and the American Newspaper Publishers Association each promote ethical codes to govern the actions of their respective media members.

The audiences for the mass media typically are large (from thousands to millions of persons), heterogeneous (that is, comprising many different sorts of people) and anonymous (not individually known well to the media organizations and their personnel). Media thus focus on commonalities among this mass:

- *Common Venue:* Newspapers and radio are said to be local media in the U.S., focusing on immediate communities or regions.

- *Common Interests and Actions:* Magazines, radio and cable television channels seek out comparatively narrow interest groups: hobbyist magazines for those who raise cats or buy compact audio disks (CDs); radio stations each providing a slightly different character of popular music (heavy metal rock, rhythm & blues, old favorites, country & western, etc.); cable television programs appealing to medical doctors (Lifeline Network), news addicts (Cable News Network), sports (ESPN), old movies (The Movie Channel).

The transfer of information to an audience in mass communication is efficient due to the large numbers reached at once. Interpersonal communication is limited to the size of theaters and the carrying power of human voice. But the audience met face-to-face is typically homogeneous (similar in some major respect—members of a particular neighborhood, interest group or club, for example). In this situation, a message may be more carefully crafted to reflect specialized interests. More can be usually be assumed in terms of what the group will understand and appreciate by way of examples or appeals to various values and beliefs.

Perhaps one of the most frustrating characteristics of mass media is the comparative lack of feedback received. The communicator in a face-to-face setting can tell almost instantly from facial expressions, questions (or their lack), and other responses if he/she can be understood and whether the message provokes interest and appreciation. Media depend on a host of limited mechanisms for feedback: letters to editors, broadcast ratings, readership studies, circulation and subscription statistics and the findings of special audience surveys, to name but a sampling. These are often expensive and inexact techniques. Letters to editors usually come from those with extreme positions on issues, broadcast ratings typically assess household set tuning, not the attention and appreciation of individuals, and circulation data may indicate dissatisfactions, but little intelligence about just what displeases the audience. None of these techniques are really very good at suggesting what new programs or subjects might be exploited. Most of them delay feedback, needing weeks of analysis before sense can be made of the date and corrections instigated.

One of the most obvious characteristics is that media technology limit the senses which are affected by a message. Few mass media besides comical attempts at "odor-vision" and "shake-o-rama" as failed movie theater inducements, can do much with touch and smell. Radio obviously is blind and television until recently offered only a monaural, low fidelity sound track. Recent improvements in broadcast television such as stereo sound and higher quality notably enhance realism, but even the most advanced theater cinema equipment pales in sensory terms to actual presence at an event.

An important point to consider is the realism with which we endow the partial sensory experience gleaned from the media. Well-produced radio programs such as Orson Welles' 1938 classic *War of the Worlds* caused some upset and panic among suggestive listeners who thought this Halloween Eve broadcast was a true news report of extra-terrestrial invasion. Viewers of television news give this experience a higher realism and credibility than the same events reported in print. Obviously, they can "see" the event as would an observer. But often the at-home viewer fails to account for the highly edited and restricted view of "real" events television news portrays. On one hand this is a tribute to production skills which minimize the problems of portraying events over mass media, on the other, it can be dangerous to assume that one has a full picture of an event from the partial view permitted through television and other media.

Media, with mass audiences, have to craft messages aimed at broad segments of the population. Critics of media complain of programming keyed to the "lowest common denominator" and the greatest mass appeal which deny minority interests in the stampede for audience numbers. Face-to-face communication, contrary, allows specialized communication to the comparatively small audiences. But as new media forms proliferate, this old distinction is not as clear as it once was. Desktop publishing, permitting sophisticated printing on low budgets, now put high quality newsletters and brochures within reach of very small interest groups. Electronic, on-line publishing, such as videotex and other text-on-computer screen systems, allow individually crafted news summaries and information retrieval. Cable television now allows broadcasters to focus economically on interest groups narrower than what traditional over-the-air network broadcasting could sustain with specialized channels for medical help, sports, world news, the arts and so on.

Mediated communication is expensive. Complex economics of advertising (over-the-air commercial broadcast, press), user fees (print subscriptions, cable TV fees) and government/citizen subsidy (public radio and television in the U.S., national public broadcast systems in other nations) sustain our mass media. Interpersonal communication can be low-to-no cost. Though as the cost of business meetings and conventions escalate, the business community is seeking out technologies such as teleconferencing to save money. The expense and scarcity of experts in developing nations, agricultural scientists, for example, are difficult to use efficiently in solely face-to-face encounters. Countries like India have resorted to radio and television satellite relays to "spread" these rare experts across the vast distances and population of their lands. Media, thus, can mean a cost savings on a per person reached basis. In many instances, mass media are the only cost-effective means of reaching large audiences.

Finally, media must be "programmed"—that is special skills are needed to create messages with make best use of a medium's capabilities. To be sure, face-to-face communication requires considerable skill if it is to be effective. But part of most individual's learning is routinely directed to interpersonal communication skills. A minimum is necessary for simple survival with peers and family.

Skills with mass media require specialized training and perhaps an artistic bent which no amount of formal training can instill. Think for a moment of the skill and gamesmanship which go into scheduling shows on television, the use of graphics and design in printed publications, the design of sets and lighting in television and, of course, scripting or writing actual content. Much of university work in mass communication is spent learning the basics of such skills.

The Rise of Mass Media and Some Basic Influences on Society

We will investigate at many points in this book the obvious (and not so obvious) influences of the media in everyday life. But, to begin with, it's very important to consider how media have both become a response to needs of modern society and, at the same time, have created it in important ways.

One of the most broadly influential statements of this influence are the ideas of Harold Innis, a Canadian historian and economist who spent the latter years of his scholarly life considering all forms of human communication from a base in economic history. Innis argued that communication and communication technologies are central to social change; indeed, that the evolution of Western civilization over the centuries was guided by the dominant media of communication. How so? Innis (1951) argued that any given medium is *biased* in terms of time and space. Paper (e.g. letters and decrees) is light and easily transported and thus helped extend administration over great distances. They are *space-binding,* holding in a network of control, so to speak, vast areas. Media which were difficult to transport were typically more durable and would last over great periods of time—clay or stone tablets, for example. These were *time-binding.* They didn't work well for the day-to-day administration needs of bureaucracy (they were heavy and hard to inscribe), but could safeguard history and religion over the years due to their permanence.

In traditional societies, speech is the dominant form of communication. Innis argued that the impermanence of speech—its transitory nature—fostered traditions in a society which through ritual and story-telling could preserve the past. Much of the energy of such societies in spent in preservation and thus are biased towards time, or are time-binding. Religion, based in these traditions, would thus hold great authority, a power vested in great part by the dominant medium of oral communication.

Writing, by contrast, lead to different societies. They were usually space-binding, favoring the growth of secular authority and institutions. They were future-oriented towards technology and expansion. The written media allowed the extension of power over great distances (sending of messages from the central government to the provinces) and the revision of practices to fit changes in technologies (issuing a new set of written instructions). The authority became central, secular, and based in the present and its plans for expansion.

Innis believed the written culture was inherently unstable, lacking as it did a foundation in tradition. What worked best was balance—the time-binding of religion and its oral traditions and the space-binding of the secular state with its control extended by written message. Printing, of course, greatly strengthened the written culture, altering religion and other folkloric institutions to the needs of the economy and state. Religion has declined as politics and its implementing technologies have risen.

It is perhaps not so important that we accept the conclusions of Innis' arguments (he worries considerably about the nihilistic tendencies in modern, Westernized society and oral traditions on the brink of extinction). Rather, we should appreciate the combination of subtlety and power which communication and dominant media have in shaping the organization of society, a stand argued for so well by Innis.

Since Innis, others have argued historically about the society-shaping influences of information, whether from mass media or not. Landes, in his book *Revolution in Time* (1983), speaks to the development of time-keeping across the centuries. From monastic bells to present-day atomic clocks, the need to synchronize the events and interplay of skills in a progressively modernizing and interdependent society is a recurrent theme. In medieval times, markets were possible in part because timepieces allowed merchants to convene in a common venue to trade. Later, improved timekeeping technology allowed complex navigation and better armament. Good clocks became essential to accounting (tabulating hours worked), military maneuvers (synchronizing troop movement) and computers (sequencing computational tasks).

Beniger (1986), in his discussion of the *control revolution* speaks to a broad range of information technologies, including traditional mass media, which drastically altered societies of the Western world during the 19th century. The industrial revolution brought many changes through steam power and, later, electricity and oil, which gave a much higher rate of productivity from each worker. Human energy was magnified by machines.

The organization of work also changed. The stop-start pace of craft work was replaced by the continuous flow of raw materials through assembly-line manufacture into products, and, in turn, the complex distribution of manufactured products through retail outlets. This system, involving many people and organizations, had to be coordinated by communication activity. All involved in the creation and consumption of products needed information to function properly. Suppliers of raw materials needed information from factories on their requirements, while manufacturers increasingly needed to predict marketplace demand for their goods. Information tools and skills ranging across market research, production control, management information systems, complex accounting and telecommunications grew to meet the needs of management. The consumer, too, because part of this system. Advertising regulated demand along with pricing policies. Factories and retailers could not turn casually to other pursuits such as farming to fill pauses in consumer demand or the supply of raw materials or parts. Commercial mass media along with telecommunications thus became part of a complex communication network which arose to meet the management needs of the industrial revolution.

Others, such as the early 20th century sociologist Robert Park (1923), have suggested that newspapers allowEd a semblance of village life to be recreated in the anonymity of the modern city. The immigrant press at the turn of the century gave newcomers to the U.S. a sense of linkage with their past, yet assisted them to find their place in the rapidly expanding cities of industrial America. Note how many of us see news and entertainment personalities on TV or in the press almost as close acquaintances. These people are used to being greeted on the street by their first name from individuals they have never met before in person. Specialized broadcast services have taken the place (though not completely) of the emigre press of a century ago. Cable television and FM radio provide programming to a variety of ethnic and national groups—Hispanics, Japanese, Koreans, Blacks and so on.

The press as a forum of national and community debate is a recurrent theme in journalism research. Baldasty (1989), for example, examined the changes in the American press over the 19th cenury. For the first half of this period, the press served the needs of political parties that provided their base of financial support. Small towns might support several newspapers, each of which took a particular ideological slant on issues. As the close of the century approached, advertising became the support mechanism for newspapers, freeing them from the need to ideologically cater to political parties. The imperative for objective reporting of "facts" became a cliche of proper journalism. But reliance on advertising brought another ideology into editorial content: the views of business and the service of large commercial advertisers. While the press often operated with the interests of the community in mind, these could be easily confused with the needs of the business community of which the newspapers were part. The political ideology of the early 19th century was largely replaced by a commercial creed by the century's end.

In more recent times, Stamm (1985) has examined the modern community press for its ability to create a sense of community belonging to mobile Americans—those who have recently moved into a community. Problems of severing old ties, of finding needed services and institutions, of understanding and participating in local issues and events could be assisted by the community press for these individuals.

While some evidence shows that the local press does contribute to identification with and positive beliefs about the local community, it appears that the reverse is also true. Ties to the local community also contribute to interest in and readership of local news. For example, studies show that those who are the most "settled" (i.e., have lived in the community longest and expect to stay) are the most likely to be the subscribers and readers of local newspapers. Thus it seems the community media are appreciated more by those settled into local life rather than those newly arrived. But this view may be overly simple. It also appears that "settlers" (i.e., those recently arrived, but planning to stay) are the most actively engaging in *becoming* new subscribers and readers. The media often work in subtle ways, in one instance promoting our integration, in the next, simply reinforcing our belonging acquired through a variety of other means (co-workers, merchants, neighbors, schools, for example).

Others, such as Philip Tichenor (1973), have studied the community media as a forum for local issues. The press often serves to reinforce the *status quo* of the community. It can be a difficult forum to enter for those who would upset and challenge community complacency. Perhaps aiding this "stand pat" attitude of many community media is a strong interest by much of the audience for "soft" news which tells of personalities, home repair hints, comics and psychological advice in solving common emotional problems. All too often, "hard" stories run contrary to commercial interests and those of community leaders. Hard news can upset readers who, if readership studies are to be believed, yearn for "good news" stories. The play-off of "hard" verses "soft" news is increasingly critical as broadcast network and especially print media deal with slow audience growth. Both seek a pleasing formula in their news product to attract a large audience.

As some development researchers suggest, community-building through the media may really work mainly for those in developing societies. A recurrent phenomenon in development is the growth of cities, through farmers and peasants leaving their subsistence rural life and migrating to urban areas. Daniel Lerner (1967) argued that for economic development to accelerate or "take off," a sequence of changes must take place. Urbanization had to be present at modest levels, as did literacy. With this base, mass media would help foster a continuing cycle of urban migration and industrialization. Those remaining in country villages would increasingly be told of the advantages of the city and of an alternative, more materially advanced life. What got presented was too often an urban view of luxury, success and attainable consumerism. What resulted, sadly, was frequently uncontrolled migration to urban slums by people poorly skilled to survive and unable to afford the glittering products the media advertised. Few will dispute the importance of the mass media in the fabric of urban life. Many, however, will debate its claim on scarce resources in developing societies against providing other needs such as housing, health care and education.

News Transmission in Society

The apparent realism of news conveyed by mass media—particularly television—is belied by the numerous steps a given story must survive as it makes its way from the events themselves to the attention of a media audience. "Gatekeeping" is a term signaling the selection of stories to report—of excluding input to fit time or space available for transmission. The volume of "news" available is immense. Assignment editors hardly ever have enough reporting and editing staff to cover the wealth of possible stories. More rare yet, is to have enough skilled reporters to cover long term issues or do investigate reporting of quiet corruption. Even when focused on major daily events— fires, earthquakes and murders—there is too much going on for truly complete coverage.

How much is filtered out in the news transmission process? A study by Cutlip (1954) examined stories taken from the Associated Press trunk wire and subsequently reported to readers in Madison, Wisconsin. With a start of over 100,000 words reported by affiliates into the AP, only 2000 made it to the attention of Madison readers (see Figure 4.1). How much was remembered by the readers after, say, a day, would likely be just a few key facts from the most important stories. Film or videotape editors discard hours of material to get just a few minutes for showing on the air. Cut ratios which allow a tenth or less of material originally filmed on the air are not uncommon. Think how long it actually takes to resolve a major city council issue or control a major fire. Then time how much of this activity makes it on the air. Few stories with film or videotape occupy more than two minutes of precious air time. So it isn't just the severe selection of stories to report, but also just how much of a given story gets portrayed which concerns researchers of gatekeeping.

Central to gatekeeping study are the reasons why certain stories are passed on to the audience and others are discarded or given limited treatment. A number of reasons have been given beyond the sufficiency of reporting staff:

Place Into AP	Words 125,000	Excluded 0%
To Trunk Wires	57,000	50%
State Wire	13,352	89%
Daily News-paper	9,000	92%
To Readers	2,000	98%
Retained by Readership	?	?

Figure 4.1. Gatekeeping on the AP Trunk Wire (after Cutlip, 1954).

a. Editors appraisals of community preferences and taboos. Pre-1960s papers in much of the Old South ignored news from the black community. In Washington state, a small town editor-publisher scandalized the region by printing the names of local rape victims from court records. The suburban press often has been criticized for its avoidance of "hard," unpopular issues and its concentration on social news.

How good are editors at appraising community tastes? It varies, of course. But studies done with editors have shown a preference for "important" political, economic and crime stories while the audience, when asked, wanted more coverage of local, neighborhood events, social news, features (sports, emotional advice) and consumer tips. Readership studies, carried out by research groups or universities, have provided much new direction for the news media. This "marketing" approach to journalism, according to Doug Underwood (1987), is increasingly the norm as circulation growth becomes fiercely competitive. The issue, of course, in this change is the subordination of an editor's judgment as to what the community needs to what the community apparently wants.

Even when it's decided to cover a story, other preconceptions come into play. What does the public "expect" to see or read about a political contest, a traffic accident, a courtroom drama or a parade? One landmark study by Kurt and Gladys Lang (1960) examined the television portrayal of a major parade in contrast to how the parade was seen by first-hand observers. Those watching the parade on television exaggerated the size of crowds (cameras were positioned where crowds were most expected; telephoto lenses "squeezed" the scene, making it appear more crowded), the noise level (selective microphone placement and mixing allowed some control over apparently "spontaneous" applause), and adulation of the parade's focus, General MacArthur (cameras selected out smiling faces, people waving).

These distortions are often defended as necessary to make a story appealing, interesting. Beginning journalists are taught to write engaging "lead" sentences to their practice stories. The "lead" conveys not only basic information to a reader who may only scan a few lines of each story, but also tries to spur interest, encouraging the reader to continue on. Broadcast TV news tries for visually exciting stories for the same reasons of attracting audience interest. But these needs may distort (or ignore) what is of central importance, or change emphasis considerably. Take news of state legislatures as an example. Editors know that most citizens are concerned about their taxes, but few are directly impacted by, say, deterioration in state care for the aged. What is reported, given this preference, usually are the taxation consequences of improving state services, not the needs of the elderly. Reporting of mental health matters often emphasizes spectacular, sordid events—ritual murders, torture. Consider the reporting of a few years ago of the Jonestown massacre, Ted Bundy or the "Son of Sam" killer. The adequacy and funding of mental health care was not a large part of these stories.

b. *Editors' biases, sources and social networks.* Warren Breed (1955) in a classic study examined social control in the newsroom. What he was observing was the social pressure of editors and the reward system that operated. Reporters gradually came to learn the preferences of editors (often, in turn, reflecting those of owners or publishers) in order to get their stories published with minimal editorial changes. Promotions, and the psychological rewards of being "one of the team" also are potent forces shaping a reporter's individual judgment to the norms of the organization.

News reporters also often work specialized assignments or *beats*. In short, they may spend more time in company of their sources of information—police, county officials, state government—than with their co-workers. After time, friendships can form (indeed they may be essential to getting inside information or leads to emerging stories) compromising one's independence from news sources. On one hand, it can be hard to criticize friends, question their judgment or challenge their honesty. On the other, to not form friendships can cost valuable advice, background stories and access to difficult-to-contact sources. Reporting effectively, honestly can be a difficult balancing of professional responsibilities and emotions.

c. *Production conditions:* Mass media are encumbered by their technologies. Script or copy must be written, film or tape must be edited, remote broadcasting equipment must be set-up in the field, and sources contacted and interviewed. All this takes time. An orchestrated mayhem often is apparent in broadcast newsrooms as air time approaches and as news personnel shift from gathering news to the actual job of reporting it on air.

Similarly, newspapers must do final editing, typesetting, page layout and plate-making in order to ready the presses. Delivery vans and other circulation jobs must move swiftly to distribute the printed product to the consumer. All of this takes time. As deadline times approach, the late-breaking story must be of great importance to pull attention from production tasks and the full docket of stories already locked in place. Earlier in the day, there is some concern with filling available air time or newspaper space (the "newhole") with stories of interest. The criteria of importance is more relaxed, some stories being chosen as "throw-away" items to make space or room for important material possibly arising near the deadline time. Fortunately, computerization of much of the newspaper production process and broadcast editorial/videotape work has enabled somewhat the late breaking story to make it into print or on the air.

The judgment of gatekeepers, typically, is a mix of reasons as suggested above. Determining where they arise and for what reasons can be a difficult sort of research to do. People, even editors, can be blind to their prejudices and work constraints. Researchers have to follow information through news organizations and do patient interviewing often to find subtle selection criteria for stories. A study by Giffard (1989) centered on the debate over the withdrawal of U.S. funding for UNESCO. By careful computer matching of key sentences contained in stories printed in major U.S. newspapers against U.S. State Department press releases, UNESCO releases and "canned" editorials sent to newspapers by conservative organizations, the overwhelming method of reporting this key event was simply to take State Department press releases and typeset them word-for-word. Smaller newspapers often ran canned editorials from conservative groups under the editor's name. The primary editing done was simply to cut the length of the story (working from the last paragraphs forward) to fit the space available to print.

Why did this happen? Much of the reason, of course, may have been time and work pressures. The convenient press release or newswire copy required little time to prepare for the presses. But press releases and interviews

94

giving UNESCO's views were also available. There was a strong trust of official government sources of information and of newswire copy, reinforced, perhaps, by a sameness of outlook toward UNESCO. Balanced reporting lost out. Few UNESCO press releases made it unscathed (or at all) into the media, depriving the public of a critical point-of-view in this debate.

Social Functions Served by Mass Media

We've suggested recurrently in this chapter the importance of mass media in society. Its functions as described years ago by Lasswell (1948) are pervasive and powerful:

a. *Surveillance of the Environment:* The mass media extend one's senses in time and space. We are informed of news events in other regions and countries where direct experience is impossible. Broadcast media particularly leave us with the illusion of direct participation in remote events, but really give us a highly compressed and synthetic picture. We often rely on a journalistically defined world for our impressions. Perhaps this partly explains the enthusiasm Americans can feel for Soviet citizens on tourist visits when it's discovered that cold war tensions of the news world don't prevail that often between individuals on a face-to-face basis. Yet, in spite of the misimpressions that can happen, the media can capably warn us about problems or direct our attention usefully to things we cannot experience in person.

b. *Interpretation of the Environment:* We've just alluded to this point in part. The media define what is news, what we should pay attention to. Obviously, no two individuals will agree completely on what this should be. A common complaint, however, is that the news media are too event-oriented; they play-up the surprising, sudden and showy events, underplaying less exciting, time-consuming issues such as the economy or white collar corruption in the business world. Some broadcasters, aware of the short time they give to stories, have lengthened their news periods to allow some depth to key stories. "Pseudo events" or "manufactured" news creeps into editorial coverage heralding such doubtful events as beer drinking contests, the "world's largest" pizza and billboards containing radio disk jockeys who have elected to live there a month on behalf of charity.

c. *Correlation of Events:* The news media, when they perform at their best, are able to link seemingly separate events into general patterns which may signal wholesale corruption of police or complex shifts in the economy. In short, they can tie events and link information together, making valuable interpretations based on what they have discovered. The Nixon Watergate exposé was based on interconnecting many seemingly unrelated events—a minor burglary, Mexican bank transactions, and comments on secret White House tape recordings.

d. *Transmission of Culture:* Our cultural heritage as conveyed by the mass media has interesting implications. Think if in two or three millennia archaeologists happened upon a vault of prime-time television programs from the present. They would: see depicted the resolution of impossible human problems in just 53 minutes (a commercial TV hour, less commercials); see solutions which were often violent or involved motor cars recklessly driven; see a world largely of police, quarreling lawyers and the emotionally extreme (soap operas); assume the world was dominated by a place called Los Angeles: and conclude that we were a society dominated by things rather than ideas. Yet part of our modern culture is what the media reflect (however distorted) back to us. Themes are emphasized that play on media conveyed standards of right and wrong, the work ethic, fair government and parental responsibility among many others.

The media also give us a view of ethnic traditions and nationalities which make-up a society. For many years in the U.S., blacks, women and others were often portrayed in demeaning, stereotyped roles. For example, blacks frequently played maids, unskilled workers, entertainers or sports stars. Women were all too often portrayed as servile and dependent on men or used as sex objects. Both groups often found themselves in the support roles of dramatic programs or the crowd shots of commercials.

Finally, media give us a view of where our culture has been and how we have changed. Recall times when old, long-gone TV programs were rerun, or old advertisements were reprinted. Clothing, cars, fashion, popular music and so on seemed at once distinctly familiar and terribly out-of-place with present life. This feeling suggests the power of media to span time and give us a view of how we once were. Does our media view of history disclose the failures of our culture as vigorously as the triumphs? Probably not. Most societies probably resist having the dark side of their past revisited. The unjustified WWII internment of Japanese-Americans wasn't widely or accurately depicted on U.S. TV until the 1970s, nor were the century-old civil rights problems of blacks carefully examined until the 1960s. But the film and tapes of those times, in part because of their distortions and omissions, form an invaluable record of where we have been as a culture.

The Mass Media and Mass Communication

At the beginning of this chapter, we emphasized the dominance of traditional mass media in research and criticism of society's efforts at mass communication. In recent years, this equating of mass media with mass communication has proven troublesome as the variety of media forms merge and multiply with changes in technology and social need. Take for example *videotex*, a system of distributing personalized information from central computer data bases to subscribers through telephone lines or cable television. The media product is unique for each individual. The consumer interacts with the computer similarly to asking questions of a librarian.

Small audio cassettes, the sort used for dictation and personal listening of music, were one of the essential media in instigating popular support of the 1979 Iranian revolution. The spiritual leader of the revolt, the Ayatollah Khoumani, then exile in Paris, communicated to millions in far-away Iran by cassette. Motorcyclists passed along the small tapes among mosques, bazaars and homes where the grassroots of the revolution met (Katirayi, 1987). New tapes were frequently smuggled into the country, swiftly duplicated and them distributed.

Rural China has used "media forums" to spread limited issues of newspapers and radio receivers amongst an immense population. Forum leaders (called cadres) interpreted the media, translating it into local dialects, answering questions and giving local examples to supplement stories. Folklore groups toured remote villages, giving plays on simple health practices interspersed with entertainment. In short, the dividing line between the mass media and individual media increasingly is blurred. New media, *personal or "small" media* are gradually making their way into use.

Mass communication thus should be viewed more as an institution than as simply particular technologies. Society needs information to exist as an organized community. Collective behavior—organizing, forming of institutions, providing services, merging specialized skills—is probably central to a good definition. This activity may be informal as with the Iranian revolution, crudely skilled as with the Chinese rural media forums or a personal, high-tech dialogue as with computer-based videotex.

Key Terms

assignment editor
collective behavior
community press (also, community media)
control revolution
correlation
cultural transmission
face-to-face (also, word-of-mouth)

feedback
gatekeeping
hard news
industrial revolution
lead sentence
mediated
newshole
personal media (also, "small" media)
programmed
Robert Park
rural media forums
sensory modes
slant
soft news
space-binding
surveillance
take-off
time-binding
UNESCO
videotex

Summary

Basic characteristics distinguished mass from interpersonal communication. Media are *mediated* by technology: presses, transmitters, telephone exchanges, for example. This characteristic impacts other differences such as audience size, speed, sensory modes available and so on.

Media require complex skills, producers, directors, writers, artists, performers and so on. They must be programmed. Policies must be developed to govern media. And money must be raised (or charged) to meet high costs of operation.

Audiences also differ between mass and interpersonal communication: size, homogeneity, distance, anonymity and opportunity for feedback.

Media have exerted basic influences on society. Innis, for example, contrasted space-binding and time-binding media. Modern societies, he felt, increasingly favor space-binding which allow communication easily over great distances but at the expense of durability with time. Much of traditional culture is, he feared, being lost to media which deteriorate easily or can't preserve messages.

Beniger's discussion of a 19th century "control revolution" speaks to the need of industrializing societies to control and synchronize a complex flow of activity from the extraction of raw materials through manufacturing, distribution and consumption. Advertising, for example, helps control consumption. Telecommunications regulate the flow of materials and goods among all these activities.

Robert Park and others saw the press as a key to creating organization and a sense of participation in large cities, especially in such highly mobile societies as the U.S. Others, such as Baldasty, Tichenor and Stamm examined the evolution of an early 19th century partisan political press to a 20th century advertising-supported business. Rather than agents of political activism and change, the press increasingly, it could be argued, became a reinforcer of the *status quo*.

Gatekeeping research examines how stories are selected for coverage by the media. Selection can occur for many reasons, including staff size, editors' preferences and appraisal of community needs, the biases and prejudices of editors, space or time available, time of day and so on.

Social functions of the media, as described by Lasswell, include surveillance, interpretation, correlation and cultural transmission.

Mass media does not fully encompass all that is implied in the term ''mass communication''. Small or personal media can survive without large organizations or complex technologies. Some newer media forms are less like traditional broadcast or print media and more like a dialogue with another person. Computer based information systems such as videotex, arguably, are like this. In China and other third world countries, simple organizational techniques have been used to spread and enhance the influence of mass media. Radio forums are one such example.

References

Baldasty, G. J. (1989). The Transformation of the American Press in the Nineteenth Century. (In press)

Beniger, J. R. (1986). The Control Revolution. Cambridge: Harvard University Press.

Breed, W. (1955). Social control in the newsroom. *Social Forces,* 33, 326–335.

Cutlip, S. (1954). Control and flow of news—From trunk to TTS to reader. *Journalism Quarterly,* 31–31, 434–436.

Giffard, C. A. (1989). Unesco and the Media. New York: Longman.

Innis, H. (1951). The Bias of Communication. Toronto: U. of Toronto Press.

Katirayi, B. (1987). Oral public communication in the Iranian immigrant community: Toward reconceptualization of mass communication. Ph.D. dissertation, University of Washington.

Landes, R. (1983). Revolution in Time: Clocks and the Making of the Modern World. Cambridge: Belknap Press.

Lang, K. and G. Lang (1960). The unique perspective of television and its effect: A pilot study. In W. Schramm (Ed.) Mass Communication. Urbana: U. of Illinois Press.

Lasswell, H.D. (1948). The structure and function of communication in society. In L. Bryson (Ed.) The Communication of Ideas. New York: Institute for Religious and Social Studies.

Lerner, D. and W. Schramm (1967). Communication and Change in Developing Countries. Honolulu: East-West Center Press.

Park, R. (1923). The natural history of the newspaper. *American Journal of Sociology,* 29, 273–289. See also, R. Park (1925). Immigrant community and immigrant press. *American Review,* 3, 143–152.

Stamm, K. (1985). Newspaper Use and Community Ties: Toward a Dynamic Theory. Norwood, N.J.: Ablex.

Tichenor, P., J. Rodenkirchen, C. Olien and G. Donohue (1973). Community issues, conflict and public affairs knowledge. In P. Clarke (Ed.) New Models for Communication Research. Beverly Hills: Sage.

Underwood, D. (1987). When MBAs rule the newsroom. *Columbia Journalism Review,* March/April, 23–30.

5 Mass Communication Effects

Introduction

Probably no truism is so firmly entrenched in the communication research literature as the proposition that the effects of mass communication are limited and minimal. We shall have occasion in this chapter to challenge the notion of minimal effects, but more importantly you will see where the idea came from, and why current thinking about mass communication effects is shifting away from the minimal effects position.

But before we can firmly grasp any proposition about the effects of mass communication we must have some idea of what is meant by "effects." When people talk about mass communication effects they have many different things in mind ranging from awareness of some new product to the decision to vote for a particular candidate. If we are going to be able to say anything at all about communication effects it will be necessary to first say which particular effect we mean.

The enormous variety of (possible) mass communication effects can be divided up a number of ways. For the sake of simplicity, we will use only two basic divisions. First, we will distinguish *primary effects* from *secondary effects of communication.* Second, we will divide secondary effects into *cognitive changes* and *behavior changes.*

Primary Effects	*Secondary Effects*
Exposure	Cognitive changes
Attention	• knowledge
Comprehension	• attitudes
	Behavior changes
	• buying
	• voting

Primary Effects

The primary effect to be expected from any effort to communicate should be some evidence that communication has occurred. However, we have become so accustomed to the idea of using communication to achieve other ends that we often forget that communication in and of itself is a worthwhile end. In our view it is primary. If we are to accomplish anything else as a result of communicating, it is generally necessary to first succeed at communicating (Figure 5.1). We do not take for granted, as many do, that communication occurs (automatically) from each and every attempt.

We could apply this basic distinction to a familiar kind of interpersonal communication effort. You call up a friend to ask her if she would play tennis with you on Friday. The first "effect" you must achieve is to get her to answer the phone. Next, you must be sure that she can hear you clearly. Then, you must present your request in a way that she can understand. And, finally, you want her to say, "Yes, I'd like to play." The first three results are primary effects. The last is a secondary effect of communication—i.e., even if you communicate effectively she may still say, "no, I have to work Saturday."

This example brings up an important reason for separating primary effects from secondary effects of communication. We seldom have much control over secondary effects of communication; we might think that we do, but in fact the receiver is in the driver's seat. There is a simple reason for this: secondary effects involve the receiver's behavior, which is under his/her direct control. It does not make much sense therefore to judge communication efforts as "failures" when they do not result in desired behavior on the part of the receiver. Getting through, being heard, and being understood can be judged as "effective communication" in its own right.

Exposure and Attention

If we were to translate these communication effects into a mass communication context, close parallels could be identified (Figure 5.2).

It is safe to say that the three communication effects listed in Figure 5.2 form the primary basis on which the mass communication industries evaluate their own performance. The use of exposure is evident in the concern of print media with "circulation," and "readership," and in the concern of broadcast media with "audience shares." These are all ways of saying "we're getting through." "We're reaching an audience of this many people." Usually, such exposure figures are also broken down into *audience segments* in order to keep track of the numbers of each kind of reader, listener, or viewer.

Figure 5.1. Primary Effects Come First. From THE WORLD OF QUINO by Joaquin S. Lavado. Copyright © 1986 by Joaquin S. Lavado. Reprinted by permission of Henry Holt and Company, Inc.

Interpersonal	Mass Communicaton
getting through	exposure
being heard	gaining, holding attention
being understood	comprehension

Figure 5.2. Some Communication Effects—
Interpersonal and Mass Communication
Parallels.

It is more difficult, and more expensive, to observe attention to a message. In interpersonal communication, we tend to monitor attention continuously (i.e., those of us who care whether the other person is listening). But how do you monitor the attention of thousands, or even millions, of receivers? This is not the kind of thing that media are able to do routinely. (Please note: as communication technology advances, it may become routine.) But they do make special efforts, at great expense, to collect such information.

A well-known example of monitoring (for exposure and attention) is the "Nielson ratings" used by the television industry. At the present time, Nielsen ratings are based on two observations: (1) an electronic device connected to the television set can determine when the set is turned on and what channel it is tuned to at any given time; (2) a viewing log kept by the household provides a record of who was watching during each time block the set was on. The log is sometimes treated as if it were a record of attention to individual programs. However, to do so requires that you assume that all those listed in the log were watching continuously during the time block.

Because this is widely recognized as a dubious assumption, Nielsen and others are experimenting with hand-held electronic devices that allow the viewer to record responses to a program while it is being broadcast. The use of such a device makes it feasible to obtain a description of the viewer's attending behavior for any given program, provided the viewer is willing to cooperate. So far, however, the use of these devices has been limited by the industry's narrow conception of what constitutes viewing behavior. Their monitoring efforts have been focused almost entirely on "like/dislike" responses to programs and ads—the proverbial tip of the iceberg.

Communication researchers have adopted more sophisticated measures of attention. One of these is electrical monitoring of brain waves (called EEG). Brain wave measures rely on the fact that alpha waves *drop* during brief periods of focused attention; thus peaks of attention will show up as dips in the charting of alpha waves. Another measure is *reaction time*. This is based on the amount of time it takes an individual to respond to a random signal (e.g., a "beep") while attending to a message. The greater the person's attention to the message at the time the signal appears, the *longer* the reaction time will be. The use of measures such as these have allowed researchers to determine some of the structural characteristics of messages (e.g., scene changes) that are associated with higher levels of attention (Reeves & Thorson, 1986).

Comprehension

Even when a message reaches the audience and gains attention, it still may not be understood. As interpersonal communicators, we generally know when we're not being understood. In mass communication, however, often we do not know—feedback is limited, there is no practical way of checking the comprehension of a vast, remote audience. Still, this communication effect is so important that it cannot be ignored altogether. Mass communicators have devised ways to take comprehension into account. They can try to construct messages according to principles that maximize the probability of being comprehended, and if they are still not sure, they can pretest the message on a sample of the target audience.

Volumes of research have been published on the characteristics of written messages that are associated with reader comprehension. One of the most ambitious programs has been the effort to devise *readability formulas* that could be used to predict comprehension. The idea behind such formulas is to use readily observed characteristics of messages such as word length and sentence length and complexity to predict the ease of reader comprehension. In fact several such formulas have been devised (Dale & Chall, 1948; Flesch, 1948; Gray & Leary, 1935), and most predict comprehension with a high degree of accuracy.

Unfortunately, readability formulas have rather limited applicability. They can tell you if a sample of writing will present comprehension difficulties, but formulas are not communication principles—they can't tell what you should change to make the message more readable.

This probably seems puzzling, but there is an explanation. Let's suppose you apply the Flesch formula to several samples of writing from a local newspaper, and obtain scores which indicate a high level of difficulty. You could safely conclude that many members of the audience would not comprehend these stories. What should you do? If you take the formula literally, you should rewrite the stories substituting shorter words and shorter sentences because this is what this particular formula is based on. But there is a fallacy in this reasoning. World length and sentence length predict reading difficulty, but they do not (by themselves) cause it. Word length and sentence length are efficient predictors of reading difficulty simply because they are highly correlated with dozens of other factors which contribute to comprehension. Actual improvement in comprehension depends on all other factors, not just word length and sentence length.

Without taking readability formulas too literally, some valuable lessons can be drawn that are widely applied in writing for the mass media. The main lesson is keep it simple (Flesch, 1946). Don't write to impress the reader. Strive instead for clarity.

The designers of commercial advertising follow this advice. But when hundreds of thousands of dollars are to be invested in production and the purchase of space and/or time, pretesting is generally employed as well. The key elements of an advertising message can be tested in storyboard form before investing in production. Comprehension is tested by asking questions about each element in the message: what does it mean to the reader? The reader is encouraged to put the meaning into his/her own words, not merely repeat the message. If something is not being comprehended, or is totally misunderstood, the readers' efforts to paraphrase provide valuable clues for revising.

Recent research on comprehension has turned from print media toward comprehension of visual media—especially television. So far, a "viewability" formula has not been devised to predict visual comprehension of television, but researchers are beginning to study the process. Among other things, these studies are beginning to show that comprehension of the television message is a function of two things: (1) content of the message: (2) cognitive behavior of the viewer.

This means that comprehension of television does not appear to be a straightforward learning process. The viewer is not so much learning the message as *transforming* it. This *transformation process* is illustrated in a recent study of viewers of the "Dallas" series (Livingstone, 1987). Livingstone compared the results of a content analysis (see chapt. 1) of Dallas themes with viewers' interpretations of the major Dallas characters. She found that viewer interpretation sometimes differed from the (actual) portrayals of characters on the program. For example, a major theme of the series (as determined by content analysis) was the conflict between morality and the corrupting power of wealth. This conflict theme was borne out by JR Ewing who is subject to the moralizing influence of his family on one hand, and the corrupting power of organized business on the other. However, most viewers did not perceive the moral conflict. Instead, they saw JR as set against the rest of his family as an unambiguous force of immorality.

According to Livingstone, these results show how the viewer's comprehension of television turns out to be a *transformation of meaning*. In this case viewers comprehended JR Ewing in a manner somewhat more consistent with their own "implicit personality" theories. Apparently we are prone to stereotyping television characters in terms of a few durable personality traits, just as we do people in real life.

Figure 5.3. A Transformation of Meaning. From THE WORLD OF QUINO by Joaquin S. Lavado. Reprinted by permission of Henry Holt and Company, Inc.

Secondary Effects

We turn our attention now to what happens as a result of communication. That is, if primary efforts occur (e.g., exposure, attention, comprehension) what consequences follow from this? Will another person be "persuaded" to change his mind to agree with the position we're advocating? Can we convince them that they ought to vote for our candidate, and actually get them to do it? Traditionally, these are the kinds of "effects" that have fascinated those interested in the effects of the mass media. Stamm (1973) likened this view of effects to the goals of early alchemists who sought to transform less desirable metals into gold. . . .

"The . . . communicator, too, begins with a material of lesser desirability—the un-lovely human mind, in many instances wholly lacking in . . . the awareness and . . .

values. The communicator hopes to add something to the cognitive material that will elevate it. . . .'' (p. 228).

Uses and Gratifications

Currently, one of the most popular ways to view effects of communication is as ''uses and gratifications.'' According to Swanson (1979) the basic idea behind this approach is that of the *''active audience''*—the view that audience members actively form intentions and create expectations of mass media. This view is offered in contrast to the ''passive audience'' conception of most effects theories, in which individuals respond mechanically to messages and passively absorb their content. In other words, individuals use media content to serve purposes of their own. These purposes are thought to originate with the needs and wants of the individual; when such wants or needs are satisfied through communication, the effect is termed a ''gratification.''

Studies of such effects are currently widespread, and date as far back as early studies of motives for watching quiz programs, and the gratifications obtained from listening to soap operas on the radio (Herzog, 1942). Recent studies have sought to identify and catalog the variety of gratifications reported by newspaper readers and television viewers. For example, here is a list of ''television gratifications'' (Blumler & Quail, 1969).

(1) To judge what political leaders are like.

(2) To see what a candidate would do if elected.

(3) To keep up with the main issues of the day.

(4) To help make up my mind how to vote in an election.

(5) To use as ammunition in arguments with others.

(6) To judge who is likely to win an election.

(7) To enjoy the excitement of an election race.

(8) To remind me of my candidate's strong points.

As you can see, these ''gratifications'' are derived from reasons given for watching political content on television. But what is the significance of such a list? Is it simply a partial inventory of effects, real and/or imagined? By itself such a list has little or no significance. Its significance must be established through relationships to other aspects of human behavior. For example, researchers have tried to demonstrate that the above gratifications are related to the probability of voting, and to the voter's ability to correctly identify candidate's stands on issues. This is very much like searching for the ''side effects'' of an original ''effect'' (the gratification).

But there may be additional significance to the study of uses and gratifications. By analyzing the reasons people give for communicating, we may come to a deeper understanding of how mass communication is useful and could be made more useful. The significance of such understanding is readily appreciated if we consider the case of a new communication technology like videotext (see Chapter 9). In this country, a "profitable" application of the technology has yet to be found. The question of what to do with videotext has been approached largely by asking, "what (content) would people be willing to pay for?" The answers to this question have been of little help to the developers of videotext.

The answer to how to develop videotext may lie in a different question, a question such as, "What conditions in the lives of individuals give rise to wants and needs that can be satisfied through communication?" The point is that we can't understand how and why individuals benefit from mass communication by looking (only) at effects (such as financial profit) that are desired by mass communicators. We must, at least, examine what's going on in people's lives that gives rise to their use of media, and we must consider outcomes that are satisfying to receivers.

Viewed historically, the current emphasis on effects as viewed by the receiver can be seen as the correction of a previous imbalance in communication theory and research. Until very recently, research on effects of communication concentrated almost exclusively on effects that were of interest to persons and organizations who wished to use mass communication for manipulative ends. Inherent in this imbalance was an ethical issue—whether it's right for mass communication research to be preoccupied with effects desired by the few, the powerful, while neglecting effects of concern to the many (the members of the audience).

While the correction of this imbalance is a laudable goal, it has not been an easy one to achieve. Despite the current popularity of "uses and gratifications" research, there are weaknesses in current research that are widely recognized. On one hand there are serious questions about the validity of present methods of observing and classifying such effects. On the other, the topic also lacks a coherent theory from which to derive fruitful hypotheses.

Observations of "uses and gratifications" have customarily been based upon self-report measures—i.e., the individual is asked to report effects that resulted from exposure (to certain messages in a certain medium). But as McLeod and Becker (1974) have noted, the validity of such reports depends on the individual's ability and willingness to tell the researcher why he does what he does with the media. These authors use "companionship" as an example of a gratification that might be reported by certain people. How might the researcher try to verify that this a valid report? That is, how could we obtain some assurance that such an effect had actually occurred?

McLeod and Becker's point is that too often such reports are simply accepted at face value. No assurance of validity is sought. They suggest that at a minimum researchers should ask whether the use (e.g., "companionship") is being reported where we have reason to expect it. For example, if the researcher could identify a group of lonely people, then they should report "companionship" as a media use more often than a cross-section of the public. But, you should ask, why should we expect this difference? This is where theory would come in. It would provide the reasons why such a difference should be expected—i.e., it is not just a hunch based on your own past experience, but a hypothesized difference based on a theoretical argument.

Stamm et al. (1976) attempted to apply such an argument to studying use of newspapers. Their concern was to identify (anticipated) uses of newspapers that would be associated with a transition from non-subscriber to subscriber. They reasoned that new residents to a community would experience "communication needs" that could be satisfied by subscribing to a local newspaper; thus, the anticipated effect could lead to subscribing. Support for this idea was found. For example, individuals high in *surveillance need* were likely to become newspaper subscribers in their new community.

To re-emphasize a previous point, the practical importance of such studies of "anticipated effects" is that they can point the way to improving what the media provide. For example, instead of being solely concerned with what attracts the most readers, a newspaper can concern itself with meeting anticipated effects that are important to certain groups of readers. In the case of new residents, this would also allow newspapers to fulfill an acknowledged responsibility, the integragation of the individual into the social and political fabric of the community.

An Effects Trinity

As we turn our attention to effects of communication in the domain of the sender, there are three effects that come immediately to mind, so prominent are they in the annals of persuasion research. These three are knowledge, attitudes, and behavior. Researchers have devoted decades in the effort to document presumed effects of communication on knowledge, attitudes and behavior. Later in this chapter we will see how these efforts have affected ideas about mass communication effects, but first we need to discuss what these terms mean.

We tend to take for granted that the meaning of such familiar terms is clear. But unfortunately these terms have been used in many different ways, often in ways that are not sufficiently precise for scientific research. This is perhaps best illustrated by beginning with the term "attitude."

In everyday usage, and much scientific usage as well, the term attitude is so broadly defined that it overlaps with both knowledge and behavior. We can show this by analyzing a widely used scientific definition:

"An enduring system of positive or negative evaluations, emotional feelings and pro or con action tendencies with respect to a social object" (Krech, Crutchfield & Ballachey, 1962, p. 177).

The reference to a "system of evaluations" implies that attitude is based on knowledge, since evaluations can hardly be made in a vacuum without taking anything into account. In fact, the reference to evaluation implies that the social object was compared to some alternative in terms of some standard of comparison. You can try this out yourself. Think of some "social object," (e.g., free trade) and ask yourself what you would need to know in order to evaluate its desirability in comparison to some alternative.

You've probably noticed yourself that the reference to "pro or con action" implies that attitude (somehow) takes in behavior. It does, in the sense that attitude is supposed to reflect the individual's movement toward or away from an object. For example, an individual with a "favorable attitude" toward free trade should say positive things about free trade, vote in favor of free trade, vote against measures that would restrain free trade, and so on.

Herein lies the attraction of "attitude" as a concept: if you know an individual's attitude you can predict his behavior (i.e., theoretically you can). Therefore, it follows that if you want to change someone's behavior the way to do it is by changing that person's attitude. And this is where communication comes in—the way to change someone's attitude is by communication (persuasively, of course).

Although the concept of attitude has held a central place in theories of mass communication and persuasion for many years, its popularity is beginning to fade. The concept is too global, and some of its central propositions have failed; for example, the proposition that attitude is a reliable predictor of behavior (Festinger, 1964).

Some researchers have abandoned the concept together, turning instead to study the effects of mass communication on knowledge. Still others have suggested that the concept be redefined, broken down into more precise components that can be studied separately.

Many of those who have abandoned the search for attitude effects have sought to replace it with another kind of effect called *agenda-setting*. The rationale for this switch in focus was given by Cohen (1963), who said that the media may not be successful at telling people what to think (i.e., attitude), but they are stunningly successful in telling its audience what to think about. This latter effect has come to be known as agenda-setting, and appears to be more closely related to knowledge than to attitude.

While the focus on agenda-setting supposedly represents a clear break from the attitude concept, there has in practice been some carry-over. In practice, it hasn't been that easy to keep knowledge separate from attitude. This can be illustrated by analyzing a popular approach to measuring agenda-setting effects. In principle, if an agenda-setting affect is going to be observed the researcher must compare "what the press is

111

thinking about" to what members of the audience are "thinking about." The latter, called the "public agenda" is measured by presenting survey respondents with a list of issues and asking them to rank the importance of these issues. Thus, the "agenda" of an individual respondent might look like this:

Vietnam war	1
Race relations	2
Crime	3
Campus unrest	4
Inflation	5
Pollution	6
Poverty	7
Sex & morality	8
Drugs	9
Women's rights	10

(Adapted from Funkhouser, 1973)

What does such a ranking reflect? Does it reflect what the respondent knows about these issues? That would be hard to say. The rationale of the agenda-setting hypothesis argues that issues that are given more prominent media coverage (e.g., as measured by no. of newspaper articles) should receive a higher ranking. Why? Because the individual reader will be more often exposed to those issues which receive the most frequent coverage, and will therefore be more familiar with those issues. Is that a useful way to define what we mean by knowledge, that knowledge is one's familiarity with an issue?

There are alternatives that may be more productive. For example, Carter (1965) offered a redefinition of attitude that divided the concept into two parts—*salience and pertinence*. According to Carter, the evaluation of any object is based on both:

1. Salience—the psychological closeness (e.g., familiarity) of the object.

2. Pertinence—a relationship between the two objects based on some means of comparing them.

Salience arises largely from accumulated experience with our environment—e.g., the longer we know a friend, the closer we tend to become. Pertinence is more cognitive—a product of how we think about things. Our evaluation of a friend based on salience is one thing; our evaluation based on comparisons with other people may be quite another.

We can begin by applying these distinctions to a typical consumer choice situation. Let's say it's time to buy a new bottle of shampoo, and you are about to purchase "Brand X," a brand that you have been using for several months. How can we describe your "attitude" toward Brand X in these terms? First, your *salience* for Brand X should be stronger than toward other brands that you have not used. There is not much that

112

communication can do to change this component of attitude—i.e., reduce the salience of Brand X, because communication cannot readily modify experience you've already had. (Communication might be used to raise the salience of a less familiar brand, but even that would be an incremental process requiring repeated exposure to a positive message.)

The *pertinence* component of attitude does not come into play unless there is a second object (Brand Y) with which Brand X is compared, and some *attribute* on which they can be compared. For example, what if you think, as you reach for old, familiar Brand X, "I started to notice a few flakes of dandruff last week. I wonder if I should get something different this time?" Now you are led to compare Brand X with Brand Y in terms of ability to control dandruff. The result of this comparison (i.e., "Brand Y will give me dandruff control where Brand X doesn't") is called a *pertinence discrimination.*

To the extent that consumer choices reflect a "habit," they are probably based on salience—sticking with something familiar. But choices sometimes involve the cognitive component of attitude, and then communication can play a more prominent role by supplying the attributes on which a comparison can be made, or providing the comparison itself. In the realm of advertising communication, ads that provide this kind of information are called *comparative ads.*

Now let's apply these ideas to the public agenda measure. The report of importance rankings tells us nothing about pertinence—i.e., about relationships among the issues based on some means of comparing them. Putting it differently, we have a report of what's important (i.e., salient) without any explanation of why one issue ranked of higher importance than another.

This brings up a question. Which would be a more significant mass communication effect, the ability of media to increase the familiarity of certain issues over others, or their ability to determine the reasons why certain issues are thought to be more important? Whatever your answer to this question may be, it should be clear that the latter effect has more to do with the cognitive component of attitude.

Theories of Effects

Empirical research on the effects of mass communication has a relatively brief history in this country, beginning in the 1930s with a series of studies on the effects of motion pictures (Charters, 1933). During this time assessments of the potency of mass communication have vacillated wildly. Initial assessments conferred almost unlimited effects, followed by a reassessment which assigned minimal effects, and another reassessment which swings back toward stronger effects. For historical perspective, it is helpful to think of these as three distinct periods (not as three distinct "theories"):

1930–1950	Unlimited effects
1950–1970	Minimal effects
1970–80s	Moderate effects

The assessment of effects has vacillated for a number of reasons, of which three are particularly significant:

(1) The types of effects studied has changed;

(2) Methods of study have changed;

(3) Conditions have changed.

Early studies tended to look for changes in behavior and attitudes. For example, the early film studies looked for evidence of delinquent behavior that could be attributed to viewing motion pictures. These kinds of effects seem to be relatively uncommon, or at least uncommonly difficult to document. More recent research has emphasized cognitive effects, which seem to be more susceptible to media influence.

Methods of study have changed from an emphasis on anecdotal evidence and case studies to more systematic methods such as surveys and experimentation. Often surveys have not substantiated effects claimed by studies using anecdotal evidence and case histories. At other times, controlled, experimental studies have been able to detect effects that are all but impossible to observe with surveys conducted outside the laboratory.

It also appears that effects change over time, as social, political and economic conditions change. An excellent example is the effect of political campaigns on voting behavior; it appears that the effects of recent campaigns has increased due to the weakening of ties to political parties. As a result, studies of recent campaigns show greater effects than studies conducted in the 40s and 50s.

Unlimited Effects (1930–1950)

What did "unlimited effects" mean—did it really mean UNLIMITED? Not exactly. This is a characterization of early views based on efforts to reconstruct the assumptions of that period. Other characterizations have been offered—e.g., "magic bullet theory," and "hypodermic theory." Whatever the label, the underlying assumptions seem to be the same, that:

• A direct correspondence exists between the content of a message and its effects;

• the cards are stacked in favor of the communicator because receivers don't have the social or psychological resources to resist skillful persuasive efforts.

Some scholars have speculated on why such assumptions might have been accepted during that period. Lowery and DeFleur (1983), for example, have suggested that prevailing assumptions about the nature of individuals and society would have been consistent with an "unlimited effects" view of mass communication. Psychology viewed the individual as non-rational, controlled largely by instincts. Sociology had conceived of a post-industrial "mass society" devoid of close interpersonal ties, which left the individual isolated and vulnerable to outside influence.

But perhaps it is more to the point to inquire what kind of evidence was available at the time that would have been consistent with such a bullish view of mass communication effects. Three events—the "War of the Worlds" radio broadcast, the Kate Smith war bond campaign, and WW II propaganda—are often cited as examples of the "unlimited" influence of mass communication. On close inspection, however, it is difficult to see how these experiences could have supported such a view of communication effects.

The effects of the 1938 Orson Welles radio broadcast were extensively studied by Cantril and did not support the anecdotal impression that the majority of listeners had responded in panic. To be sure, there was ample evidence of panic, but it was not universal.

> "The panic began well before the broadcast had ended. Terrified people all over America prayed and tried frantically, in one way or another, to escape death from the Martians. The reaction was strongest in the New Jersey area (in a single block, more than 20 families rushed out of their houses with wet handkerchiefs and towels over their faces) but people were affected in all sections of the country" (Lowery & DeFleur, 1983, p. 66).

Figure 5.4. Unlimited Effects. From the *Journal of Communication,* 1984, 34(3) p. 68 © 1984 *Journal of Communicaiton.* Used with permission.

Cantril's (1940) analysis identified a number of reasons why some people panicked and others did not. For example, many people tuned in late, thereby missing the explanation that the program was a fictional dramatization not a news broadcast. Among those who tuned in late some panicked, but others stopped to verify the authenticity of the broadcast (the CBS switchboard was flooded with such calls).

Thus, if anything, Cantril's analysis shows that mass communication effects are far from simple and direct. Only a superficial analysis could give that impression. The same can be said about other (apparent) instances of "unlimited" effects. The Kate Smith campaign convinced only a small percentage of its audience to buy war bonds, and failed miserably in its major objective of explaining that war bonds would help curb wartime inflation. Shils & Janowitz (1948) found that the social cohesiveness of the German army rendered Allied propaganda surprisingly ineffective right up to the end of the war.

The most impressive effort to develop evidence for the unlimited effects view is found in a program of experimental studies initiated during WW II and continued by Hovland and others at Yale thereafter. These studies started from the position that mass communication messages have a variety of effects, the only question being how best to design a message in order to maximize its effect. The findings of this research program certainly demonstrated that communication can have effects, but it also showed that there were important qualifications—e.g., what was "effective" for some members of a group did not always work on others.

The first sign of complications emerged in studies of films ("Why We Fight") that were designed to motivate Allied troops for the invasion of Europe to reclaim territory occupied by the Nazis. Surprisingly, the films had no effect on the men's motivation to fight, although some other kinds of effects were observed. There were substantial effects on knowledge of events leading up to the war, and modest effects on certain opinions about the war effort (Hovland et al., 1949). Thus, there did appear to be limits to the kinds of effects that could be expected from persuasive messages.

Perhaps an even more important discovery from the film studies was the evidence that effects did not depend solely on the content of the message. For example, those soldiers who held opinions in opposition to the ones being advocated by the films were less likely to be influenced. The importance of this discovery is that it suggested simple cause-and-effect explanations did not work; one could not predict effects from characteristics of the message alone. It appeared that characteristics of receivers had to be taken into account as well.

This became even more evident as a program of experimental research on persuasion was continued at Yale after the war (Hovland et al., 1953). The search for simple laws of persuasion was continued, and once more frustrated by the discovery of *mediating conditions.* This made it very difficult to resolve such questions as whether "primacy" was superior to "recency," because there was no simple answer. The answer depended upon the operation of a variety of mediating conditions.

Message	Rel. to Position Advocated	Size of Effect
1-sided	favorably disposed	large
1-sided	opposed	small
2-sided	favorably disposed	very small
2-sided	opposed	large

Figure 5.5. Illustration of a "mediating condition." In this case the size of effect due to a message is mediated by the receiver's relationshp to the position advocated in the message.

For example, what is heard first (i.e., "primacy") seems to have the most effect if receivers have less initial interest, while what is heard most recently will have more effect if initial interest is high. A two-sided message is more effective when receivers are unfavorably disposed to the position advocated, a one-sided message more effective if they are favorably disposed.

This discovery of mediating factors is very relevant to practical questions that are continually being asked about communication effects. When designing any kind of message, the professional can always profit from asking what characteristics of receivers (or other factors) are likely to make a difference in the effect of the message. Or, when raising concerns about the impact of televised violence (or other media fare) we can get quickly beyond simplistic ideas which posit uniform effects over a vast audience.

So far we have tried to establish a basis for the unlimited effects model from research conducted within that framework. We have seen, however, that most of this research does not seem to be very consistent with unlimited effects; the researchers by and large did not find what they were looking for. Given the lack of supporting evidence, we are hard pressed to explain the origins of the unlimited effects model. We feel at least two other possibilities are worth considering. First, there seems to be a recurrent tendency to overestimate the effects of any new mass medium. In 1929 public concern prompted the Motion Picture Research Council to sponsor research to investigate harmful effects of motion pictures on youth. Later, when comic books became a popular medium, public hysteria was directed toward them as a cause of delinquency and other anti-social behavior (Wertham, 1954). The fear of comics no sooner subsided than it was replaced by fear of the effects of a new medium—television. Fear of television has not yet subsided, the most recent manifestation being concern about the effects of music videos.

It is also conceivable that there never was an unlimited effects model in vogue during 1930–50. Instead, the model was constructed later as a convenient "straw man" with which to bolster the credibility of a limited effects model. Certainly, there is no explicit reference to an unlimited effects model in the earlier literature. It first appears as a contrasting position to the limited effects model which originated in the 1950s (DeFleur, 1970).

It is probably more useful, and more accurate, to regard the unlimited effects model as a simplistic way of thinking about communication effects that is still in use today. Anytime that the effects of media are said (or feared) to be uniform and direct, as in stimulus-response, this model is being invoked. It is important to recognize such thinking, and to question its validity. For example, you might hear someone assert that the lyrics in popular music are turning young people into drug addicts. Such an assertion leaves room for many questions; for example, what about the effects of all the lyrics that warn young people against drugs? Whatever the statement, the question that always applies is, "Exactly how does that work?"

Limited Effects (1956–1970)

While the origins of "unlimited effects" are dubious, the source of the limited effects model is well known. It originated in the mind of Joseph Klapper, formed the basis of his doctoral dissertation at Columbia University, and was later published in "The Effects of the Mass Media" (1960). Klapper's conclusions were based on a review of effects research done up to that point in time, most notably studies of publicity campaigns, election campaigns, and experiments on the design of persuasive messages. In Klapper's view, the results of all this research pointed to one conclusion:

> "When the media offer content in support of both sides of given issues, the dominant effect is stasis, or reinforcement, and the least likely effect is change or conversation."

Certainly, the results of the Cincinnati UN campaign seemed consistent with this view (Hyman & Sheatsley, 1956). A massive media bombardment modeled after allied propaganda efforts during WW II was used to promote citizen participation in establishing a United Nations organization. Despite extensive use of all the available media—radio, newspapers and leaflets, the campaign had little impact on public participation. It appeared that the campaign had only been successful in reaching those who were already knowledgeable and supportive of the UN concept.

Studies of election campaigns during the 40s and 50s yielded similar results. One of the most well-known studies—"The People's Choice"—described effects of the 1940 Roosevelt-Wilkie presidential campaign in Erie Ct., Ohio (Lazarsfeld, Berelson and Gaudet, 1948). The study was carefully designed to interview a representative sample of voters as several points during the campaign, beginning in May and ending right before the election in November.

The researchers' attention was focused on the campaign's effect on voting behavior. They were looking for evidence of *conversion*—i.e., voters who had been persuaded to desert their candidate and switch sides. They found that only about eight percent of the voters made a switch during the study period, and not all of these switches could be attributed to media influence.

Since over half of the voters had already decided who to vote for very early in the campaign, and few changed their minds, it seemed that the major effect was to:

". . . allay the partisan's doubts and to refute the opposition arguments which he encounters in exposure to media and friends—in short, to secure and stabilize and solidify his vote intention and translate it into an actual vote" (Lazarsfeld et al., p. 88)

In retrospect, the limited effects interpretation of the early election studies can be explained in a couple ways. First, the timing of the studies must be considered. The Erie Ct. study (and subsequent Elmira study, 1948) were done during a period in American politics when party loyalty had a strong influence on voting decisions. As we shall see in Chapter 7, media effects have since increased as party loyalty has declined. Second, we have to keep in mind that these early studies assessed the influence of the media largely in terms of a certain kind of effect—a change in voting behavior. As subsequent studies have shifted attention to other kinds of effects (e.g., cognition) the influence of political campaigns has seemed more substantial.

Not-so-limited Effects (1970 to Present)

The current perspective on mass communication effects, in some quarters at least, can be aptly described as "not-so-limited." No doubt some scholars held to this view before 1970, having never accepted the model advocated by Klapper, but little was published on an alternative perspective until the 70s.

In retrospect perhaps the first significant blow to limited effects was struck in 1960 with Freedman and Sears review of the evidence on selective exposure (see Chapter 2). Selective exposure was a key to the limited effects model, but as we have seen the evidence bearing on this hypothesis is often contradictory. Freedman and Sears found as much evidence contradicting the hypothesis as supporting it. There was really very little basis for saying that people consistently go out of their way to avoid information with which they disagree. If the major premise for arguing limited effects is faulty, then how can the model stand?

Perhaps the model continued to stand because it was not directly challenged. Certainly it took several years before the import of the Sears and Freedman review was widely appreciated. In fact, numerous textbooks continued to advocate the selective exposure hypothesis long after its validity had been challenged (Chaffee & Miyo, 1983).

But this was only the beginning. The more direct challenge to limited effects came from other quarters. Studies were published which reported effects from information campaigns that would not have been expected under limited effects (see Chapter 6, sheltered workshop campaign). Studies of the impact of televised violence began to suggest that effects on behavior were not limited to those already predisposed to behaving aggressively (see Chapter 8).

Recent studies of the political effects of mass communication have also posed a direct challenge to the limited effects model. Most notable are recent studies of the impact of political campaigns, and the extensive literature on "agenda-setting" effects (discussed above).

The political impact of media will be discussed in a later chapter, but it is appropriate to mention here some findings that suggest effects are not limited to reinforcing an existing vote intention, as claimed by Klapper (1960). Studies of the presidential debates (Kraus, 1962) and of political advertising campaigns (Atkin et al., 1973) began to reveal exceptions to the truism that voters only pay attention to messages from their own candidate. In the case of debates and spot advertising, it was clear that voters were about equally exposed to both major candidates and recalled information about both candidates. Other studies showed that televised debates and political advertising could have major impacts on how candidates were perceived by voters (Patterson & McClure, 1976).

An agenda-setting study in the tradition of the famous Yale experiments provided a convincing demonstration of the impact of newscasts on the perceived importance of political issues. According to the agenda-setting hypothesis, it should make a difference which issues are emphasized in evening television newscasts. Specifically, those issues which receive the most prominent coverage should (as a result) take on greater importance to viewers. A group of yale researchers tested this prediction experimentally (see Chapter 1).

In one experiment the researchers altered videotapes of network newscasts to produce one version that contained stories dealing with weaknesses in U.S. defense capability and a second version with no defense stories. Participants in the study were exposed to one or the other version of the newscasts. Those who were exposed to the "defense" version showed a substantial increase (.90) in their ratings of the importance of defense relative to seven other issues. Those who saw the "non-defense" version rated defense as less important compared to other issues (e.g., pollution and unemployment).

This raises a question about why recent studies have provided stronger evidence of media effects than the studies which led to Kapper's limited effects model. This is a very complex question, and the difficulty in answering it reveals why a single, unified theory of media effects is so difficult to achieve. One possibility is that the influence of media changes over time. For example, recent political campaigns may have had more effect because voters became more susceptible to influence (see Chapter 7), and because new and more effective communication techniques were developed (e.g., debates and candidate advertising). Another reason is broadening of the research agenda to include several kinds of effects (of communication) that had not been considered in the earlier research. For example, the systematic search for agenda-setting effects did not get underway until 1972.

We do not feel that the rejection of the limited effects model signals a return to the view of media as tools with unlimited power to manipulate their audiences. It reflects instead a more balanced view in which *certain* kinds of effects do occur, but only under the right circumstances.

This new model has important implications for both practitioners and consumers of mass communication. To practitioners it means that communication programs must be carefully planned and designed, and even then effects cannot be taken for granted. The chances for success are enhanced by incorporating audience research into planning and follow-up evaluation of any communication program (e.g., an information campaign). To consumers it means that not all of the cards are held by communicators who would manipulate then for their own ends. Effects which are not in the best interest of media consumers are less likely to occur, but not altogether improbably. This is why ongoing research to monitor media impact is essential to protecting the interests of consumers. For example, some research indicates that parents are warranted in restricting children's access to certain kinds of television programming.

Key Terms

"Active audience"
Agenda setting
Alpha wave
Attitude
Beta wave
Brain waves
Communication effects
Comprehension
Conversion
Limited (minimal) effects
"Magic bullet theory"
Mediating conditions
Nielsen rating
Not-so-limited effects
Pertinence
Primacy
Primary effects
Reaction time
Readability formula
Recency
Reinforcement
Salience
Secondary effects
Self report
Unlimited effects
Uses & gratifications
Validity

Summary

Secondary effects of communication are generally the most sought after, but their occurrence depends upon achieving primary effects such as comprehension of the message.

The most basic definition of "effective communication" entails not attitude or behavior change, but the primary effects of exposure, attention and comprehension.

Brain waves as a measure of attention depend upon the empirically established correspondence that alpha wave activity *drops* during brief periods of focused attention.

Reaction times are *longer* during periods of focused attention.

Readability formulas are reliable predictors of message comprehension, but they cannot tell a writer how to revise a message to make it easier to read.

Comprehension involves *transforming* a message into a meaningful interpretation; the result of this process depends on both the content of the message and the cognitive behavior of the receiver.

According to the "uses and gratifications" view of (secondary) effects, effects depend upon the purpose of the receiver rather than the intent of the sender.

The uses and gratification approach poses the question: "What conditions in the lives of individuals give rise to wants and needs that can be served through mass communication?"

The value of uses and gratifications as an approach to communication effects has (so far) been restricted by the questionable validity of self report measures.

A major reason for the interest in attitude change as a communication effect has been the assumption that attitudes predict behavior, yet many studies have shown that this assumption often fails to hold.

The (global) concept of attitude can be divided into more specific components such as: (1) the familarity of an object (salience), and (2) relationships discriminated between objects (pertinence). Some components have been shown to be more susceptible than others to change via communication (e.g., pertinence more than salience).

The "unlimited effects theory" of communication effects was based on the ideas of (1) direct correspondence between message content and effects, and (2) receivers with weak social and psychological defenses.

The acceptance of a limited effects model was in part a result of the discovery of *mediating conditions*—i.e., the discovery that the effect of a message depends upon factors in addition to content of the message (e.g., different messages are differentially effective on different kinds of people).

According to Klapper's limited effects model the dominant effect of communication is reinforcement, and the least likely effect is change in attitude or behavior.

A major premise underlying limited effects—selective exposure—has received inconsistent empirical support, thus opening the door to the currently accepted view of not-so-limited effects.

The tendency for recent research to overturn limited effects is due to: (1) changes in media influence over time; (2) improved communication techniques; (3) improvements in the ability of research to identify and detect effects.

References

Atkin, C. K., L. Bowen, K. G. Sheinkopf and O. B. Nayman (1973). Quality vs. quality in televised political ads. *Public Opinion Quarterly, 27,* 209–224.

Blumler, J. G. and D. Mcquail (1969). Television in Politics. Chicago: U. of Chicago Press.

Cantril, H. (1940). The Invasion from Mars: A Study in the Psychology of Panic. Princeton, N. J.: Princeton U. Press.

Carter, R. F. (1965). Communication and affective relations. *Journalism Quarterly, 42,* 203–212.

Chaffee, S. H. and Y. Miyo (1983). Selective exposure and the reinforcement hypothesis: an integenerational panel study of the 1980 presidential campaign. *Communication Research, 10,* 3–36.

Charters, W. W. (1933). Motion Pictures and Youth: A Summary. New York: Macmillan.

Cohen, B. C. (1963). The Press and Foreign Policy. Princeton, N.J.: Princeton U. Press.

Dale, E. and J. S. Chall (1948). A formula for predicting readability. *Educational Research Bulletin, 27,* 11–20, 37–54.

DeFleur, M. L. (1970). Theories of Mass Communication. New York: McKay.

Festinger, L. (1964). Behavioral support for opinion change. *Public Opinion Quarterly, 28,* 404–417.

Flesch, R. (1946). The Art of Plain Talk. New York: Harper & Row.

_____ (1948). A new readability yardstick. *Journal of Applied Psychology, 32,* 221–233.

Funkhouser, G. R. (1973). The issue of the sixties: an exploratory study in the dynamics of public opinion. *Public Opinion Quarterly, 37,* 62–75.

Gray, W. S. and B. E. Leary (1935). What Makes a Book Readable, with Special Reference to Adults of Limited Reading Ability: An Initial Study. Chicago: U. of Chicago Press.

Herzog, H. (1944). Motivations and gratifications of daily serial listeners. In P. Lazarsfeld and Stanton (eds.), Radio Research; 1942–43. New York: Duell, Sloan & Pearce.

Hovland, C. I., A. A. Lumsdaine, and F. D. Sheffield (1949). Experiments on Mass Communication. Princeton, N.J.: Princeton U. Press.

_____, I. Janis, and H. H. Kelley (1953). Communication an Persuasion. New Haven: Yale U. Press.

Hyman, H. H. and P. Sheatsley (1947). Some reasons why information campaigns fail. *Public Opinion Quarterly, 11,* 413–423.

Klapper, J. T. (1960). The Effects of Mass Communication. New York: Free Press.

Kraus, S. (1962). The Great Debates. Bloomington: Indiana U. Press.

Krech, D. and R. S. Crutchfield (1948). Theory and Problems of Social Psychology. New York: McGraw-Hill.

Lazarsfeld, P., B. Berelson, and H. Gaudet (1948). The People's Choice. New York: Columbia U. Press.

Livingstone, S. (1987). The implicit representation of characters in Dallas: a multidimensional scaling approach. *Human Communication Research,* 13, 399—420.

Lowery, S. and M. L. DeFleur (1983). Milestones in Mass Communications Research. New York: Longman.

McLeod, J. M. and L. B. Becker (1974). Testing the validity of gratification measures through political effects analysis. In Blumler & Katz (eds.), The Uses of Mass Communication. Beverly Hills: Sage.

Patterson, T. and R. D. McClure (1976). The Unseeing Eye; The Myth of Television Power in Natural Elections. New York: G. P. Putnam's Sons.

Reeves, B. & E. Thorson (1986). Watching television: experiments on the viewing process. *Communication Research,* 13(3), 343–361.

Shils, E. A. and M. Janowitz (1948). Cohesion and disintegration in the wehrmacht in World War II. *Public Opinion Quarterly,* 12, 280–315.

Stamm, K. R. (1973). Conservation communications frontiers: reports of behavioral research. In Schoenfeld (ed.), Interpreting Environmental Issues. Madison, Wis.: Dembar Educ. Research Services.

_____, K. Jackson, and L. Bowen (1976). Antecedents to newspaper subscribing and using. Presented to Association for Education in Journalism, College Park, Md.

Swanson, D. (1981). A constructivist approach. In Nimmo and Sanders (Eds.). Handbook of Political Communication. Beverly Hills, CA: Sage.

Wertham, F. (1954). Seduction of the Innocent. New York: Rinehart.

6

Advertising and Public Information

Introduction

Every day each of us is the target of dozens of non-personal messages from outside agencies. Each message has been carefully designed with particular effects in mind. Often the audience has been studied beforehand, and this knowledge applied to structuring the message and selecting the media most capable of reaching the intended audience. These efforts are the product of major communication enterprises known as advertising and public information programs. It is important for all of us to understand what lies behind such efforts, not only because we are their constant targets, but also because many of us will become involved in the planning and design of advertising or public information.

Since we plan to discuss these as separate topics, let's begin with distinguishing them. Although they have much in common, there are grounds for separating them. At first glance it may appear that advertising can be separated from information programs on monetary grounds—advertising is usually paid for. The sponsor of an advertising message must normally pay for the opportunity to transmit that message over a particular medium. Information campaigns, on the other hand, sometimes get free time or space (e.g., in the form of public service announcements—PSAs).

This distinction breaks down, however, when we get beyond a superficial comparison. Not all advertising is paid for, if we consider as advertising the free publicity that organizations obtain through press releases and other devices. Furthermore, there is not enough free space available to provide for every legitimate request, which means that the opportunity to transmit public information must often be paid for.

The essential distinction between *advertising* and *public information* must therefore rest on something else. Rice and Paisley (1981) have suggested what we think is a more useful distinction by defining public information as containing an element of "reform."

By reform they mean any change in the individual's behavior that is intended for the benefit of the individual (and/or society).

We can contrast this with the major purpose of advertising, which is not reform but the monetary gain of the sponsor. This is not to say that advertising is of no benefit to us as receivers. It undoubtedly is of some benefit. Advertising lets us know about new products and services, and may even give useful comparative information. But advertising would not be conducted in the absence of a benefit to the source (i.e., the sponsor).

It's generally easy to apply this distinction to messages that we see and hear in the mass media. The great bulk of messages about products is obviously advertising. Messages urging us to get more exercise, change our diet, stop smoking, protect the environment, and so forth are generally in the category of public information. But there are less obvious cases as well. Sometimes "public information" turns out to be advertising wearing a thin disguise. For example, a lumber corporation expounds on the values of forests and the need to protect them. The intended benefit of such a message is to improve their own image. Some cases are much more difficult to decipher. A hospital, which has a drug treatment program, publishes a message telling parents how they can identify drug use in adolescents. Clearly there may be some benefit to the hospital that published this message. But is this its major purpose? It is conceivable that a hospital would be more concerned about the adolescent drug problem than the profits from their treatment program. Such a message is as much in the realm of public information as it is in the realm of advertising.

Models of Advertising Effects

Probably few people would doubt that advertising has effects. As a student in a communications class argued, "They wouldn't keep spending so much money on it if it didn't work." The argument has merit, assuming that advertisers have documented the effects of their efforts. They have, or at least they have tried to, and it seems the more important question is not *whether* advertising has an effect, but *how* it has an effect. There is considerable disagreement over how it is that advertising works.

High Involvement

The traditional model of how advertising works—called the *high involvement model*—is very straight-forward, almost mechanistic. It describes advertising as working through a hierarchy of steps beginning with "awareness" and ending with "purchase" of a product (Lavidge & Steiner, 1961; see Figure 6.1). This model seems to represent an idealized conception of the communication process a "rational" consumer would employ—e.g., knowledge precedes liking, and conviction precedes purchase.

From the perspective of this model, the ideal advertisement (or ad campaign) would be one that takes the receiver though each of these steps in the order shown. For example, the advertiser cannot skip steps and try to take the receiver from "liking" directly to "purchase." Each preceding step is viewed as necessary and sufficient to the subsequent step.

One can imagine that advertising, as a communication process, might work this way. But it does seem like an awfully lot of work; one has to wonder whether every purchase decision merits so much effort. Information seeking costs time, money and potential frustration. Therefore, the kind of thorough information-seeking posited under this model may not predominate. For example, Bucklin (1965) reported that only 5–10 percent of shoppers for shoes, accessories & appliances sought information prior to shopping. Chaffee & McLeod (1973) observed that even when information was readily available the consumer may ignore it rather than try to cope with it.

The high involvement model also seems much too rigid; wouldn't a "real-world" communicator require more flexibility? Possibly, the high-involvement model is (only) an apt description of how advertising works under certain limited conditions. For example, it would seem that the consumer would have to attach considerable importance to the purchase decision (to merit all this effort), and that the advertising message would have to be perfectly timed to intercept the consumer when he/she is actively seeking information about the product.

The high-involvement model can be regarded as an application of the familiar "limited effects" model to advertising (Robertson, 1976). According to Bauer & Bauer (1960):

> ". . . influencing people via communication is a most difficult business . . . Typical communication experiments, including advertising tests, show that only a few percentages of the people exposed to the communication ever change their mind on anything important" (emphasis ours).

Step 6   PURCHASE

Step 5   CONVICTION

Step 4   PREFERENCE

Step 3   LIKING

Step 2   KNOWLEDGE

Step 1   AWARENESS

Figure 6.1. High Involvement Model of Advertising Effects.

Low Involvement

In contrast with the high involvement view, advertisers have begun to assume that (1) not all purchase decisions are important to the consumer; and (2) advertising messages often reach consumers who are not in the market for the product at the time. One such model—called the *low-involvement model*—has been proposed by Krugman (1965). Krugman's point is that many choices between brands of consumer goods are of

Step 6   ATTITUDE CHANGE

Step 5   TRIAL

Step 4   RECOGNITION

Step 3   CHOICE SITUATION

Step 2   "UNCONSCIOUS" LEARNING

Step 1   EXPOSURE

Figure 6.2. Low Involvement Model of Advertising Effects.

no great importance. Therefore, there is no requirement that the consumer has to process a great deal of information in order to reach such a decision. For example, in choosing a brand of pasta, one might leap directly from "awareness" (i.e., brand recognition) to "purchase."

Krugman's model suggests that advertising often works something like that (see Figure 6.2). The consumer is exposed to an ad, but does not make a "connection." That is, since he has no use for it at the time, the information is of no particular relevance. Of what consequence is such an exposure? Under the high involvement model it would be of no consequence, since recall (learning) of the content would be unlikely. But according to Krugman, recall is not important, since the consumer can proceed directly from awareness to trial, and awareness can be maintained through repetition. Let's say, for example, you are not a wine drinker, so you don't pay much attention to wine commercials. But it happens you are invited to a friend's home for dinner, and etiquette dictates that you bring a bottle of wine. You find yourself at the store trying to select something, and at this point, says Krugman, the recognition of a familiar label or symbol may lead to a purchase (unless there's a wine clerk handy to help you out). In Krugman's model "attitude change" (i.e., "liking") occurs after purchase, not before as in the high involvement model.

The difference between the communication processes represented by these two models can be formulated as an *involvement hypothesis*. According to this hypothesis, the receiver's level of involvement is a critical mediating condition (see chapt. 5) for communication behavior. The contrast in behavior hypothesized between low and high involvement is shown in Figure 6.3. This difference has been characterized in various ways. For example, high involvement has been associated with "greater depth of information processing," and with "central route processing" (Petty & Cacioppo, 1979). Low involvement has been associated with "uncritical processing," and with "peripheral route processing."

A major application of the involvement hypothesis has been to explain differences in the way people process advertising messages from difference sources—i.e., print vs. television.

Low Involvement	High Involvement
right brain processing	left brain processing
relaxed, inattentive	active, focused
alpha brain waves	beta brain waves
uncritical evaluation	critical evaluation
poor recall	good recall

Figure 6.3. Involvement as a Mediating Condition for Processing of Advertising Messages.

Television Versus Print

Krugman's model has sometimes been considered a "theory" of effects that is primarily applicable to television advertising, which leaves print advertising in the domain of the high involvement model. Some effort has been made to try to document differences in brain wave patterns between print and television. If print is the more involving medium of the two, then *high beta* readings should be found for print messages and high alpha readings for television.

An initial study by Krugman (1971), who measured the brain waves of a single subject during exposure to three tv commercials, seemed to support this idea. Krugman reported that the measure showed mostly "slow waves," which could mean alpha, but could also mean delta (sleep) or theta (reverie) waves.

Krugman also interpreted a study by Appel, et al. (1979) as supporting the low involvement hypothesis for television. Appel had reported that beta activity diminished over time during exposure to tv commercials, but did not conclude from this that tv viewing was an alpha wave (right brain) activity. Krugman was clearly speculating that given long enough viewing times beta waves would eventually turn off altogether, and only the right brain would remain active.

Fact and speculation do not always agree. A much more thorough study by Miller (1985), failed to find anything exceptional about brain wave patterns during tv viewing. In fact, it was not alpha waves but beta waves that predominated, a pattern that has been observed for a variety of other waking state activities. Miller's findings held for a variety of television programs.

This was "bad news" for the idea that there are involvement differences that correspond closely to the medium used to deliver the advertising message. On the other hand, it's always good news for science when a hypothesis can be that cleanly rejected, because it means research can be rechanneled into more productive ideas. Meanwhile, the interest in brain wave measurement continues because of its unique ability to monitor information processing behavior without disturbing the cognitive processes of the receiver. Recent work has confirmed that there are significant correlations between alpha wave activity and measures of recognition and recall (Rothschild, et al., 1986). Because increased attention to a commercial is accompanied by a drop in alpha power, alpha measures are negatively correlated with recognition and recall. This suggested that brain wave measurement is a useful indicator of information processing.

What may be more useful, however, is the ability to continuously monitor attention to commercials. Alpha power measures taken at half-second intervals clearly show that attention to commercials is anything but constant (Figure 6.4). Rothschild, et al. (1986) report the following findings:

(1) Some scenes gain and hold attention. The onset of the scene is accompanied by a sharp drop in alpha and recovery of alpha is slow.

(2) Some scenes gain attention but do not hold it. A sharp drop in alpha at the beginning of the scene followed by rapid recovery.

(3) Other scenes never gain attention. A scene change occurs with no drop in alpha.

Further research on brain waves may be used to answer a variety of practical questions about relationships between message design and attention. For example, it appears that motion leads to higher levels of attention, since motion is accompanied by a drop in alpha. But does that mean information presentation should accompany motion? Or should motion precede the presentation of information? If so, by how much?

Standards of Effectiveness

In the previous chapter we raised a distinction between primary and secondary effects of communication, which we will now apply to the question of advertising effectiveness. How should one gauge the effectiveness of advertising? This is a question that must be answered daily by researchers working within the country's major advertising agencies. Typically, major clients want evidence of effectiveness before, not after committing themselves to any particular creative design. So the problem is one of evaluating the merits of a design before-the-fact, not one of verifying a sales effect after-the-fact.

The advertiser's attention at this stage is normally directed to primary effects, reflecting the belief that advertising must communicate in order to sell. The two most common methods of testing ads—on-air and theater tests—use tests for *recall*. In addition theater tests, but not on-air, often incorporate measures of *comprehension* and *attitude change*. The latter you will recall is a secondary effect of communication, not a primary effect.

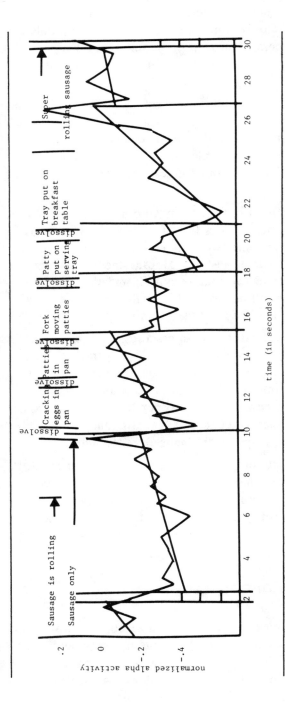

Figure 6.4. Plot of Normalized EEG Data in Half-Second Increments for Sausage Commercial. From *Communication Research*, 1986, 13(2), p. 207 © 1986 *Communication Research*. Used with permission.

131

In the on-air technique of copy testing, the ad is aired live surrounded by program content and other advertising clutter. Then, the day after, people in the broadcast area are called to find out what they remember. The key measure (of recall) is the number of people who remember the commercial. Generally, advertisers assume that a high recall score means greater sales effects than a low score, but as we'll see shortly that is not always the case.

Theatre testing involves bringing respondents into a controlled facility and exposing them to the test ad, which is embedded in a short program along with other ("control") commercials. Attitude is measured by asking respondents to indicate their preference for a list of brands that will be given away later as "prizes." Comprehension is measured through a series of tailored questions about the respondents' understanding of specific parts of the message.

Often the information on comprehension is critical to making a correct evaluation of an ad's effectiveness. Hodock (1976) has described a test of three shampoo ads using both on-air and theater tests. As often happens, the two tests conflicted. The on-air test showed satisfactory recall (19 percent) for all three test ads. But the theater test showed the greatest amount of positive attitude change for commercial C, and the comprehension questions revealed that young males identified strongly with the actor in this commercial. (He was young, virile, and had the kind of look they wanted for their hair.)

Nevertheless, management decided to trust the on-air scores, and developed a rationalization for selecting commercial A. But when the product was tracked later in test markets, several respondents indicated they would not buy the product and that they disliked the advertising. Obviously, it was time to take a closer look at communication effects. When the ad was discussed with a new group of respondents, the advertisers discovered that the actor in this commercial came across as arrogant and "phony tough," and his hair did not convey the look respondents themselves wanted.

The moral of this story seems to be that copy testing is a very tricky business. At present, there does not seem to be any one test that can tell an advertiser all he needs to know. Negative reactions to ads may not show up in recall tests. In such cases, there is no substitute for a careful, detailed analysis of what is being communicated (since this cannot be predicted in advance).

Advertising Strategies

Advertisers employ a variety of strategies to try to maximize communication effects: repeating the message, varying the content ("appeal") of the message, and selecting the target audience for the message. The planning of an advertising campaign involves all these strategic considerations, plus the selection of media best suited to reaching the target audience(s).

The frequent repetition of advertising messages is something that we're all familiar with. Perhaps you've wondered why advertisers elect to do this. According to Severin and Tankard (1988), there are several reasons. It may take several repetitions just to reach all (or most) members of the target audience. And repetition may achieve multiple exposures, which helps the audience to remember the message. Thus, there are two questions an advertiser must address: (1) how many repetitions will it take to reach all members of the audience? and (2) what is the optimal number of exposures.

Typically, media planners will construct an "advertising schedule" comprised of several ads aired at different times over a period of several days. Exposure data for the individual ads can be obtained from media rating services, and used to calculate the "*reach*" of the schedule—i.e., the percentage of the audience exposed one or more times. If the media planner is also concerned with obtaining an optimal number of exposures, then "*frequency*"—the average number of spots in the schedule seen by the typical viewer, will also be calculated. First, the ratings for the individual spots will be summed to obtained the "*gross ratings points*" (GRP) for the schedule. Frequency can then be obtained by dividing GRP by reach. For example, if the GRP for a schedule equals 280, and reach equals 100, then frequency would be estimated as 2.80. The typical viewer will see an average of 2.8 spots out of the schedule.

If the intention of the above advertising schedule were to reach every member of the audience once, then the results show it to be wasteful—more spots than necessary were purchased. But is one exposure enough? One view that is currently popular among advertisers says that the optimum number of exposures is three (Krugman, 1972). From this perspective, the above schedule is nearly optimum rather than grossly inefficient.

Why are three exposures enough? According to Krugman, the first exposure to an ad results in recognition ("what is it?"), the second in assessing personal relevance ("what of it?"), and the third serves as a reminder. The third exposure also marks the dividing line between attention and disengagement (second and third reminders are not accepted).

But does this mean that three exposures will always be enough? Not exactly. According to Krugman, recognition will not always occur on the first exposure, nor will relevance always be achieved on the second. Conceivably, many more than three exposures could be required to obtain the three that really count. But from a practical standpoint, it is probably inadvisable for a media planner to design a schedule for more than three exposures. Not only will many of these additional exposures be wasted (on some people), but too much repetition can have undesirable effects. For example, in the case of political spots, too much repetition resulted in decreased liking of the candidate (Becker & Doolittle, 1975).

The content ("appeal") of an advertising message can be varied endlessly. Because of this, the design of advertising copy is often thought of as primarily a "creative" communication task. More often than not, however, the type of appeal to be employed is carefully selected based on type of product, characteristics of the target audience, communication medium, and so forth. The role of creativity is largely limited to the implementation of a particular kind of appeal.

Given the numerous kinds of appeals available, an exhaustive treatment is not possible here. Before one gets too involved in identifying and sorting out the various kinds of appeals currently in use, there is a more basic question. Does a difference in appeal make any difference in communication effects? The basic faith of the copy writer, of course, is that it does. The answer that research gives, however, is a qualified "yes." It makes a difference sometimes, but not always, and it can be devilishly difficult to predict what kind of a difference (in appeal) will make a difference in effect.

You may recall from Chapter 5 that efforts to find "magic keys" to persuasion led to the discovery of mediating conditions. For example, sometimes a "one-sided" message was best; other times a "two-sided" message proved more effective. The principle of mediating conditions can be readily extended to advertising appeals.

Let's begin with the question of noncomparative vs. comparative advertising appeals (which is roughly parallel to one-sided vs. two-sided messages). Recently there has been a trend toward greater use of comparative ads based on the notion that they are more informative. But keeping in mind the principle of mediating conditions, you should be skeptical that this would be a general rule. The astute question would be, "when is it better to use noncomparative advertising, and when is it better to use comparative ads?" There are many possible ways to answer this question, but one way would be in terms of the "involvement" concept we discussed earlier. Comparative ads are more useful to consumers who have high-involvement in a choice, since they are more likely to consider alternative brands (Bowen, 1974). According to a study by Levine (1976), the use of comparative ads for packaged goods (where involvement is low) results in misidentification of the sponsor, and generates increased skepticism toward advertising claims.

The use of "fear appeals" offers another good example of the principle of mediated effects. The basic idea is that a fear appeal provides a source of motivation for complying with an advertiser's request (e.g., "did you know you have millions of germs in your house? . . . . we have this spray that kills germs on contact. . ."). But is a fear appeal always appropriate? And if it is, how strong should the appeal be? The stronger the better?

The question of the strength of a fear appeal has proven to be very complicated indeed. For many years the accepted answer to this question went contrary to expectation, and was based on an experiment by Janis & Feshbach (1953). This experiment provided evidence that compliance with a message was inversely related to the strength of the fear appeal. That is, a low fear appeal (in their experiment) was more effective than a high fear appeal.

The explanation that has been given for this is that comprehension of the message is a mediating condition; possibly a strong fear appeal could produce so much emotional tension that the receiver becomes defensive and distorts the meaning of the message. However, this explanation did not fit some later studies (e.g., Leventhal & Niles, 1964), which found a direct relationship between compliance and strength of the fear appeal. These authors suggested that a strong fear appeal is effective, providing it is accompanied by convincing recommendations for coping with the source of fear. This, of course, is exactly what most advertisers try to do.

Audience Segments

In order to apply the mediated effects principle to the design of advertising campaigns, it is clearly necessary to obtain some relevant facts about the groups with whom you are trying to communicate. Since the effectiveness of an appeal will depend on such things as past experience, patterns of buying behavior, personality, and so forth, the planning of any extensive advertising campaign involves an intensive study (called a "Market Segmentation Study") of prospective consumers. The purpose of the market segmentation study is to isolate distinctive groups of consumers, study each group in depth, then devise message appeals tailor-made to the segments selected for the campaign.

The key concept here is the *segment*. Basically, a segment is simply a group of individuals who have certain key characteristics in common, but differ from other groups on those same characteristics. There are a wealth of characteristics that may be used to define market segments. It is up to the advertising researcher to determine which characteristics are relevant to communication about the product. For example, some researchers would feel that the following characteristics are crucial to defining segments (Percy, 1976):

(1) Consumer needs and desires, especially as they relate to the brand and product under study.

(2) How perceptions of the brand and product relate to the benefits desired.

(3) Product use and buying behavior

(4) Attitudes toward the brand, and perceptions of the similarities and differences between brands.

(5) Background characteristics and personality.

Let's see then, how this kind of information might be used in the development of message appeals. For example, Percy (1976) has described the use of a "personality profile" to identify two market segments:

SEGMENT 1—unsure of themselves and abilities, seek continuity and stability in their environment, and are apprehensive of ill-defined and risk-involving situations. Try to avoid decision-making situations, dubious about results of expending effort or becoming involved.

SEGMENT 2—Determined to do well and usually successful. They have quiet confidence in their own abilities and self worth, and welcome challenges in disorder and complexity. They are adaptable and resourceful and comprehend problems and situations rapidly and incisively.

According to Percy, these segments seem to call for advertising appeals differing greatly in "tone," which is a way of saying that you need to talk to them differently. In Percy's opinion, segment 2 should be responsive to a direct message, while segment 1 would require a more nurturing and reassuring message.

Of course, you may or may not agree with this interpretation. The segments may be based on empirical fact, but their interpretation is highly subjective. It simply gives the copy writers a basis for asking, "how should I go about communicating with people like that?" If a useful interpretation is made, it will show up on measures of communication effectiveness when the copy is tested (using on-air and/or theater testing).

Subliminal Advertising

Given the time and effort that goes into the design of advertising messages, which may in spite of everything, still not get through to the consumer, advertising hardly seems like the powerful weapon envisaged under the "unlimited effects" model. There seems to be no magic bullet, no powerful persuader, just a group of professionals using the tools at their disposal to communicate as effectively as possible. Still, the notion persists that there is some "magic" behind advertising, secret methods which, because they are secret, render the consumer defenseless and vulnerable.

According to Wilson Bryan Key (*Subliminal Seduction,* 1972; *Media Sexploitation,* 1976) one secret weapon is subliminal advertising—the notion that people can be influenced by messages they are not aware of receiving. According to Key, many ads contain *embeds*—concealed words and other objects such as the word "sex" and representations of male and female sex organs. Key proposes that receivers unconsciously perceive these embeds and are influenced by them to desire the product. However, he has not presented any evidence on the effects of subliminal messages; he has simply presented examples of ads supposedly containing "embeds."

For evidence of effects, we first turn to James Vicary and his Subliminal Projection Company. Vicary (1957) claimed that projecting the message "Eat Popcorn" and "Drink Coca Cola" at 1/3000 of a second to movie audiences resulted in a 50 percent increase in popcorn sales and an 18 percent increase in Coca Cola sold. Unfortunately, a detailed account of this demonstration has never been made available, so it cannot be assumed that even the most rudimentary scientific precautions were taken.

Vicary's report leaves many questions unanswered. If we assume, for the sake of argument, that exposure to the embedded messages was the cause of increased popcorn and cola sales, how did this come about? Are we to suppose that the concealed message triggered an already established response, and that members of the audience suddenly arose like automatons to satisfy a sudden craving? Or, are we to assume that the message was stored in long-term memory and recalled during the intermission? And, for those who bought their refreshments before the movie, how can these sales be considered an effect of Vicary's message?

We know of only two other public demonstrations with subliminal messages (subliminal messages have been banned from U.S. broadcast media for several years). These demonstrations have also yielded unclear results. In 1956, the British Broadcasting Corporation (BBC-TV) transmitted the message "Pirie breaks world record" at a speed assumed to be subliminal. Some viewers reported they had noticed something, but this may mean only that the message was not subliminal for everyone in the audience. A U.S. television station (WTWO in Bangor, Maine) experimented with subliminal public service messages, but no effects were detected.

For more rigorous evidence bearing on subliminal persuasion, one must turn to the psychological literature. Here you will find efforts to precisely define what is meant by a subliminal stimulus, as well as much more guarded interpretations of the potential power of subliminal perception.

In psychological terminology, "subliminal" has a technical definition. It means *below the limen*—that is, below the threshold of perception. But how is this threshold defined? Psychologists define the limen as the stimulus value which gives a response 50 percent of the time. Therefore, a subliminal stimulus would be any value which gives a response less than 50 percent of the time.

It is very difficult to predict with any precision what the exact limen will be for a given person in a given time and place. Defining a limen for a mass audience comprised of individuals with widely varying thresholds is even more difficult. Apparent instances of "subliminal perception" may simply be due to wide differences in thresholds (that is, some people will routinely detect sounds and images well below the limen for most people). As we mentioned, psychologists are very cautious in their interpretations of subliminal phenomena. Some, but not all, psychologists agree that under certain conditions the phenomenon of subliminal perception does occur. But mostly they believe that subliminal perception has little power to influence behavior.

Here's an example of an experiment widely accepted as showing evidence of subliminal perception. In this study, the researcher (Huntley, 1953) began by obtaining photographs of the hands and profiles of his subjects, as well as handwriting and voice samples. As evidence of subliminal perception, Huntley noticed a tendency for his subjects to assign higher ratings to their own samples. But curiously, most subjects could not correctly identify their own samples even after they were told they were present in the series.

Such demonstrations are certainly intriguing, but what use is to be made of them in advertising? Advertisers are not taken solely with the possibility of communicating at the subliminal level. What intrigues advertisers (and, conversely, frightens consumers) is the possibility that subliminal communication has the power to influence behavior. Valid demonstrations of such power are hard to find. For example, we would have to take the Huntley experiment to step further and demonstrate that subliminal association of the personal samples with some product resulted in increased desire for that product According to McConnell et al. (1958), very little is known about the effects of subliminal perceptions:

"... anyone who wishes to use subliminal stimuli for commercial purposes can be likened to a stranger entering into a misty, confused countryside where there are but few landmarks."

In other words, there is no conclusive evidence that deep-seated, long-established behavior can be changed as a result of subliminal messages.

Advertising and Children

As a complement to concern about the all-powerful advertising message, we also have concern directed toward the more vulnerable members of the audience—children. Children are the major target group for certain kinds of advertising (e.g., toys and breakfast cereal), but recent research has demonstrated that they are not as defenseless as originally thought.

Much of the research on advertising and children has been based upon the *developmental model* of the French child psychologist, Piaget. According to Piaget's model, the cognitive development of children proceeds through an orderly sequence of "stages." Each stage is characterized by a unique set of cognitive abilities (see Flavell, 1963).

Communication researchers have been interested in the developmental model because of the close association between cognitive capability and communication. Cognitive abilities are necessary for communication. For example, we might ask at what point children can discriminate between advertising and other kinds of messages? Or, at what point can they began to critically evaluate the claims of advertising? Using Piaget's model, communication researchers have predicted that these skills would begin to appear between the ages of two and 11 during the "preoperational" and "concrete operational" stages of development.

To understand the basis for this prediction, you'll need a little more background on Piaget's model. Specifically, what cognitive abilities are associated with these two stages of development (Ward & Wackman, 1973)?

Preoperational—characterized by "centration" and "perceptual boundedness." The preoperational child tends to focus on one dimension of a situation while failing to make use of other equally relevant dimensions. He/she responds primarily to the immediate, perceived environment, to accept what is immediately perceived as the only reality.

Concrete operational—able to mentally manipulate elements in his perception, to imagine possibilities other than what is immediately perceived. Able to focus on more than one dimension of a situation and to perceive relations between dimensions (i.e., "decentration").

Ward and Wackman (1973) discussed the implications of these two stages to children's processing of advertising messages. They felt that preoperation children (aged 2–7) would focus on the visual content of ads and miss the verbal content, while the concrete operational child would process both visual and verbal information. Thus, the preoperational child might be able to discriminate between advertising and other kinds of messages (on television, e.g.), but probably only in terms of gross visual differences, while the concrete operational child might discriminate on the basis of differences in intent.

Differences such as these have been found in studies reported by Ward & Wackman (1973) and others. For example, preoperational children do not seem to understand the purpose of commercials, while concrete operational children often do. Preoperational children often are not certain whether commercials "always tell the truth," while concrete operational children generally answer "no."

In subsequent studies (Ward, Wackman & Wartella, 1977) researchers began to suggest that even very young children often reach a stage of cognitive development which enables then to "filter" advertising messages. In one study, 18 percent of kindergartners, 73 percent of third graders, and 90 percent of sixth graders were found to have a filtering capability—i.e., when asked "what is a TV commercial," they explicitly stated that commercials try to sell products. Furthermore, the researchers demonstrated that possession of a filtering ability *mediated* the effects of advertising on the children. For example, children classified as "filters" often went beyond the immediate advertising message and raised questions about performance and functional attributes of the product.

The discovery of this mediating condition for children's advertising suggests that even children are not defenseless victims of advertising messages. It also suggests that critical abilities might be further developed, if given a little encouragement. Ward, Wackman & Wartella (1977) suggested that both advertisers and children would benefit from separate campaigns to encourage positive habits and values among children (e.g., as in one cereal company's campaign to encourage children to eat a complete breakfast).

Information Campaigns

Earlier in this chapter we distinguished "information campaigns" from "advertising" by noting the essential difference in purpose. Advertising is driven by a profit motive, while information campaigns seek reform. Such campaigns are the bread and butter of many public agencies and countless non-profit organizations. Often communication affords the only (or primary) means by which the goals of reform can be achieved. For example, you can't legislate conservation or preventive medicine; you have to convince people that such practices are in their own best interest.

Minimal Effects

Despite the ubiquitous deployment of information campaigns as a panacea for change, the outlook for success has for some time been pessimistically portrayed in the communication literature. The last word on the effects of information campaigns was (for some time) "minimal." The sponsors of information campaigns, however, don't seem daunted by this assessment. Perhaps they haven't read about minimal effects; or, if they have, perhaps they thought their campaign would be the exception. But before we explore the basis for optimism, let's examine the source of minimal effects.

One of the early landmark pieces on information campaigns (Hyman & Sheatsley, 1947) seemed to anticipate Joseph Klapper. Titled "Some reasons why information campaigns fail," the article detailed several reasons why information campaigns could not expect to duplicate the persuasive effects of communication demonstrated in laboratory studies. The authors illustrated these "reasons" with a number of real-world campaigns that had not achieved their desired effects.

The reasons for failure can be boiled down to just two: (1) selective exposure, and (2) resistance to change. According to Hyman & Sheatsley, the persons most likely to be reached by an information campaign are those who are already well informed and who have attitudes favorable to the object of the campaign. The phenomenon is often illustrated with the (now) well-known example of the Cincinnati United Nations Campaign (Star & Hughes, 1950). The City of Cincinnati was bombarded for days with an intensive campaign to promote the idea of the United Nations and to encourage active participation in local discussion groups. Despite these efforts, major segments of the population remained unaware of the campaign and consequently were unaffected by it.

According to Hovland (1959), information campaigns often attempt to change "socially significant attitudes," which are deeply rooted in previous experience and involved strong personal commitment. Such attitudes are not readily changed. Under circumstances of this sort, campaign message content is perceived selectively—or rejected altogether. Numerous examples of "resistance" have been reported in the literature. Studies of the wartime Mr. Biggot cartoon series revealed that many readers failed to see the absurdity of prejudicial attitudes the series was designed to satirize (Cooper & Jahoda, 1947). More recent studies of the "Archie Bunker" television series have yielded similar results. Many in the audience identified with Archie and interpreted his prejudicial views as correct (Wilhoit & de Bock).

The dynamics of resistance have also been described by Tichenor et al. (1974) concerning environmental attitudes. In a study of Minnesota citizens, widespread concern was voiced about environmental problems, but this did not extend to acceptance of a general environmental ideology. Instead, attitudes toward specific environmental control measures seemed governed by individual self-interests. A citizen living within 10 miles of suspected nuclear contamination of river water from a power plant disassociated himself from the issue, claiming that radioactivity was largely a big city issue—downstream. Why? The plant was a local employer.

Not-so-minimal Effects

There is another way to look at these "reasons for failure." One can view them simply as mediating conditions that must be taken into account if an information campaign is to succeed. One need not view them as insurmountable obstacles which doom every information campaign from the start. If the current outlook on information campaigns is more rosy, it is because of the belief that new communication strategies can be developed which keep us from repeating failures of the past.

If we take this approach, then there is every reason to examine information campaigns that succeed—as well as those that fail. No doubt an article titled, "Some Reasons Why Information Campaigns Succeed" would be instructive, unless no examples were to be found.

One of the earliest discoveries of an effective campaign strategy is attributed to Kurt Lewin (1958), who was looking for ways to deal with the food rationing problem in WW II. One approach was to encourage housewives to use unpopular cuts of meat—sweetbreads, kidneys and tongue. Lewin believed that women who publicly said to an assembled group that they would change to unpopular cuts would be more likely to do so than those merely listening to a lecture. A check some time later found that 32 percent of women having made a public commitment to change were complying while only three percent of those merely listening had done so.

This discovery has been the basis of many information campaigns since. The rationale is that resistance to change can be overcome if one believes other members of the group agree with the change taken. More recent applications of this technique are anti-smoking campaigns. Printed instructions on how to quit smoking were largely ineffective. But smokers who received the same instructions in a supportive group were able to quit smoking for significant periods of time (McAlister & Kenigsberg, 1975).

The use of televised messages to help people stop smoking has likewise produced limited results. Programs were broadcast to reach thousands of smokers, but only a few hundred viewers reported they stopped smoking for more than a few days (Dubren, 1977; Best, 1978). To enhance the effectiveness of a televised campaign, one might arrange for group communication which provides social reinforcement, much like group therapy settings used in Alcoholics Anonymous or the discussion groups used to reinforce the teaching of new farming practices by radio in developing countries (Rogers & Shoemaker, 1971). McAlister (1976) adapted the "radio forum" technique to a televised anti-smoking campaign with encouraging results. A similar approach has been used in Finland on a national scale. Some 30 to 40 thousand participated in volunteer-led groups, with about 10 thousand eventually crediting the program with helping them drop smoking for more than a year (Puska et al., 1979).

Audience Segments

As with advertising, the design of successful information campaigns usually requires the identification of different groups, or "segments," which make up the audience. Once this is done, communication strategies can be developed that will be more effective with each group.

In his *situational theory* of public communication, Grunig (1980) defines these segments in terms of:

(1) whether or not members of the audience recognize a given situation as *problematic*. For example, some individuals viewed the Nestle infant formula controversy as a problem (i.e., stopped to think about it), but many did not.

(2) whether or not audience members are *involved* in the situation. Even those who view a situation as a problem don't necessarily connect themselves with it.

(3) whether or not the audience member feels he has any *personal control* over the situation—i.e., could do something about it if he wanted to.

(4) whether the audience member thinks he has a *solution* that would help resolve the issue.

Although Grunig's model allows him to define 16 different audience segments in terms of how they relate to public issues, he finds that for most purposes it usually suffices to distinguish four:

(1) *Non-Publics*—those who do not recognize a problem;

(2) *Latent Publics*—those who recognize a problem, but do not see themselves as involved;

(3) *Aware Publics*—those who recognize a problem and see themselves as involved, but have not taken any action.

(4) *Active Publics*—those who have acted to do something about a problem which involves them.

The value of distinguishing audience segments in these terms is that it tells you something about the probable communication behavior of different groups in the audience. According to Grunig, members of *aware* and *active* publics more often seek and process information, and usually have formed their own ideas about the problem. Members of active and aware publics should be reached through specialized media that can provide in-depth treatment of the issue (without the expectation that their attitudes can be changed). Members of the latent publics, since they do not actively seek information, have to be reached through mass audience media such as prime-time television.

We can see the potential application of these definitions if we consider a recent situation, such as the Exxon oil spill in Alaska. Environmental groups would be interested in reaching members of the latent public (for this issue) to try to raise their awareness and concern about oil spills. For that purpose they should turn to such media as general circulation magazines and television. They should not assume that their audience is particularly interested in oil spills, or that they have formed any definite ideas. At the same time, the oil companies (especially Exxon) are faced with a situation where they must communicate; if they fail to, members of aware and active publics will seek out and get all their information from other sources.

Overcoming Selectivity

If a campaign is to be more than minimally effective, selective exposure must often be overcome. In an earlier chapter we analyzed the selective exposure hypothesis, and concluded that selective exposure is seldom psychologically motivated by a desire to avoid unwelcome (i.e., "dissonance-producing) information. It seems to be more a problem of making the information relevant than one of overcoming psychological defenses. For example, in the anti-smoking campaigns discussed above, once smokers are convinced they should quit smoking, instructions and advice on how to quit become relevant.

A campaign that overcame selective exposure and achieved effects on both knowledge and attitudes was reported some twenty years after the Hyman and Sheatsley classic (Douglas et al., 1970). In juxtaposition to the earlier article, the title seemed almost boastful: "An Information Campaign That Changed Community Attitudes." The purpose of this study was to see if a media campaign would be effective in preparing a local community for the social innovation of a "sheltered workshop" for the mentally retarded. This would be accomplished if the campaign could promote greater knowledge of mental retardation as a community problem, and a positive shift in attitudes toward mental retardation.

Two comparable communities (Reedsburg and Richland Center) were selected for the study. A vigorous information campaign was conducted in Reedsburg, consisting of news stories, feature stories, advertisement, posters, public meetings, speakers, etc. Richland Center served as the "control group"; no campaign was conducted there. Measures of knowledge and attitudes were taken in both communities before and after the campaign. Greater before-to-after change was predicted in Reedsburg, a prediction that was strongly substantiated.

Why should this campaign have succeeded where others had failed? The authors offered three primary reasons:

1. The campaign succeeded in reaching over 90 percent of Reedsburg citizens (thus, selective exposure was not a strong mediating factor);

2. The topic was not highly controversial; thus, strong resistance or local "backlash" was not aroused.

3. Campaign messages were relayed interpersonally, supplementing and extending their effects.

A more recent example of an effective public information campaign is the Stanford Heart Disease Prevention Program (SHDPP). In this campaign a community-based approach was used to examine the potential of media to influence diet, exercise, and smoking habits (Farquhar et al, 1977). The media messages were combined with intensive face-to-face interaction among groups of "high risk" individuals. Not only did the campaign result in greater knowledge of heart disease risk factors; the campaign participants also made changes in diet, reduced smoking, with resulting decreases in blood pressure and cholesterol.

The designers of the SHDPP attribute its success to a few major factors: (1) extensive use of audience feedback in message design; (2) stimulation of interpersonal channels; and (3) the emphasis on "community-based intervention," which reflects the recognition that change occurs *within a social structure* (Maccoby & Alexander, 1980).

Overcoming Knowledge Gaps

Another reason why information campaigns are said to frequently fail is that *knowledge gaps* between different groups in society are increased as a result of mass communication campaigns. For example, it is well known that on many topics those of higher socio-economic status (SES) tend to have more information than those of lower SES. Efforts to provide additional information to a mass audience may increase this difference in knowledge between high and low SES groups. Many times this is a serious drawback because the very people who could benefit most from the additional information are in the low SES group. A case in point is the public television series "Sesame Street," which was intended to help educationally disadvantaged children. Evaluators of the series concluded, however, that the program had been of most benefit to children who already had an educational advantage (Ball & Bogatz, 1975).

According to experts on information campaigns, it can be difficult to design campaigns that have an opposite effect—i.e., *reduce* rather than widen knowledge gaps. To do so a communication campaign would have to:

(1) get the attention of people who would just as soon not pay attention;

(2) achieve exchange of information with people who are unused to or uninterested in receiving information;

(3) provide motivation which seems to be missing (Hawkins, et al., 1987).

According to Hawkins, et al. (1987), this requires a radical shift in the way that people think about communication campaigns. It means shifting the focus from information that experts want to convey to *answering questions that individuals may want to ask.* (This has much in common with the "uses & gratifications approach" discussed in Chapter 5.) The problem with such an approach is that it implies tailoring information to answer the specific questions of individuals with different problems and backgrounds—the very kind of communication service that campaigns designed for mass audiences are ill-equipped to provide.

An experimental interactive computer campaign for adolescents—Body Awareness Resource Network (BARN)—has been developed at the University of Wisconsin to reach those adolescents most in need of health information—those experimenting with risky behaviors (e.g., drugs, smoking, sexual intercourse). According to the campaign's designers, computers may be better suited to this kind of effort than traditional mass media (Hawkins, et al., 1975). The branching logic of interactive computer programs allows them to tailor information to the requests of individual users. The information is also available when and where the individual chooses (i.e., synchronicity).

The BARN campaign has incorporated some unique features. It provides interactive programs covering five areas—alcohol and other drugs, human sexuality, smoking prevention and cessation, stress management, and body management (Figure 6.5). For example, with the body management unit, the user participates in an adventure game in which proper diet and exercise choices allow one to conquer obstacles and continue the quest. With the smoking unit, he/she can practice with situations he or she might experience, or decide what should happen next to short "soap operas."

Preliminary evidence indicates that BARN has been successful in reaching those adolescents most in need of health information—not just the "good kids" who avoid risky behavior. BARN was used more by those students who were previously experimenting with risky health behaviors than by those who were not experimenting (Hawkins, et al., 1975). BARN not only attracted more experimenting students, but the

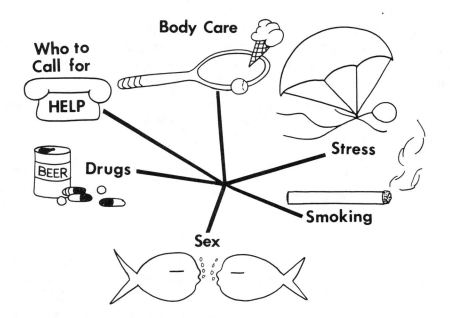

Figure 6.5. Structure of BARN Interactive Campaign for Adolescents. From *Journal of Communication,* 1987 37(2), p. 25 © 1987 *Journal of Communication.* Used with permission.

students discriminated among the programs once they got into BARN; they selected those programs most relevant to their own behavior. For example, students who were sexually active were much more likely to use the Human Sexuality program than those on other topics.

In conclusion, recent evidence does support the idea that carefully planned and executed information campaigns can achieve more than minimal effects. The persistence of the public information industry in continuing to mount such campaigns therefore appears to rest on more than an implicit faith that they produce desired effects. In fact, most campaign planners can no longer afford the luxury of assuming effects on faith. The sponsors of expensive campaigns more often than not insist on careful follow-up research to document effects. For example, a metropolitan electric power utility was told that continued Federal funding of numerous information programs designed to promote energy conservation depended on rigorous documentation of their effectiveness. Outside evaluation by a team of communication researchers resulted in further funding of some programs, and the discontinuation of those whose lack of results did not justify the expense.

Key Terms

(Audience) segment
Advertising
Alpha level
Beta level
Concrete operational stage
Developmental model
Frequency
Gross rating points
High involvement model
Interactive media
Involvement hypothesis
Knowledge gap
Low involvement model
Market segmentation study
Message appeal
Preoperational stage
Public information
Publics
Reach
Situational theory
Socioeconomic status (SES)
Subliminal
Subliminal message
Subliminal perception

Summary

Public information campaigns are intended to benefit the individual or society, while advertising is intended to benefit the sponsor.

The high involvement model of advertising communication assumes that the consumer is rational and the decision important enough to justify a great deal of information processing effort.

The low involvement model assumes that not all purchase decisions are important, and that advertising messages often are not relevant at the time they are received.

According to the involvement hypothesis, the receiver's level of involvement makes a difference in how messages such as ads are processed.

Efforts to establish that TV is a low involvement medium have (so far) shown that there is nothing very distinctive about brain wave patterns that occur during TV viewing.

Brain wave patterns are, however, useful for monitoring attention to messages, and have shown clearly that attention to advertising messages is anything but constant.

The major techniques for evaluating the communication effects of commercials are theatre tests and on-air tests.

According to Krugman, the optimum frequency for an advertising schedule is "three" because three exposures marks the dividing line between attention and disengagement.

A basic faith of the advertising copywriter is that message appeal makes a difference, but in practice the effectiveness of a given appeal is hard to predict.

In the design of advertising campaigns, market segmentation studies are used to identify characteristics of specific groups of consumers on which to base development of tailor-made message appeals.

Psychologists agree that subliminal perception does occur under certain conditions (not fully understood), but they disagree with claims that subliminal messages have great power to influence behavior.

Children's ability to comprehend television advertising is closely related to their stage of cognitive development. Research shows that even at a very early age children attain a level of cognitive development that allows them to critically evaluate the claims of commercial messages.

Early research on public information campaigns identified two major reasons for campaign failure: (1) selective exposure, and (2) resistance to change. Recent campaign research shows that selective exposure can be overcome by targeting messages to specific publics. Resistance to change can be overcome by linking mass media to interpersonal support networks.

One drawback of public information campaigns is that they may increase knowledge differences between low and high SES groups. Some recent campaigns have avoided the "knowledge gap effect" by shifting their information focus to answering questions that individuals may want to ask (rather than telling people what "experts" have decided they should know).

References

Appel, V., S. Weinstein & C. Weinstein (1979). "Brain activity and recall of TV advertising." *Journal of Advertising Research,* 19, 7–15.

Bauer, R. A. (1964). The obstinate audience. *American Psychologist,* 19, 319–328.

Bauer, R. A. and A. H. Bauer (1960). America, mass society and mass media. *The Journal of Social Issues,* 16, 3–66.

Becker, L. B. & J. C. Doolittle (1975). How repetition affects evaluations of and information seeking about candidates. *Journalism Quarterly,* 52, 611–617.

Best, J. A., L. E. Owen and L. Trentadue (1978). Comparison of satiation and rapid smoking in self-managed smoking cessation. *Addictive Behavior,* 3, 71–78.

Bowen, L. and S. H. Chaffee (1974). Product involvement and pertinent advertising appeals. *Journal Quarterly,* 51, 613–621.

Bucklin, L. P. (1965). The informative role of advertising. *Journal of Advertising,* 5, 11–15.

Chaffee, Steven H. and J. M. McLeod (1973). Consumer Decisions and Information Use. In S. Ward and T. S. Robertson (Eds.). Consumer Behavior: Theoretical Sources. Englewood Cliffs, N.J.: Prentice-Hall, pp. 385–415.

Clancy, Kevin J. and Lyman E. Ostlund (1976). Commercial Effectiveness Measures. Vol. 16, No. 1. Pp. 29–34.

Cooper, E. and M. Jahoda (1947). "The Evasion of Propaganda: How Prejudiced People Respond to Anti-Prejudice Propaganda," *Journal of Psychology,* 23, 15–25.

Douglas, D. F., B. H. Westley and S. H. Chaffee (1970). "An Information Campaign that Changed Community Attitudes." *Journalism Quarterly,* 47, 479–487, 492.

Dubren, R. (1977). Evaluation of a televised stop-smoking clinic. *Public Health Reports,* 92, 81–84.

Farquhar, J. (1978). The Community-Based Model of Life Style Intervention Trials. *Am. J. Epidemiol,* 108, 103–111.

Flavell, J. H. (1963). The Developmental Psychology of Jean Piaget. Princeton: Van Nostrand.

Grunig, J. (1980). Public response to corporate communication about public policy issues. Presented to Operations Research Society of America, Colorado Springs, Colorado.

Hawkins, R., et al. (1987). Reaching hard-to-reach populations: Interactive computer programs as information campaigns for adolescents. *J. of Comm.* 37(2), 8–28.

Hodock, Calvin I. D(1976). Predicting On-Air Recall from Theatre Tests. *Journal of Advertising Research,* 16, 25–32.

Hovland, Carl I. (1959). Reconciling Conflicting Results Derived from Experimental and Survey Studies of Attitude Change. *American Psychologist,* 14, 8–17.

Hovland, C. I., I. L. Janis and H. H. Kelley (1953). Communication and Persuasion. New Haven, Conn.: Yale University Press.

Huntley, C. W. (1953). Judgments of self based upon records of expressive behavior. *Journal of Abnormal & Social Psychology,* 48, 398–427.

Hyman, H. H. and P. B. Sheatsley (1947). "Some Reasons Why Information Campaigns Fail." *Public Opinion Quarterly,* 11, 412–423.

Key, W. B. (1972). Subliminal Seduction: Ad Media's Manipulation of a Not-So-Innocent America. Englewood Cliffs, N.J.: Prentice-Hall.

_____ (1976). Media Sexploitation. Englewood Cliffs, N.J.: Prentice-Hall.

Krugman, H. E. (1965). The Impact of Television Advertising: Learning without Involvement. *Public Opinion Quarterly,* 29, 349–356.

_____ (1972). Why three exposures may be enough. *Journal of Advertising Research,* 12, 11–14.

Krugman, H. (1971). "Brainwave measures of media involvement." *Journal of Advertising Research,* 11, 3–9.

Lavidge, R. and G. A. Steiner (1961). A model for predictive measurements of advertising effectiveness. *Journal of Marketing,* 25, 59–62.

Leventhal, H. and P. Niles (1964). A field experiment on fear arousal with data on the validity of questionnaire measures. *Journal of Personality,* 32, 459–479.

Levine, Philip (1976). Commercials that name competing brands. *Journal of Advertising Research*, 16, 7–14.

Lewin, K. (1958). Group decision and social change. In E. E. Maccoby, T. M. Newcomb and E. L. Hartley (eds.), Readings in Social Psychology. New York: Holt, Rinehart and Winston.

Maccoby, N., & J. Alexander (1980). "Use of media in lifestyle programs." In *Behavioral Medicine: Changing Health Lifestyles,* eds. P. Davidson & S. Davidson, pp. 351–70. New York: Brunner/Mazel.

McAlister, A. and M. Kenigsberg (1975). Methods and modalities for smoking cessation training. Presented to Assoc. for the Advancement of Behavior Therapy, San Francisco, CA.

McAlister, A. (1976). Toward the Mass Communication of Behavioral Counseling. Ph.D. Dissertation, Stanford University.

_____ (1981). Antismoking Campaigns: Progress in Developing Effective Communications. In Rice and Paisley (Eds.) Public Communication Campaigns. Beverly Hills: Sage Publications, Inc.

McConnell, J. V., R. L. Cutler & E. B. McNeil (1958). Subliminal stimulation: an overview. *American Psychologist*, 13, 229–242.

Miller, W. (1985). "A view from the inside: brainwaves and television viewing." *Journalism Quarterly*, 62(3), 508–514.

Percy, Larry (1976). How market segmentation guides advertising strategy. *Journal of Advertising Research*, 16, 11–22.

Perry, Michael and Arnon Perry (1976). Ad recall: biased measure of media? *Journal of Advertising Research*, 16, 21–25.

Puska, P. et al. (1980). The North Karelia Project. Kuopio, Finland: University of Kuopio.

Rice, R. E. and W. J. Paisley (1981). Public Information Campaigns. Beverly Hills, CA.: Sage.

Robertson, T. S. (1976). Low Commitment Consumer Behavior. *Journal of Advertising Research*, 16, 19–24.

Rogers, E., with F. Shoemaker (1971). Communication of Innovations: A Cross-Cultural Approach. New York Free Press.

Rothschild, M., E. Thorson, B. Reeves, J. Hirsch, and R. Goldstein (1986). "EEG activity and the processing of television commercials." *Communication Research*, 13(2), 182–220.

Severin, W. J., and J. S. Tankard (1988). Communication Theories: Origins, Methods, Uses. New York: Longman.

Star, S., and H. Hughes (1950). A Report on an Educational Campaign: The Cincinnati Plan for the United Nations. *American Journal of Sociology*, 55, 389–400.

Tichenor, P. J., G. A. Donohue, C. N. Olien and J. K. Bowers (1974). Environment and public opinion. In Schoenfeld (ed.) Interpreting Environmental Issues. Madison, WI.: Dembar Education Research Services.

Vicary, J. M. (1957). Reported in Advertising Age, Sept. 16, p. 127.

Ward, S. and D. B. Wackman (1973). Children's information processing of television advertising. In P. Clarke (ed.) New Models for Communication Research. Beverly Hills, CA.: Sage.

Ward S. and E. Wartella (1977). How Children Learn to Buy. Beverly Hills, CA.: Sage.

Wilhoit, G. C. and H. de Bock (1976). 'All in the Family' in Holland. *Journal of Communication*, 26, 75–84.

7

Mass Communication and Political Campaigns

Introduction

In this chapter we want to gain some insights into the role and effects of mass communication in political campaigns. As a focal point for this chapter, we would first like to point out that ideas about this have changed significantly since 1960, when Klapper based his "minimal effects" model partly on a study of the 1940 and 1948 election campaigns (Lazarsfeld, Berelson & Gaudet, 1944; Berelson, Lazarsfeld & McPhee, 1954). As you have already seen, the influence of the minimal effects model has extended until the present time, but data which would throw an entirely different light on the effects of mass media election campaigns were already being collected during the 1960 Kennedy/Nixon campaign, the very same year that Klapper's model was published. This was indeed a pivotal year in our understanding of the effects of political campaigns.

Based on the election studies done before 1960, you probably would have agreed with Klapper—the effects of mass communication did appear to be minimal. Two major studies had been reported: (1) a study conducted in Erie Ct., Ohio of the 1940 Roosevelt/Wilkie campaign; and (2) a study conducted in Elmira, New York of the 1948 Dewey/Truman election.

The results of these studies were very similar. The 1940 study compared May and October voting intentions and found that only 8 percent changed their intentions, and even this 8 percent was "low" in attention to the media campaign suggesting that these conversions were probably due to some other cause. The 1948 study found an even lower (August to October) conversion rate of 3 percent, and once again it was not clear that these conversions could be attributed to the media campaign.

Based on election studies done after 1960, it is doubtful that you would go along with a minimal effects model. A vast number of studies could be cited that document a wide variety of effects attributed to political campaigns. We haven't the space here to summarize all these studies, nor would that serve our purpose. It is far more revealing to begin with a question: why do studies done from 1960 to the present yield such different results?

Actually, there seem to be a number of reasons:

- Media and communication tactics have changed.
- The political environment has changed.
- Research paradigms have changed.

We turn now to discussing each of these changes and the way in which they have contributed to the changing view of political communication and its effects.

Media Changes

Nineteen-sixty marked the first nationally televised broadcast of presidential debates, and the context for several studies that uncovered evidence contrary to minimal effects. Some observers feel that this change in media from a print-dominated to a television-dominated campaign has been the major reason for increased effects. In fact some have gone so far as to say that television has altered the process of political communication in the United States (Robinson, 1977).

The shift to a television-dominated campaign actually began before 1960 with the introduction of televised political advertising in 1952. The beginning of nationally televised debates followed in 1960. Then in 1963 the major networks insured that television became a major source of political news by expanding their evening news broadcasts (from 15) to 30 minutes. Let's look more closely at how each of these changes may have enhanced the impact of election campaigns on the electorate.

Political Advertising

The 1952 campaign saw General Dwight Eisenhower staring uncomfortably out at the television audience, reading his lines in a halting voice. A voice off camera asked, "General, if war comes is this country really ready?" "It is not," said the General (Devlin, 1986). Although this 1952 spot seems primitive by today's standards, the rationale behind the 60-second spot remains much the same today. The basic idea was to capsulized a 45-minute speech in 60 seconds. The loss in depth of information would (from the candidate's point of view) result in several advantages (compared to the original speech):

1. One could now afford to broadcast the "speech" over television, with the result that a much larger audience could be reached.

2. A short, simple message would be more easily remembered.

3. The message could be rebroadcast repeatedly thereby both increasing the size of the audience, and enhancing recall through multiple exposures.

It was not until the 1970s that researchers became seriously concerned with measuring the effects of these television spots. By this time there was beginning to be concern that spots ads in combination with television news coverage of campaigns would shift the focus of campaigns from issues to personalities. The implication of this was that a major effect of television would be to change the basis on which people voted. People would now vote for "personalities," rather than voting on the basis of issues.

While studies of political advertising have provided evidence for a variety of effects, the notion that advertising encourages personality voting has never received much support. The research literature contains several studies showing that exposure to political advertising is positively related to political knowledge, including awareness of issues (e.g., Atkin, Bowen, Nayman & Sheinkoppf, 1973; Kaid, 1976; Mendelsohn & O'Keefe, 1976; Hofstetter & Buss, 1980). In addition, studies of the content of televised spots have shown, surprisingly, that they contain as much information about issues as they do about the personalities of the candidates (Joslyn, 1980). One study reported that over 40 percent of the television ads in the 1972 presidential campaign were "issue-oriented." In comparison with print media ads, the television spots were no less issue-oriented (Bowers, 1972).

At this point the reader is asked to recall a principle that we have emphasized in previous chapters—the effect of a message is not due to content alone. There are, as we have said, "mediating conditions." In the case of candidate advertising, one important mediating condition is the voter's candidate preference. By a process of *selective perception*, voter's see in a candidate's message what they want to see. For example, they can select out the positive qualities of a preferred candidate, and the negative qualities of an opposing candidate (even from an ad supporting that candidate).

Another important mediating condition may be the way that voters think about candidates. It is often suggested that political ads influence the way that voters think about candidates. For example, the concern that political advertising leads to voting choices that are "personality-bound." It may work the other way around. That is, the way that voter's think may shape the kind of effect that a spot ad can have. According to a recent study, the effect of an ad on candidate popularity was not solely a function of its content; instead, the type of appeal used by the ad sometimes shifted the individual into a cognitive mode that effectively blunted the effectiveness of the advertising (Zandpour & Bowes, 1984).

Televised Debates

Some of the earliest evidence contrary to a minimal effects interpretation of election campaigns was discovered by researchers who sought to document effects (if any) of the 1960 Kennedy/Nixon debates. The popular conception of these debates is that they were a turning point in the campaign, and the most significant factor in Kennedy's victory. Some would carry this characterization even further, flatly stating that Nixon lost the election because "he did not look good on television."

The evidence does not fully support this popular conception, although the debates may have moved enough undecided voters to account for Kennedy's margin of victory. It would be a mistake to conclude, however, that the debates went entirely in Kennedy's favor. Both candidates gained substantial numbers of "undecided" voters during the debates (Kennedy—17 percent, Nixon—16 percent). It is only when we consider the loss of undecided voters who would normally vote Republican that Kennedy gains a clear advantage. Nixon lost about 8 percent of the undecided Republican voters after the 1st and 4th debates, reducing his net gain to 8 percent. Kennedy lost only 1 percent of undecided Democratic voters (after the 3rd debate), leaving his net gain at 16 percent.

This movement of undecided voters toward a voting commitment is termed "*crystallization*" (as opposed to "conversion," which involves reversing a previous commitment). Crystallization has emerged as a very important effect in recent campaigns. It was observed as well in the 1940 and 1948 election studies, but was accorded little attention because of the emphasis on conversion effects.

In addition to the "crystallization" effect, a number of other effects were observed for the 1960 debates. But before we discuss these it is worth noting that there are some reasons for expecting more than minimal effects. It was not just that the audience was large; seventy-million adults watched the first debate. It was also the composition of the audience. The audience was varied, attracting persons from all walks of life. But most important, in terms of the selective exposure hypothesis, the debates were watched by equal numbers of Republicans and Democrats, and equal numbers of Kennedy and Nixon supporters. Since the candidates appeared together, how could the viewers help but be exposed to information about both candidates?

In fact viewers seemed to learn about both candidates, not just the candidate they supported. One study of the debates tested panels of pro-Kennedy and pro-Nixon voters on their knowledge of factual items concerning both candidates (Carter, 1962). There was no difference in knowledge.

Nixon supporters recalled what both candidates had said, and so did Kennedy supporters. Here was direct evidence that the "minimizing" influence of *selective exposure* did not apply to this new form of campaign communication.

While studies of the debates contradicted the selective exposure principle, there was evidence of selective perception. We have already seen that viewers acquired infor-

Attribute

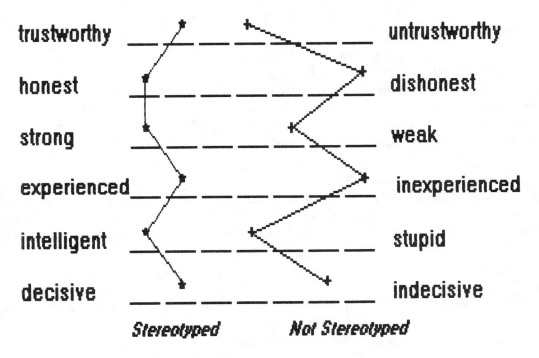

Figure 7.1. Stereotyping of Candidate Images.

mation about both candidates. But what use did they make of the information? One possible use would be to construct "images" of the candidates. Selective perception seemed to operate in the construction of these images because viewers constructed more strongly stereotyped images of their own candidates. What this means is that viewers selected attributes of their own candidate that they developed into a consistent, homogeneous picture (see Figure 7.1).

No less than 31 separate studies were conducted of the 1960 debates (see Krauss, 1962). In subsequent elections featuring presidential debates they have remained a popular subject of injury. For example, the 1976 Ford/Carter debates became the subject of another volume of effects studies. These studies have continued to provide challenges to Klapper's minimal effects model. One of the more significant studies of the 1976 debates sought to directly test some propositions from the minimal effects model (Chaffee & Miyo, 1978). Specifically, the model predicts that voters view the debates primarily for "reinforcement" of voting intentions—e.g., to reassure themselves that their party had nominated a candidate for whom they could vote. Thus, the debates should not provide a new basis for candidate choice; the information acquired should be assimilated in a way that supported a choice that had already been made.

Chaffee and Miyo reported that in fact this kind of "minimal effect" did apply to some debate viewers—"occasional" viewers (who did not watch all the debates). These viewers tended to vote along party lines, and only watched enough of the debates to confirm that intention.

However, for "regular" viewers of these debates the primary function did not appear to be reinforcement (as predicted by minimal effects). Instead, the debates facilitated *"informed voting"*—voting in conformance with the policy positions that candidates took on important campaign issues. Differences between candidates on key issues served to "crystallize" the voting intentions of "regular" debate viewers; they tended not to vote on the basis of party loyalty or candidate personalities.

A number of debate studies have found that watching the debates influences voters' images of the candidates. As noted above, the 1960 debates resulted in increased stereotyping of the candidates. The 1976 debates produced a similar effect. In 1984 the study of image effects has taken a step further with the discovery that the Bush/Ferraro (vice presidential) debate also influenced the meaning of the voter's image (Stamm et al., 1985).

In this study voters were polled before and after the debate to determine:

(1) Which *attributes* (e.g., "aggressive," "shallow," etc.) they applied to the candidates; and

(2) How they *characterized* the candidates on each of these attributes.

The study found differences in both components of the image. First, let's take Bush. After the debate viewers more often described Bush as "indecisive." But perhaps more importantly, Bush's indecisiveness took on different meanings as a result of the debate. Before the debate, his indecisiveness was seen as one of his *qualities,* or as a *failing.* But after the debate "indecisiveness" took on more ominous implications; it led voters to characterize him as *risky,* even *dangerous.* Similar changes occurred in Ferraro's image. Both before and after the debate voters often perceived Ferraro as "insensitive." But once again debate viewers changed their perceptions of what this attribute meant. After the debate Ferraro's insensitivity often meant that she was dangerous (prior to the debate this characterization was not even present in the sample).

Campaign News Coverage

While we have given emphasis to the political impact of candidate advertising and televised debates, according to Robinson it was the network's switch from a 15– to a 30– minute format that fundamentally altered the process of political communication in the U.S. How? By changing the audience for political information. The audience for television news is drawn more heavily (than print media audiences) from the less educated and less politically active members of the electorate. These individuals, according to Robinson, are more susceptible to media influence.

There are, however, a number of reasons why not everyone would agree with Robinson's assessment of the political influence of television news. First, Robinson's description of the television news audience is a bit overdrawn. While it is correct that all demographic groups make substantial use of television during presidential campaigns (Wade & Schramm, 1969), the use of television for political information still differs sharply between demographic groups. For example, college graduates use television more regularly for political information than do high school graduates (McCombs, 1973).

Second, is it true that television news has more influence on the less-educated, less active members of the electorate? Perhaps, but again this should not be over-stated. One can argue that this group is more likely to vote on the basis of personalities, and that television news provides mainly that kind of information about candidates. But too much of this argument hinges on the fallacy that effect is synonymous with content.

The notion that television campaign coverage does not contribute much to the voter's knowledge of issues had been accepted for a variety of reasons. Television as an information source appears to have some built-in defects. TV news flies by quickly, with viewers having no opportunity to control the pace, or to go back over parts of the message. And as mentioned in Chapter 6, a great deal of television exposure is "incidental," suggesting that viewers would not pay close attention or think very much about what they see.

This reasoning appeared to be supported by studies that showed weak associations between TV news viewing and political knowledge, perhaps because much news viewing represents incidental exposure. However, this conclusion changes if we examine the effects of instrumental exposure (see Chapter 6). When people pay close attention to television news, there is a substantial positive effect on political knowledge (Chaffee & Schleuder, 1986; Culbertson & Stempel, 1986). Thus, it would appear that the contribution of television news goes beyond information about candidate personalities.

Media Reliance

Along with the belief that television is a largely ineffective channel for political communication, we find the notion that television is also the *only* source of political information for most Americans. This is the so-called *media-reliance* hypothesis, which explains why many Americans don't (seem to) know very much about politics—because they rely on television.

In reality the evidence does not support this hypothesis. Still, there is confusion over this point because different definitions of "television reliant" have been employed.

For example, if 32 percent of a population names television as their "first choice for political information," should all these people be classified as tv-reliant (McLeod & McDonald, 1985)? Obviously not, since this information by itself does not tell us that all these persons rely on television as their sole source of political information. It turns out that most of these persons also name newspapers as a major source of political information. In fact the majority of Americans rely on more than one source (Chaffee & Schleuder, 1986).

The idea of millions of Americans totally reliant on television for political information is largely a myth. Even if we grant that a sizable percent (but far from a majority) rely largely on television, this should not imply that this group is largely ignorant of politics as a result. As we have seen, there is little or no difference in political knowledge between those who rely largely on television and those who rely largely on print.

While it is inadvisable to make glittering generalizations about the impact of television news, there are some more specific questions about the impact of television on politics that can be answered. These include the following: (1) Does the broadcasting of poll results contribute to a "bandwagon effect"? (2) Does the broadcasting of early voting returns influence the choices of those who have not yet voted? (3) Does television news help set an "agenda" of issues which influences how voters evaluate candidates? (4) Does television news contribute to "video-malaise"—a sense of being unable to influence political processes?

Effects of Poll Results

The idea that publicizing election poll results could affect voting behavior goes back many years; it was a matter of concern before television became a primary medium of political information. If the impact of poll results is of greater concern now, it is not only because they are publicized over television, but because the use and publication of polls has itself become more widespread. On the one hand, polls have become an almost indispensable tool of the modern campaign. On the other hand, they have also become a tool to the political reporter—an accepted means of generating political news.

This makes obvious a point that is often overlooked because of our concern with the possible impact on voters. But perhaps the major impact of polls is to be found on those who use the tool. Certainly the findings of polls have major impact on how candidates conduct their campaigns. And they have had a major impact on how reporters cover campaigns. For example, the ready access to poll results (in some cases on a day-by-day basis) facilitates the use of a "horse race" analogy in covering campaigns because journalists always have plenty of information on how the "horses" are running.

But what about the impact, if any, on voters? Might there be an impact on voter turnout? And could there be an effect on voting preference?

Polls are thought to reduce voting turnout. The turnout could be reduced in two ways: if supporters of the trailing candidate(s) give up, and/or if supporters of the leading candidate become over-confident. Unfortunately, very little research has been done on the question of turnout, none of it conclusive (Mendelsohn & Crespi, 1970). So we are left with many questions. Is turnout more likely to be affected the larger the margin between candidates? Or, perhaps, do most voters disregard poll results because they distrust them, or because their motives for voting require them to vote regardless of whether they vote for the winning candidate?

Polls are also thought to influence voters to cast their ballot for the winning candidate—the so-called *bandwagon effect*. If a bandwagon effect occurs, this increases the margin of victory for the candidate who is leading in the polls. To take a recent example, polls taken up to two days before the New Hampshire presidential primary in 1988 showed Robert Dole leading George Bush by a healthy margin. If a bandwagon effect were operative, then Dole should have won the primary by an even larger margin (since poll results were extensively publicized). But to the contrary, Bush actually won the primary by a margin of 9 percent. Interestingly, polling done on the day of the primary revealed that as many as one-third of Republican voters made up their minds after the final poll predicting Dole's victory. So if ever there was an optimum situation for a bandwagon effect, this would appear to be one. Yet a bandwagon effect clearly did not occur.

Studies designed to detect bandwagon effects have been made in a number of other campaigns, going all the way back to 1948 when all the major national pollsters reported that Dewey was leading Truman. Almost none of these studies yielded convincing evidence of a bandwagon effect (Mendelsohn & Crespi, 1970).

One notable exception is a study which predicted an effect provided that the poll reports an unexpected split in opinion within one's own *reference group* (Atkin, 1969). Notice the difference in reasoning here. It is not simply a matter of who is reported to be leading that is significant. Instead, the occurrence of a bandwagon effect is dependent on two factors: (1) whether the poll results are relevant to one's own reference group (for voting); and (2) whether the results are contrary to expectations. Under these conditions, Atkin found some evidence that voters shift their intentions to vote for the candidate supported by their reference group (e.g., other college students).

Let's see if we can apply this to the 1988 New Hampshire presidential primary. You'll have to imagine that you're a Republican college student voting in that primary, that you expect most Republican college students would favor Bush, and that you receive poll results showing that most such students actually favor Dole. In such cases there should be a bandwagon effect toward Dole. And, conceivably, there could have been among this particular group of voters. The point is that a bandwagon effect uniformly influencing all voters is highly unlikely, and clearly did not occur in New Hampshire or in the other elections where it was sought.

Early Voting Returns

In addition to using polls to predict the outcome of an election, media also use early returns. For example, in presidential contests voters on the East Coast go to the polls first because of time zone differences. Thus, it is possible that election outcomes could be predicted based on early returns before many of the West Coast voters reach the polls. Again, there are two concerns: (1) Projections of election winners based on early returns could discourage turnout from those who have not yet voted; and/or (2) voting preference might be influenced. The influence of early returns on voter turnout has been studied in several presidential campaigns, including the 1964 (Johnson/Goldwater), 1968 (Nixon/Humphrey), and 1980 (Carter/Reagan) campaigns. Of these, the 1968 campaign can be disregarded because the outcome was so close that a winner could not be predicted from early returns. Five studies were conducted on the two remaining campaigns. None found an effect on voter turnout that could be attributed to broadcasting early returns and prediction of winners (Fuchs, 1966; Jackson, 1983; Lang & Lang, 1968 & 1984; Mendelsohn, 1966). Only one of the studies (Jackson) found a decline in voter turnout, but the author indicated this decline was likely due to Carter's concession speech which was broadcast before the polls had closed on the West Coast.

A popular interpretation of these voter turnout studies is that a *"law of minimal consequences"* applies (Lang & Lang, 1968). Strong among the reasons people vote is a sense of citizen duty, an obligation of citizenship, no matter how lopsided early election returns may be for or against one's favorite candidate. One voter commented:

> "I wanted my vote in this election counted, even though I knew I was on the losing side . . . we should treasure our vote." (Mendelsohn & Crespi, 1970, p. 202).

A second reason early predictions have little influence is the small number of persons potentially open to influence. Only those who put off voting until late in the day and watch an early projection of election winners could conceivably be discouraged from voting. For example, in a sample of 1,724 voters interviewed the day before and the day after the 1964 presidential election, only 130 voters were identified as having watched forecasts of a strong Johnson victory before having voted (Mendelsohn & Crespi, 1970).

We have already seen that there is no evidence of a "bandwagon effect" attributable to publicizing poll results generally. Thus we should expect few effects of this sort based on polls of early election returns.

Before giving up on the bandwagon effect, perhaps we should look for it among "undecided voters." Perhaps election forecasts helped these people decide on or "crystallize" their vote. There is little firm evidence for such an effect in past elections.

Although these studies indicate no evidence of turnout or bandwagon effects in previous elections, some observers feel this does not foreclose the possibility in the future.

"If the expectation of a close race had been wide-spread and if many people were undecided about whether to vote or how to vote, large numbers of people might delay going to the polls until they had first heard how the election was going." (Lang & Lang, 1963, p. 165).

Setting the Political Agenda

We have discussed previously (Chapter 5) the hypothesis that media can influence which issues are perceived as important by their audiences—the so-called "*agenda setting*" effect. Considering that "issues" publicized through the media are generally political in nature, we are led to treat agenda setting as a political effect of media. Certainly, those issues which receive public attention and discussion are likely to become objects of political action, and may as a result eventually have resources directed to dealing with them.

Another way to look at agenda setting is to view it in the context of a political campaign. We might ask, "Does it make any difference (to the course of a campaign) which issues achieve prominence in the minds of voters?" It would seem that the answer to this question must be "yes." At least the normative view of democratic elections is that voters take these issues into account when making up their minds how to vote. If this is the case, then candidates should strive to establish the importance of issues that reflect well on their candidacy and, conversely, seek to remove issues that reflect unfavorably.

But, of course, candidates do not have that much control over the "issue agenda" that is created through the news coverage of print and broadcast media. Thus, it is possible that media could influence the course of an election by which issues they choose to give prominent coverage. The extensive coverage of Senator Hart's extra-marital affair during the 1988 campaign is a case in point. There would not be much question in many people's minds that the intense publicity which made this a campaign issue resulted in his early withdrawal from the race. Because of this issue "public opinion" seemed to turn against Hart.

We could probably think of many such anecdotes, but anecdotes by themselves can be misleading. Is there any other evidence that agenda setting effects "snowball" in this way? Or, is this just another plausible effect (like the bandwagon) for which there

161

is little or no solid evidence? Surprisingly, what evidence exists indicates that a decidedly "unfavorable press" was incapable of swaying the course of an election. We are referring to Ronald Reagan's landslide victory of 1984. It was generally agreed Reagan had been the object of predominantly hostile election news by television newspeople, who spotlighted issues damaging to Reagan's record (e.g., Adams, 1984).

However, in view of Reagan's victory, this hostile election news was passed off as irrelevant. The election coverage did not matter because a candidate "needs good news, not a good press" (Robinson, 1985). That is, since the news was good in 1984, it didn't matter that the election coverage was unfavorable.

If we assume that the news was good in 1984, then perhaps we can say that the media (despite their criticism of Reagan) presented an issue agenda favorable to Reagan's election. We would say that the media contributed to the landslide. This would be consistent with the conventional wisdom that incumbents are favored in "good times" (because the news is "good").

On the other hand, what if the news (like the election coverage) was not "good" in 1984? Then we would have to acknowledge a landslide victory in spite of an unfavorable issue agenda established by the news media.

This question was carefully studied with regard to early evening television newscasts over a 10-week period prior to election day (Graber, 1986). All news stories broadcast by ABC, CBS and NBC were analyzed (except those that dealt explicitly with the election). There were 918 such stories. The question was whether analysis of the content of these stories would show then to be predominantly "good news," thereby constituting an issue agenda favorable to Reagan's re-election.

Results of the study showed quite the opposite. Of the 918 stories broadcast, 49 percent were "bad news" for the United States and only 17 percent were "good news" (the remaining 34 percent were "mixed," "neutral," or "uncertain"). More than half (58 percent) of these stories were explicitly linked to the president. Moreover, the preponderance of "bad" news persisted throughout the 10-week period.

In other words, bad news abounded. It was overwhelming. So much for the notion that incumbents need "good news" to be re-elected. Perhaps, as Graber explains, one has to consider what kind of news was circulating through interpersonal channels. In contrast with negative media coverage, interpersonal exchanges may have centered on reduced inflation and unemployment, and lower taxes.

Yet another way of looking at the political consequences of media agenda setting is that media, especially television, may succeed in stirring up political controversy (Lang & Lang, 1984). By seeking out controversy and publicizing it the media might contribute to political division—e.g., the escalation of national conflict over the Reagan administration's support of the Sandanistas in Nicaragua. The potential for television coverage to act as a divisive force has been carefully analyzed in the case of the major television events leading up to the resignation of President Richard Nixon in 1974: the

Watergate hearings, the impeachment hearings, Nixon's resignation speech (Lang & Lang, 1974). After analyzing this case the authors suggested that television served as a unifying force rather than a divisive one.

How could this have been the case? Lang & Lang observed that when Nixon quit the presidency there was no public outcry. Despite the fact that Nixon had even picked his own successor—Gerald Ford, only about one in 10 Americans was unhappy with the outcome. The changeover was noncontroversial in large part because television had helped to legitimize the whole process by making it open and visible. If events leading up to the changeover had taken place behind closed doors, the authors argue, it might have ended on a more controversial note. For example, the legitimacy of Ford's succession might have been seriously challenged.

While television may have acted to prevent controversy in this case, in other cases it has been seen as an instigator of political controversy. For example, it may be that television's tendency to cover militant political demonstrations encourages the use of such tactics. In turn media coverage of these demonstrations may stir up controversy over the underlying issue. The repeated coverage of confrontation and dissent is thought to have a cumulative effect of stimulating dissatisfaction and loss of confidence in society. For example, exposure to ''bad'' news on television has been correlated with feelings that the lot of the average person is getting worse (Gerbner et al., 1978).

Creating Political Malaise

It has also been suggested that critical television coverage of politics and government has contributed to feelings of political powerlessness and increased distrust of government institutions. Beginning in 1976, evidence was presented showing a positive association between reliance on television (for political information) and expressions of political powerlessness, distrust and cynicism (Robinson, 1976). This association has been labeled *''videomalaise''* because it suggests a television-caused political malaise resulting from television's negativism in news interpretation and its emphasis on violence, conflict and anti-institutional themes.

Efforts to further document this idea have not yielded consistent results. Using a national sample of non-voters, one study found that attention to televised political news was positively associated with a variety of reasons for not voting—cynicism about candidates, distrust in candidates and government, the inability to change anything by voting (O'Keefe & Mendelsohn, 1978). Another study found that television-dependent persons were less trusting of local government officials than people who relied on newspapers (Becker et al., 1978).

But is was not entirely clear what these result meant. They did not necessarily mean that reliance on television news was a cause of political malaise. It could be that the already politically disenchanted tended to choose television (rather than other sources) for political information. There are many possible reasons for this. People with these attitudes about politics may not want to expend the extra effort of reading newspapers, and/or they may be more satisfied with the less in-depth coverage television provides.

Later studies failed to support the idea of "videomalaise," instead finding evidence to the contrary (O'Keefe, 1980; Miller & Reese, 1982). In these studies reliance on television was associated with positive political values, such as the efficacy of voting and less distrust of politicians. It is not clear why these studies yielded different results. It may be that "videomalaise" was a phenomenon bound to a particular historical period. Perhaps it has disappeared only temporarily and will appear again when conditions are suitable. Meanwhile, it is apparent that television does not necessarily contribute to political disillusion, and may in fact do the opposite.

Changing Political Environment

As a view of the political effects of mass communication, Klapper's "minimal effects" model was out-of-date almost before it was published. We have seen that sweeping changes in the nature of political communication began about the time the model was published, and help explain why "minimal effects" is not an accurate description in the face of the many innovations brought on by the televised political campaign. But there have been other changes as well, changes in the political system and in the ideas which guide communication research. We turn now to the first of these changes.

How has the American political system changed? If that question draws a blank for you, it's because the changes while dramatic in some respects have been quite subtle. They could easily go unnoticed. But if we were to compare the "political system" of the period covered by early election studies (1940s–50s) to the present system, we would see some important changes in voters and in political parties (Table 7.2). How did these changes come about? And how are they related to the political effects of mass communication?

We cannot discuss all the reasons for these changes, but you should be aware that the media—particularly television—have been implicated in every case. First, the parties are said to be weakened by the advent of television campaigns which allow candidates to bypass the parties and appeal directly to voters (Robinson, 1977). In fact, in the face of the necessity for television campaigning, the support of a party has limited utility. What the candidate needs is a campaign organization that can raise large sums of money (for the television campaign) and a campaign manager who knows how to design and execute a complex media campaign.

Pre-Klapper (1940–50s)	Post-Klapper (1961–present)
Parties vital to legitimation of candidates	Candidates succeed with minimal party support
Parties have strong ties with electorate	Parties have weak ties with electorate
Voters have stable party/candidate preferences	Voters have volatile party/candidate preferences

Figure 7.2. Pre- and Post-Klapper Differences in American Political System.

Second, the voter's relationship with political parties becomes weakened as a secondary effect of media campaigning. In most cases candidates still carry a party label, but because the party has so little control over a candidate's campaign the party label is not that informative. There do not seem to be sharp, consistent differences between candidates from different parties. How can a voter vote on the basis of party if there is no predictable relationship between party and candidates' positions on the issues? In the face of the weakening party/candidate relationship we have also seen an erosion of the party/voter relationship to the point where people today are less likely to say they belong to a party, and more likely to classify themselves as "independents" (Nie, et al., 1977).

Television has also been implicated in the increased "volatility" of voters. Voters seem to wait until much later in the campaign to make their choices, a phenomenon that contrasts sharply with findings of the pre-Klapper election studies. This seems to happen because voters have changed the way they make choices; instead of choosing on the basis of party, they seem to choose more on the basis of campaign information. And it is the weakening of the party system coupled with the constant flow of "new" information supplied by active television campaigning that has contributed to the "wait-and-see" strategy of so many voters. Large numbers of voters remain undecided right up until the last few days of major elections, and are still actively processing information about the candidates (Stamm, 1986).

These subtle changes in relationships between parties, candidates, and voters have also (apparently) rendered voters more vulnerable to campaign influence. Let's conclude this section by discussing some reasons for this.

You will recall that a central tenet of the minimal effects model was *selective exposure*. In the context of campaigns in the 1940s–50s, partisan differences were strong and most people strongly associated with a party (Chaffee & Miyo, 1983). Therefore, it would not be surprising if exposure to campaign messages was strongly tilted toward the party of choice. Generalizations such as the following are readily derived from the election studies of that time.

". . . audiences attend selectively to political information in the mass media. . . .
They were more likely to attend to messages supporting or agreeing with preferred
positions or candidates" (O'Keefe & Atwood, 1981, p. 335).

Evidence from recent campaigns, however, does not provide overwhelming support
for the selective exposure tenet. The weakening of the link between candidates and parties has resulted in campaigns that are conducted on behalf of candidates not parties.
Thus, partisanship on the part of voters, even where it still exists, is not a useful basis
for selectivity because campaign messages are seldom clearly distinguished along these
lines. In addition, many voters these days are not strong partisans, so it would not be
useful to them to select the messages of (only) one party, even if it were feasible to do
so.

The selective exposure tenet, if it applies in today's campaigns, should be based on
candidate preference rather than party preference. We might expect to find higher levels
of exposure to the voter's own candidate than to messages from the opposing candidate.
This proposition was tested in a study of the 1980 Carter/Reagan campaign (Chaffee &
Miyo, 1983). The study found that selective exposure (to party nominating conventions,
and to campaign speeches and ads) was evident, but not very strong. It was only when
the sample was divided into two groups—"parents" and "adolescents," that clear
evidence of selective exposure emerged. The adolescents were significantly less exposed
to the campaign messages of the candidate they did not support. But why should selective exposure apply to adolescents, and not to their parents? One might have expected
the reverse if selectivity were partisan-based (because parents should be the stronger
partisans). Could it be that the adolescents, who were not yet of voting age, did not feel
the same kind of responsibility for their choice; and were free to simply pay attention to
a candidate that they liked?

Whatever the reason, it seems quite clear that what selectivity remains in recent
campaigns is based on candidate preference. But this brings up another point. If selectivity is to be based on candidate preference, then it should not occur until *after* a
preference has been established. For many voters this would not be until very late in the
campaign. This points to another reason why present-day campaigns may have more
influence. Many more voters remain undecided for nearly the duration of the campaign.
During that time they are not selectively attending to the messages of one candidate,
and they are open to a "crystallization" effect as long as they remain undecided. Most
undecided voters make up their minds on the basis of campaign information, not on the
basis of partisan predispositions.

In summary, changes in the "political system" have enhanced the opportunity for
mass communication effects by largely nullifying partisan-based selective exposure, and
by keeping many voters open to "crystallization" effects throughout most of the campaign.

166

Changing Research Paradigms

It would seem, from what we have said so far, that events have largely forced researchers to take a different view of the political effects of mass communication. As the media of mass communication have changed and the political system has changed, researchers have slowly, sometimes grudgingly, revised the legacy of "minimal effects" inherited from the Erie County and Elmira studies. But researchers have done more than revise their estimates of effects; they have also begun to reach for new ways of thinking about political communication. Within the scientific community the emergence of a new way of thinking about important phenomena is termed a *"paradigm change."*

We are not arguing that a paradigm change has (already) taken place in political communication research, only that such a change is underway. The outlines of the paradigm that gave us "minimal effects" are clear. The outlines of the new paradigm are still fuzzy. Like a picture that is not sharply focused, only a few pieces in the new paradigm are recognizable at this point. Even these few pieces give us some strong clues about how the new paradigm will differ from the old.

The parameters of the old paradigm have been aptly summarized in an article on the origins of the minimal effects model (Chaffee & Hochheimer, 1985). Early election studies clearly did not follow the paradigm set down by Dewey for American social science (see Chapter 1). Nor were they consistent with the reciprocal view of communication embodied in the concept of "coorientation" (see Chapter 3). Instead, the early studies embraced what we will call the *persuasion paradigm.*

The peculiar bias of the persuasion paradigm is that effects are viewed from only one perspective—that of the sender. In the context of political communication that means the sponsors of a political campaign (i.e., a political party and/or candidate). Candidates and parties are the "senders," and it is the effects of their messages on voters that becomes the primary subject of inquiry. There is no comparable concern with what voters may be saying, or with what effects those messages might have on parties and/or candidates!

This would appear to be a very limited perspective from which to view political communication. Limited because it yields research that is mainly useful to candidates who are interested in mass communication as a vehicle for winning elections. Limited because it tells us little about how voters might be better served by mass communication. Limited because it appears to reduce political campaigning to the equivalent of marketing campaigns designed to sell a "product." Limited because voting is treated no differently than any other "consumer" decision.

This perspective on political communication was comfortable to the researchers (and researcher sponsors) during that era of mass communication research. By the 1960s many of these investigators had left the field and were being replaced by a "new breed" of communication researcher. This new breed of researcher started out as journalists by training and practice. Then, recognizing the journalism profession's desperate need for a scientific knowledge base, these professionals went back to school to earn advanced degrees in mass communication research. For the first time, the subject of political communication was largely in the hands of scientists whose primary interest lay in the role of journalism in serving the democratic process. This was the opening "wedge" that led to new perspectives and new questions about political communication.

The new breed of researcher has brought a new way of thinking about political communication. Political communication is not thought of as a persuasive process that determines which candidate gets the most votes. In fact voting is no longer the primary outcome. Instead, consistent with the role of communication in a democracy, political communication is viewed as an *informing process* between candidates and voters. The goal of mass communication is not to persuade voters to vote for a particular candidate, rather to assist them in arriving at an *informed choice*.

Within the framework of the persuasion paradigm, the "informed voter" would be the voter who knew (only) what a particular candidate wanted him or her to know. A more meaningful definition of "informed choice" would consider both what the voter wants to know and what the candidate wants her to know.

This shift in perspectives has already brought some important changes in research on political communication. One change has been a shift toward cognitive effects of exposure to political messages. Another has been a surge of new studies on the ways that voters use mass media to find out what they want to know about politics.

As the idea of "informed choice" gained importance, it was only natural that researchers should become more interested in cognitive effects. One cannot find out whether a voter is informed by assessing candidate preferences; one has to observe how voters think about candidates, about issues, and about relationships between candidates and issues. Thus, it is common to find studies relating media exposure to voter's knowledge about issues and candidates.

Some researchers have even turned the question around, and are studying how the cognitive behavior of voters affects their attention to political information. Such studies show that cognitive behavior of voters is very diverse, and this diversity makes a difference in what it means to be informed. Each voter is free to arrive at an "informed choice" in his own way. Thus, there is more than one definition of "informed"; it is all relative to the cognitive behavior of the voter.

For example, a recent study shows that some voter's arrive at their choice through a (cognitive) process of *valuation*—i.e., examining one candidate at a time. Others employ a process of *evaluation* in which they make comparisons between candidates (Zandpour & Bowes, 1984). These differences have clear implications for the kind of information that would be useful to voters. A voter who is engaged in evaluation probably could not make much use of political advertising that simply portrays what is attractive about a single candidate.

Another study has shown that voters appear to make significant changes in cognitive behavior as they go through a campaign (Stamm, 1986). At one point they may "wedge"—focus on the differences between candidates. Later, they may "hedge"—focus on qualities that make them functionally equivalent. The study found that as voter's cognitive behavior changed so did their attention to the campaign. In fact, the voter's communication activity depended on both the *stage* of the campaign and the cognitive strategy.

Such findings begin to suggest that there is much to be learned about voter's cognitive behavior if media are to do a more adequate job of informing voters. Media need to consider not only what candidates are ready to tell voters, but also what voters want to know at a particular stage of the campaign. When reporters consider only what they think is relevant, they may badly misjudge what voters need. A recent example was the news media's preoccupation with Gary Hart's extra-marital affair. The media through their prominent and persistent coverage gave the impression this was a critical campaign issue. However, when college-age voters were asked what they considered "most unattractive" about the presidential campaign, nearly 90 percent mentioned the trivializing of the campaign by concentrating on "sex scandals" (Stamm, 1988).

This broader way of thinking about media's role in political campaigns is already paying off in ways that help voters. Some major newspapers and broadcasting stations are developing new approaches to political polling that do more than keep track of candidate preference. An excellent case in point is a presidential campaign experiment conducted by *The Orlando Sentinel* during the 1988 campaign (Straight, 1988). The Sentinel designed "the Florida 100"—a poll to follow the thinking of 100 voters through the March 8 primary to November 8th. The purpose of this poll was to enable the Sentinel to cover the campaign "from the ground up, not from the plane down." Using the traditional approach to campaign coverage (i.e., following the candidates), Sentinel reporters realized they knew almost nothing about how the candidates were perceived by the voters they were supposed to be serving.

Perhaps the day is not far off when panels of voters will be linked to their media electronically, and their input used to monitor the utility of previous coverage and identify gaps in coverage that need to be filled. By contributing to these kinds of developments, communication research can (finally) be of as much benefit to voters as the persuasion paradigm has long been to candidates and campaign managers. Although mass communication has not been proved responsible for the decline of confidence in democratic institutions (such as elections), it may yet help to restore that confidence.

Key Terms

Agenda-setting
Bandwagon effect
Candidate image
Characterization
Crystallization
Early voting returns
Evaluation
Informed choice
Law of minimal consequence
Media reliance
Mediating condition
Minimal effects
Paradigm change
Partisan
Persuasion paradigm
Political malaise ("videomalaise")
Selective exposure
Stereotyping
Valuation
Voter turnout
Voter volatility

Summary

Prior to 1960 the effects of political campaigns were believed to be limited to reinforcement of existing voting intentions. A "not-so-limited" view emerged after 1960 because researchers were able to document effects that had escaped detection, and (possibly) because of changes in voters and in communication techniques.

The introduction of TV spot advertising in the 1950s resulted in a much larger audience being reached with simple, repetitive political messages.

Many observers feared that the shift toward televised campaigns would produce "personality voting," but this fear has not been supported. Television news and advertising is not as "personality bound" as its critics claimed, and TV effects are not determined solely by content.

The 1960 televised presidential debates had a number of documented effects, including crystallization of undecided voters and increased knowledge of the issue positions of both candidates.

A key study of the 1976 presidential debates showed that "limited effects" held for some viewers (those who watched only part of the debates), while at the same time many viewers became "informed voters" as a result of debate viewing.

A number of presidential debate studies have shown effects on candidate images—e.g., increased stereotyping and changes in characterization.

According to Robinson, TV's change from a 15– to a 30–minute news format altered political communication in the U.S. by changing the audience for political communication to draw more heavily from the less educated and less politically active. Despite Robinson's view, TV has been shown to make positive contributions to voters' political knowledge.

Television is sometimes claimed to be the *only* source of political information for most Americans. This is an exaggerated claim since most persons who use TV for political information also rely on other media.

The publication of campaign poll results is thought to produce a "bandwagon effect" favoring the leading candidate, but research has found no evidence that large numbers of voters are subject to such a influence.

The influence of early voting returns has been studied in several elections with only one study finding any evidence of a decline in voter turnout.

A study of the 1984 campaign indicated that even a decidedly unfavorable press may be incapable of swaying the outcome of a presidential election.

Television coverage of politics, despite its tendency to emphasize "bad news," does not appear to contribute significantly to political malaise.

In recent years American voters have become less partisan and have begun to make their voting decisions later in the campaign.

Changes in the political system have increased the opportunity for communication effects by reducing the amount of partisan-based selective exposure.

Research in political communication has begun to undergo a paradigm change in which the persuasion paradigm is being replaced by a concern with the voter's ability to make an informed choice.

References

Adams, W. C. (1984). Media coverage of campaign '84: a preliminary report. *Public Opinion,* April/May.

Atkin, Charles, (1969). The Impact of political poll results on candidate and issue preference. *Journalism Quarterly,* 46, 515–521.

Atkin, Charles, L. Bowen, K. G. Sheinkoppf, and O. B. Nayman (19730. Quality vs. quantity in televised political ads. *Public Opinion Quarterly,* 27, 209–224.

Becker, Lee, Idowu Sobowale and William Casey Jr. (1978). Newspaper and television dependencies: their effects on evaluations of government leaders. Presented to International Communication Association, Chicago.

Berelson, Bernard, Paul Lazarsfeld, and William McPhee (1954). Voting. Chicago: University of Chicago Press.

Bowers, T. A. (1972). Issue and personality information in newspaper political advertising. *Journalism Quarterly,* 49, 446–452.

Carter, Richard, (1962). Some Effects of the Debates. In Sidney Kraus (ed.) The Great Debates. Bloomington: Indiana University Press.

Chaffee, S. H., and Y. Miyo (1983). Selective exposure and the reinforcement hypothesis: an intergenerational panel study of the 1980 presidential campaign. *Communication Research,* 10, 3–36.

Chaffee, S. H., and John Hochheimer (1985). The Beginnings of Political Communications Research in the U.S.: Origins of the 'Limited Effects' Model. In Gurevitch & Levy, (eds.), Mass Communication Review Yearbook, Vol. 5. Beverly Hills: Sage.

Chaffee, S., and J. Schleuder (1986). "Measurement and effects of attention to media news." *Human Communication Research,* 13, 76–107.

Culbertson, H., and G. Stempel (1986). "How media use and reliance affect knowledge leve." *Communication Research,* 13(4), 579–602.

Devlin, L. P. (1986). An analysis of presidential television commercials. In Kaid, Nimmo & Sanders (eds.), New Perspectives on Political Advertising. Carbondale: Souther Illinois University Press.

Fuchs, D. A. (1966). Election-day radio-television and western voting. *Public Opinion Quarterly,* 30, 226–236.

Graber, D. A. (1986). Framing election news broadcasts: news context and its impact on the 1984 presidential election. Presented to International Communication Association, Chicago, Ill.

Hofstetter, C. R., and T. R. Buss (1980). Politics and last-minute political television. *Western Political Quarterly,* 33, 24–37.

Jackson, J. (1983). Election night reporting and voter turnout. *American Journal of Political Science,* 27, 615–635.

Kaid, L. L. (1976). Measures of political advertising. *Journal of Advertising Research,* 16, 49–53.

Lang, K. and G. Lang (1968). Voting and Nonvoting: Implications of Broadcasting Before Polls Are Closed. Waltham, Mass.: Blaisdell Publishing Co.

Lang, K. and G. Lang (1978). Immediate and delayed responses to a Carter-Ford debate: assessing public opinion. *Public Opinion Quarterly,* 42, 322–341.

Lang, Gladys Engel & Kurt Lang (1984). Politics and Television Reviewed. Beverly Hills: Sage.

Lazarsfeld, Paul, Bernard Berelson and Hazel Gaudet (1944). The People's Choice. New York: Duell, Sloan and Pearce.

McCombs, Maxwell (1972). Mass communication in political campaigns: information, gratification, and persuasion. In Kline & Tichenor, (eds.), Current Perspectives in Mass Communications Research. Beverly Hills: Sage.

McLeod, J., and D. McDonald (1985). "Beyond simple exposure: media orientations and their impact on political processes." *Communication Research,* 12, 3–33.

Mendelsohn, H. (1966). Election-day broadcasts and terminal voting behavior. *Public Opinion Quarterly,* 30, 212–225.

Mendelsohn, H., and I. Crespi (1970). Polls, Television, and The New Politics. Scranton: Changler Publishing.

Miller, M. M., and S. D. Reese (1982). Media dependency as interaction: effects on exposure and reliance on political activity and efficacy. *Communication Research,* 9, 227–248.

Nie, N. H., S. Verba, and J. R. Petrocik (1976). The Changing American Voter. Cambridge, MA.: Harvard University Press.

O'Keefe, G. (1980). Political malaise and reliance on media. *Journalism Quarterly,* 57, 122–128.

O'Keefe, G., and L. E. Atwood (1981). Communication and election campaigns. In Nimmo & Sanders (eds.) *Handbook of Political Communication,* Beverly Hills, CA.: Sage.

O'Keefe, G., and H. Mendelsohn (1978). Nonvoting and the role of the media. In C. Winick (ed.), Mass Media and Deviance. Beverly Hills: Sage.

Pool, Ithiel de Sola (1959). TV: A new dimension in politics. In Burdick and Brodbeck (eds.), American Voting Behavior. New York: Free Press.

Robinson, M. J. (1976). Public affairs television and the growth of political malaise, *American Political Science Review,* 70, 409–431.

_____ (1977). Television and American politics: 1956–1976. *Public Interest,* 48, 3–39.

_____ (1985). Teflon is where you find it: what network news did and didn't do in the general campaign. O'Neill Symposium paper.

Stamm, K. R., A. Burgess, M. Jordan, and S. Lim (1985). Characterizations of political candidates: a constructivist approach to political communication. Presented to International Communication Association, Honolulu.

Stamm, K. (1985). The effects of the Bush/Ferraro debate on candidate characterization. Presented to Association for Education in Journalism, Memphis, TN.

_____ (1986). Cognitive strategies and communication during a presidential campaign. *Communication Research,* 14, 35–57.

_____ (1988). Unpublished survey. Seattle: University of Washington School of Communications.

Straight, H. (19880. The real experts. *Sentinel Quarterly,* 6, 12–14.

Wade, S. and W. Schramm (1969). The mass media as sources of public affairs, science and health knowledge. *Public Opinion Quarterly,* 33, 197–209.

Zandpour, F. and J. Bowes (1984). Adversary advertising, cognitive mechanisms and candidate utility. Presented to International Communication Association, San Francisco.

8   The Effects of Mass Communicated Entertainment

Introduction

Perhaps one of the most controversial issues in the recent past has been the values and examples contained in mass media products, primarily television content. Because television commands so much time, particularly with children, governments, mental health officials, courts and social scientists have been keenly interested in whether or not there are negative effects from viewing. In this chapter, we describe some real cases where public concern has been excited, as well as competing "theories" of what effects entertainment content have. We also examine research which shows how family life and television viewing may influence each other. This may be a frustrating story, since so many ideas compete with each other without many clear winners. But firm answers can be hard to come by in a high-stakes situation where millions of dollars in program costs, audience preferences and society's right to dictate media content are involved.

Are There Effects?

It has been argued that our most time-consuming wakeful activity is the use of mass communicated entertainment. Indeed, by current reckoning, we spend as a nation well over 4 hours on average daily with television alone, the preponderance of content viewed being entertainment. Because measurement of print media is not time-dependent we don't know precisely how much additional time would be spent were all sources of media taken into account. On a world scale, the United States and Canada vie with Japan for being "highest" media consumers, followed by nations of Western Europe and Australia. As media grow in availability and sophistication in the third world, increasing amounts of time are taken world-wide with entertainment.

Figure 8.A. From *Communication Research,* Volume 17
February 1990, cover, Copyright 1990 by Sage Publications, Inc.
Reprinted by permission of Sage Publications, Inc.

Perhaps the most benign view is that we really aren't affected by this activity—that entertainment is innocuously diverting with really little influence on the important matters of our daily life. Common sense, however, should suggest otherwise. Think of conversations that include references to programs on TV or try to make a point by relating a real life situation to something seen on television. "She acts just like Roxanne." "He's as funny as Johnny Carson." "She talks like Barbara Walters". We are communicating our ideas by symbolizing them in terms of the mass media.

Think also of news stories that show people acting out in real life fictional drama seen on television. The incident of a frightened New York City subway passenger shooting four men who appeared to threaten him was foresaged in a television airing of *Pelham 345,* a story starring Charles Bronson who organized terrorized subway passengers into killing drug-crazed tormentors holding them captive on a New York City subway car. Soon after the showing of a made-for-TV movie depicting an abused wife finally murdering her drunken husband by burning him in bed, a Washington State women suffering similar circumstances committed exactly the same crime suggested to her by *The Burning Bed.* Another Charles Bronson film showing a daring prison escape facilitated by a helicopter snatching the escapees away from a prison yard was enacted for real at the Michigan State Penitentiary a few weeks later. Other incidents abound where there is a seemingly strong tie between television content (especially) and subsequent action.

Is it only television which has this effect? And are the effects always so specific? In 1986, a coalition of Congressional representatives wished to censor the content of popular music aired on radio or sold as recordings because it allegedly contained antisocial messages buried in the lyrics (In some instances the recording had to be played backwards to really "hear" the obscene message subtly coded into otherwise innocent songs). The Congressional critics argued that the constant bombardment of this music gradually eroded the moral standards of youth. Indeed, our history is filled with accounts of vigilantes or community leaders purging libraries of "dangerous" books (*Catcher in the Rye* and many other titles) over the years have been the targets of communities and special interests who see their threshold of proper community standards eroded by media content. The recurrent controversies over pornographic material simply are a continuation of the sort of community discomfort which surrounds many more legitimate media products.

The collective impact of especially U.S. entertainment products has been viewed by many developing nations as instances of "cultural imperialism". Traditional cultures, languages and art forms are seen as under attack by the slick, attractive programs and music dispensed in high volume (and low cost) by Hollywood and the popular culture centers of Northern Europe. The airing of *Little House on the Prairie* in Thailand and India, and the almost ubiquitous attractiveness of *Dallas* and *Dynasty* provokes periodic outrage from various countries where these programs have achieved a large following in preference to the local media products. Many countries enact laws to keep out "foreign" programs, others try to create their own products modeled on those from the U.S., but with native actors and plots. France, in 1986, started airing its version of *Dallas, Chateauvallon*, emphasizing sex somewhat more and underhanded business practices somewhat less than its American model.

So we have considerable informal evidence that entertainment media seem to influence everything from violent behavior to artistic expression. We know that governments try to act on these suspicions to safeguard their cultures, moral standards and language. But do we have research evidence which can give us some measure of this perceived threat?

Research Evidence on Negative Media Influence

Perhaps the oldest line of research has concerned negative effects of mass media entertainment on youth. Historically, it seems, such questions have been raised with every major new media form appearing in the 20th century. Nickelodeons, early movies, jukeboxes, dime novels, comics and radio have all been exposed in their growth days to considerable public concern over their influence on youth (Wartella & Reeves, 1985). Indeed, such measures as construction of palace-like cinemas in the 1920s, rating codes for comics and movies in the 1950s, and voluntary broadcast industry codes giving at least lip-service to wholesomeness of content, were all efforts to improve the image of these various media with the public, and particularly those who might otherwise censor or regulate content. Several major organizations in the United States—National Association for Better Radio and Television, and Action for Children's Television, for example—have as their sole purpose the prevention of negative influence from broadcast entertainment on the nation's children.

Chief among concerns is the question of violence. Impressionable children, bombarded with 4-plus hours per day of television, it's reasoned, learn much from the programs they watch. Television's critics point out that within one evening's viewing, multiple murders, assaults, lewd sex acts and verbal abuse can be seen in everything from situation comedy and cartoons to police melodramas and "action-adventure" feature films. The wide availability of home videotape players allows children to rent films unsuitable for broadcast, averting limited network standards. Cable television allows R-rated viewing on pay channels meant for "adult" viewers. Indeed, cable TV legislation in Britain prescribes that cable TV decoders have a key-operated switch to allow parents to lockout objectionable "adult" content from curious children.

With the growth of the U.S. television audience in the 1950s, concern over violence grew as well. The first response of the broadcast industry to critics was to commission research. Among the first studies were those by Joseph Klapper (1960). His research suggested TV as a *reinforcer* of violence. Mentally ill people predisposed to violence could be encouraged through media content to "act out" their feelings, but television could not be considered a cause alone in a way which would negatively affect normal people. Should broadcasters be held responsible for the actions of a few sick people? Doesn't most drama contain tension, some violence and occasionally references to sex as a legitimate part of various plots? The broadcast industry believed so, occasionally referring to the violence in *Macbeth* and other literary classics as justification.

An even more limited, benign view of media violence was proposed by Irving Janis (1961). Though Janis might repudiate this view today, his description of *catharsis* is still referred to as a distinct perspective. Janis argued that a three step process takes place:

a. *Identification with an aggressor.* Here a hero (or heroine) is settling some grudge, getting even after unjustified attack. Indeed, the content of *Rambo* films show the hero (Sylvester Stallone) continually being schemed against by crooked police, evil government officials and terrible criminals who hurt innocent people. Indeed, Rambo and the people he protects are shown as common folk wronged by cynical, powerful forces. We often identify sympathetically with this hero and his friends, recalling perhaps, the callous magistrate who showed little sympathy for our last parking infraction.

b. *Vicarious participation.* As we watch, we increasingly see ourselves in the place of actors, carrying out violence against our tormentors. The final triumph of virtue over adversity—Rambo destroys the villains in a burst of mortar fire; Superman, with powers restored, sends evildoers on a one-way trip to outer space. These turns-of-fortune often bring theater audiences to their feet, cheering and clapping. This is good vicarious participation. We feel the power and vindication of the heroes.

c. In the climatic conclusion to the presentation, we are *relieved of our tension* and hostility—both that generated synthetically in the theatre and what we had on entering from real misfortune and abuse. In short, the film or television program induces us to release our aggressive drive harmlessly in response to a film. Accordingly, we are less violence-prone and more at ease than when we entered the cinema or began viewing the television program. Media, if one accepts this view, perform a public service in presenting violent content and allowing for the fantasy, vicarious release of our violence, saving society from the real thing.

Subsequent views of television/media violence depart progressively from the benign implications of the reinforcement and catharsis arguments. There are several lines of investigation which typically confirm harmful consequences from media violence:

a. *Media present Aggressive cues:* Fundamental here is the idea that TV has two effects—arousal and learning. From media violence, people learn there are appropriate circumstances for violence—that can be can be aroused by violence. Media thus are both teacher and instigator of violent outcomes by telling us that violence is ok and encouraging hostility.

In one study (Berkowitz, 1964), students were insulted by a teaching assistant for performance on a test. Later, half were shown a film with considerable violence; other students viewed a "neutral", non-violent film. Finally, students were enlisted in a faked experiment where technicians asked them to administer high voltage shocks to the teaching assistant. Students who were both insulted and who viewed the violent film, delivered the most fake shocks (the teaching assistant was instructed to scream and writhe appropriately). Progressively lower violence came from students who were either (a) insulted but didn't see the film, (b) saw the film but weren't insulted or (c) saw a non-violent film and received no insult. In short, as both arousal (insult) and appropriate circumstances (film) were systematically reduced, violence (shocks) fell off. This idea of the media as both teacher and trigger of violent behavior is perhaps the most frightening to those fearing a strong antisocial effect from the mass media.

b. *Media present a learning model.* While this idea is contained in the research just discussed, this approach simply stresses the instructional role of television in socializing youth. Bandura and Walters (1963) argue that children model or imitate what they see on TV. If they see violence, they'll incorporate it into their behavior. Showing films of children attacking dolls produced imitative behavior by young viewers when placed in a play situation some moments later. Network executives counter that such research merely shows children can attack dolls—a far step from harmfully attacking other people.

But what of *years* of exposure to such content? This is an idea of violence aimed at how children become socialized to the world, how they establish ways of dealing with anger, negotiating with others, resolving problems and conflicts.

Perhaps viewed in this way, youthful exposure to violence may seem trivial at the time, but do the lessons presumably learned from content at, say, age 4, show-up as violent behavior when one is becoming a young adult? In one study that followed children for ten years, children with high versus low levels of viewing TV violence were compared at age 4 (Lefkowitz, 1977). There was little difference in aggressive behavior between the two groups. However, the group with high exposure at 4 years showed significantly higher aggressive behavior 10 years later at age 14. The interesting twist is that at age 14, the aggressive group didn't have a particularly high level of viewing violent content. Lessons learned from tv violence at an early age·may not really show up until later. Indeed, the suggestion here is that there is a period during which children are especially vulnerable to long-term influence from violent content.

Figure 8.B. From the *Journal of Communication,* 1987, 37(2) p. 25 © 1987 *Journal of Communication.* Used with permission.

c. *Media cultivate a view of the world.* Proponents of this view find that those viewing high amounts of television see the world as a mean and dangerous place to a greater extent than those watching less. According to research by George Gerbner (1976), high viewers continually exaggerated the actual levels of violence in society. While this possible outcome probably indicates little direct threat to the well-being of society, it does suggest that television may encourage a frightened, cautious and cynical view of the world.

d. *Media violence can create a heightened level of physical arousal*—change in pulse, stress and blood chemistry (Zillman, 1982). We react to fictionalized violence with many of the same reactions we would have to actual threat. The linkage of sex and violence is emphasized here because the physical reaction is much the same in either case.

In short, the bulk of evidence suggests strongly that media depiction of violence has harmful consequences. But it is important to recognize the shortcomings in this research before making sweeping conclusions about television violence in particular and antisocial media content in general. What are some drawbacks to keep in mind:

a. *Little of the research studies long-term effects over time.* Studies of imitative violent behavior done on samples of very small children measured "violent" acts committed with dolls and play blocks soon after violent films were viewed. How long would this effect last? Critics suggest that the influence was temporary.

b. *Many question the unnaturalness of the experiments themselves.* Children are gathered in unfamiliar surroundings to watch television and play. University students are deliberately angered over a test and subsequently offered the unusual situation of shocking their teacher in retribution. Consider that we typically watch television at home in the presence of friends or family, that we may not pay close attention to content, and that we may "switch around" trying out bits of programs during our viewing time. Much time may pass until we are frustrated, angered or afforded the opportunity to avenge some wrong committed against us. How much the content of particular programs is recalled under such circumstances is unknown.

c. *Tension and violence are a part of drama,* just as they are part of everyday life. The critical question for society (and one which is difficult to assess) is to judge when the violence portrayed is excessive and is not redeemed by a good dramatic point or values.

d. *There seem many conditions in media content which may mediate* or cancel the effects of violence shown. Let's consider a few:

- Does the violence in news, documentary and other "actuality" programs have effects similar to those noted for fictional content? Though there is not a great deal of research on the topic, what little there is suggests it may have a similar effect. Intuitively, we can see how high consumption of television news, with its orientation towards disasters, wars and crime, could evoke a feeling in viewers that the world is a violent and dangerous place.

- Would there be imitation of violence if its true consequences were shown—the distress of family and loved ones, pain, blood and gore, and the emotional and financial devastation to survivors of violence. The National Association of Broadcasters, ever mindful of not blatantly offending the public on such matters, discourages "gratuitous" or unnecessary violence in dramatic plots. Some years ago, the National Broadcasting Corporation (and later the Public Broadcasting System) aired a program entitled *Lifeline* which graphically depicted real hospital emergencies and crises. The copious bleeding of stab victims, the tears of survivors and painful screaming were all shown. The show was withdrawn, despite critical acclaim, because it was too graphic, perhaps too realistic.

The violent influence of the media, if such is really case, may not be so much due to the violence, as to its attractive portrayal. Heroes solve major problems, neutralize enemies, win wars often with violent solutions all accomplished within the 50-plus minutes of a prime-time entertainment hour. Intuitively, speedy, violent resolutions to problems may appeal to those with high frustration and poor skills at negotiation and finding other non-violent solutions.

- *Realism versus fantasy.* Does the humorous violence of cartoons have the same impact as does realistically depicted violence? There is some suggestion in the research literature that as the content and depiction become distant from the viewer's circumstances—less realistic or attainable—imitation would be less likely.

- *Verbal violence verses physical violence.* There is the suggestion in several studies (notably those of Himmelwaite) that scolding, threats and accusations frighten children as much or moreso than physical violence.

- *Justification and identification with the aggressor.* As mentioned earlier in this chapter, violent heroes are common in cinema and television. Research has rather well substantiated that people are increasingly likely to approve of violence and, experimentally, to actually do it (recall the bogus shocks administered to teachers described above) when it seems justified and the hero is a sympathetic and charismatic one.

There are complex reasons to find violence either attractive or repulsive in media content. And these seem to bear on how likely individuals are to imitate or condone violence suggested there. But the studies themselves done over the past 30 years raise a number of important issues. What is violence—is it verbal as well as physical? Does it include certain sexual behaviors as well? Can one effectively measure the level of violence in content by counting murders and rapes per hour depicted? Or are other qualities involved?

Can we say unequivocally that violent tv leads to violent behavior, or do already aggressive, hostile people view more violent content? The causal direction is important as civic organizations and governments try to decide whether violent content should be regulated or not.

What are the effects of long-term as opposed to short-term exposure to TV violence? Most studies to date have been short-term, given the cost and years of commitment from researchers long-term studies require.

Are the studies done with sufficient realism to generalize well to typical viewing situations? Are they done with sufficient controls to accurately weigh TV as an inducement to violence in contrast to the wealth of other causes of frustration and hostility in modern society?

Television Entertainment and the Family

While media violence may have been a long-standing pre-occupation of research, the broad influence of the media, especially television, on the socialization of children and family life has been a persistent concern of social scientists and government since the late 1950s. Television is typically viewed in the home, often with friends, brothers and sisters, and parents. Do the media intrude, altering how family and friends interact? And does the family intrude on the viewing in a way that alters the influence of programs compared to solitary exposure?

With research suggesting that television could promote aggressive, antisocial behavior in children, attention turned to how families controlled or mitigated this sort of influence. Researchers saw the family as a defense against bad influences from media content. What could families do to assure "safe" viewing?

A Swedish study (Linne, 1976) suggests that parents should watch programs with children, especially shows with aggressive content. By discussing what happened in the program with young children and allowing play activity, the influence of aggression can be dissipated.

In England, a survey of 450 mothers (Brown, 1975) uncovered a set of key attitudes toward television. These ranged from "protective" (TV is frequently unsuitable for children) to "liberal" (let the child develop his/her own viewing pattern) and "deliberate" (parents use tv to socialize the child and evaluate the programs with them).

An American study (Lefkowitz, 1977) followed 63 children from the age of 4 through 9 years of age. The researchers expected that 4 year olds who viewed heavy amounts of television—particularly action-adventure programs—would, given certain family patterns, be aggressive later on and be more fearful of the their world. What, then, were family patterns that would influence this outcome? Family behaviors such as parents using physical punishment to control kids and imposing few rules on watching tv contributed to later aggressiveness in children who watched the most aggressive content. What are these young children learning? The authors speculate that violence is seen as a solution to problems and conflict.

With the onset of adolescence, the relationship of children to family characteristically changes. Do the media have a role in these changes as well? McLeod and Brown (1976) maintain there are real changes in TV use and family interaction which are related. Teens watch substantially less TV with drops especially in comedy programs. But more importantly, the researchers examined two basic dimensions of family interaction. In *socio-oriented* families, parents expect children to defer to their authority, to restrain feelings and maintain harmony. *Concept-oriented* families encourage independent views of issues by children. Given these two concepts, families were divided into one of four types:

Socio-Orientation	Concept Orientation	Family Type
High	High	Consensual
High	Low	Protective
Low	High	Pluralistic
Low	Low	Laissez-faire

The consensual family tries to balance independent thinking with harmonious family relationships. These kids are in, it seems, a catch-22 situation: they can think independently so long as it coincides with parents' views. These children watch some violent content and, of all the groups, see life as portrayed on tv closest to real life. At the other extreme, laissez-faire families—ones who don't encourage either a socio or concept orientation—have children who seek direction elsewhere, from peers particularly. They tend not to be interested in either public affairs or entertainment programs.

Perhaps the most interesting instances found are the "mixed" situations where one of the two dimensions is emphasized by the family. Protective families stress harmony and "getting along" at the expense of self-expression. These tend to watch the most television and the most violent content. Television, it seems, provides an aggressive outlet for stifled expression among family members. Pluralistic families encourage exposure to new ideas and taking independent stands even when they clash with parents. These children watch less TV than average, prefer news and public affairs content and watch the least violent programming.

In a related study, Lull (1980) looked more closely at how socio and/or concept oriented families actively use TV as a tool in family interaction. For example, discussing family matters sometimes is easier. Awkward, embarrassed pauses in conversation can be masked by turning attention for a time to TV. Plots and characters in a program can make it easier to introduce parallel family problems for discussion (". . . Timmy, you act just like the Cookie Monster on 'Sesame Street'.") It can allow one to escape family interaction by isolating attention to the screen ("Don't bother me, I'm watching TV!') or be a tool to facilitate interaction ("What do you think of the 'Miss America' pageant winner?").

More in keeping with early research on radio soap operas, television can be used as lessons for everyday living—social learning. Heroes, happy families, situation comedies and action-adventure provides many with role models (have a family as happy as the Cosby's), solutions to small problems (how to "break-up" a romantic relationship) and knowledge about social institutions (how police work, for example, or what politics is about). Special news programs can substitute for school experience. Finally, as most children and parents know, TV access can be used as a reward or punishment.

Television, especially, seems a powerful force in family life: shaping how wakeful time is spent, organizing conversations, being used as a reward, as a means to isolate oneself, or as a source of advice and information about everyday life and the world.

There has been little recent attention to effects from media other than television. As new media forms capture audiences and larger shares of time, social concern will turn to their influence. They may have unique effects. For example the videocassette recorder (VCR) provides one such example. By the mid-1980s they are found in about half of American households. VCRs are more than just an occasional supplement to a typical diet of broadcast TV. They may have unique effects. For example, the specialization of content one can have through rental of tapes appealing to individual, not family interest, possibly threatens family interaction, around the television. Each family member, some suggest, may depart from the family group to view in isolation content of narrowly focused interest.

Other innovations in media—cable television in particular—also suggest this specialization of interest. When one looks historically to earlier media which evolved into specialty vehicles—general circulation magazines, for example, being replaced by special interest publications in the 1950s or the demise of "family" radio in favor of specialized interest stations at about the same time—we may indeed see the same kind of evolution away from mass appeal network television. The suggestion of much of the research in this chapter is that such change in new media forms will influence family life appreciably. Personal computers and video games in addition to videocassettes are prime candidates for a new generation of research on media and the family.

Key Terms

aggressive cues
causal direction
consensual
cultivation
justification
laissez-faire
long-term effects
pluralistic
protective
reinforcement
vicarious participation

Summary

U.S. and Japanese television consumption is the highest in the world. Common sense alone suggests that this exposure must have enduring effects.

Regulators in many countries restrict content on broadcast and other media because of supposed harmful effects it may have. For example, in the U.S., tobacco advertising is restricted from television because it may encourage new, youthful smokers.

Other nations fear the "imperialism" of U.S. television programming and popular music invading their culture, displacing or changing it in in undesirable ways.

Concern with negative effects has been longstanding and has accompanied most new media forms such as movies, radio and television.

Violence has been a persistent concern, first with cheap novels, then with radio, the cinema and television. Newer technologies, such as cable television with its threat of "adult entertainment" services being accessed by children, continue in this tradition of public concern.

A number of viewpoints contend as both predictors and explanations of media violence effects.

First among these in the 1950s was the *reinforcement* explanation of Joseph Klapper. In this view, media violence merely reinforces the tendencies of people who were already violent and disturbed. This view suggested only a minimal media influence on actual violence.

A more benign view emerged in Irving Janis' *catharsis* explanation. Under certain conditions, viewing violence could actually lessen such tendencies. To work, the audience had to identify with the aggressor and vicariously participate in his or her violence. In doing so, it could relieve its tension and hostility harmlessly.

The *aggressive cues* theory holds that media have two effects—arousal and learning. Media both triggers and teaches violence.

The *learning model* view is that children imitate what they watch. It becomes part of childhood socialization, teaching that violence can "solve" problems quickly and give one control. There is evidence that this influence is greatest for certain age groups and will not manifest as anti-social behavior until, perhaps years later.

The *cultivation* view doesn't so much teach people to be violent as it does to suggest the world is a mean and dangerous place. Fearfulness and cynacism are the primary negative effects of violent media content.

Physical arousal research tries to measure the biochemical response to violent or sexually explicit content. Our reaction to fictionalized violence and sex is similar to a real situation suggesting that we can't dismiss media sex and violence simply as fictional or unreal.

Many conditions influence the level of reaction to media violence, such as the social justification for the violence, the level of realism, or showing the consequences of violence.

There are many problems in adequately testing for effects from media violence, such as the length of exposure to violence content, the realism of experiments done, the countervailing influence of friends, etc.

Families have been studied to see if patterns of interaction and lifestyle influences TV use and violent content exposure.

As new media develop, concern with the influence of violent content persists.

References

Atkin, C. K. and B. Greenberg (1977). Parental mediation of children's social behavior. Report #4 of Learning from Television. Washington: U.S. Office of Child Development.

Bandura A. and R. H. Walters (1963). Social Learning and Personality Development. New York: Free Press.

Berkowitz, L. (1964). The effects of observing violence. Scientific American, 210, 35–41.

Brown, J. R. and O. Linne (1976). The family as mediator of television's effects. in R. Brown (Ed.). Children and Television. Beverly Hills: Sage.

Gerbner, G. and L. Gross (1976). Living with television: The violence profile. Journal of communication, 26, 2, 172–199.

———— (1971). Violence in television drama: Trends and symbolic functions. in G. Comstock and E. Rubenstein. Television Content and Social Behavior, Vol. 1: Content and Control. Washington: U.S. Government Printing Office.

Janis, I. (1961). The stimulating verses cathartic effects of a vicarious aggressive activity. Journal of Abnormal Social Psychology, 53, 381–385.

Klapper, J. (1960). The Effects of Mass Communication. New York: Free Press.

Korzenny, P. B. Greenberg and C. Atkin (1980). Styles of parental disciplinary practices as a mediator of children's learning from antisocial television portrayals. in D. Nimmo (Ed.). Communication Yearbook 3. New Brunswick: Transaction.

Lefkowitz, M. (1977). Growing Up to be Violent. New York: Pergamon Press.

————, L. Eron, L. Walden and L. Huesmann (1971). Television violence and child aggression: A follow-up study. in G. Comstock and E. Rubenstein (Eds.). Television and Social Behavior, Vol. 3: Television and Adolescent Aggressiveness. Washington: U.S. Government Printing Office.

Lull, (1980). Family communication patterns and the social uses of television. Communication Research, 7, 3, 319–334.

McLeod, J. and J. Brown (1976). The family environment and adolescent television use. in R. Brown (Ed.). Children and Television. Beverly Hills: Sage, pp. 199–234.

Wartella, E. and B. Reeves (1985). Historical trends in research on children and the media 1900–1960. Journal of Communication, 35, 118–133.

White, R. (Ed.). (1984). Violence in the media. Communication Research Trends, 5, 4, 4.1–4.11.

Zillman, D. (1982). Television viewing and arousal. in Television and Behavior: Ten Years of Scientific Progress and Implications for the Eighties, Vol. 12. Rockville: National Institutes of Health, pp. 53–67.

9
Mass Communication and the Future

Introduction

Mass communication usually depends on sophisticated technologies. And these have been developing at an accelerated pace over the past 30 years. How has this progress affected our society and its institutions? This chapter examines these questions from several perspectives: historical development, questions for the social sciences, questions for policy and regulation, and finally, questions for the study of communication itself.

Characteristics of Information Societies

Much interest in mass communications has been toward the future. The phenomenal growth of computer and telecommunications technology since the close of World War II has offered an unprecedented number of inventions for the consumer to use. Microcomputers, video cassette recorders, on-line information services for business and home use and the enormous improvements in video and audio entertainment are but surface indications of our progress toward an information intensive society.

Let's point out some of the more obvious changes:

- *The increase in easily accessible information resources.* The spread of cable television in the U.S. is one example. Once relegated to small town needs to import distant, big city stations, cable systems have formed virtual networks through satellite-distributed "super-stations" like WTBS, Atlanta, and WGN, Chicago. Premium pay services such as *Home Box Office* and *Disney* appearing in the early 1970s accelerated the growth of cable into major cities as viewers sought more variety than a handful of broadcasters could offer. Presently, about 53 percent of U.S. households are connected to a cable-like system to enhance traditional, over-the-air offerings. Other nations such as Belgium, Canada, Ireland and the Netherlands have extensive cable systems as well. More recently, computer information networks have reached beyond their core of commercial and professional users to the middle-class household. Services such as *Prodigy*, a joint effort of Sears and IBM, are trying to make "electronic publishing" successful on a mass basis. Today, we have information choices as we have never had them before.

- *The growth and affordability of microcomputers and other microchip technologies.* The microcomputing industry is a well-known success story. From its inception in 1975 as a hobbyist's toy, microcomputing has become a multi-billion dollar business. Personal computers (PCs) are commonplace in business and education and are increasingly so in the home. Look in your local bookstore or newsagent to check the many titles available aimed at helping you cope with coomputer software and hardware. Other everyday products from automobiles to television sets are increasingly reliant on "smart" technologies embodied in microcomputers.

- *The improvement in telecommunications services.* The reliability and power of telephone services world-wide have accelerated in the past 30 years. Costs, reliability and quality especially for long-distance calls have improved with the advent of satellite links and high-capacity optic fiber cables. As the volume of use increases and computer-based switching offices supercede old, mechanical exchanges, the cost of service declines. Beyond simple voice services (called "plain old telephone service" or POTS in the telecomms business), a host of new services are now available—data-encryption communications, electronic mail, pay-per-view premium TV, videotex, video teleconferencing, for example—which were largely unknown before the late 1970s. A whole class of telecommunications-based "enhanced" information services have come into being which in some instances challenge traditional mass media and in almost all instances challenge the traditional ways by which we carry out business and social communication.

- *A decline in employment in heavy industry and agriculture across developed countries of North America and Europe.* New jobs are being created in services (for example, fast-food franchises), professions (for example, medical doctors, accountants and computer scientists) and communications (for example, public relations and telecommunications). The truly high-paying jobs are shifting to those working in information industries. Traditional heavy industry workers— steel, automobiles, shipbuilding—are recurrently victims of mandatory pay-cuts, lay-offs or replacement by automation as competition mounts from Japan and the rapidly industrializing third world (Korea, Taiwan and India, for example). Knowledge of such changes probably has much to do with the choice you will make about careers and university training.

If these, then, are the surface indicators, what can we isolate as the fundamental developments responsible? In the 1960s, economists, philosophers and technologists began to appreciate that the many changes taking place in communication and information technologies were not simply a progression of the post-WWII industrial boom in the U.S., but that it really heralded something quite unprecedented and important. Daniel Bell (1976), Zbignew Brezenski (1970), Jaques Ellul (1964) and Y. Masuda (1981) are a sampling of the international scholars responding at that time. Daniel Bell summarized well these changes in his book, *The Information Society* (1976). Let's summarize and discuss some major "information society" characteristics:

A movement in national economies from goods to services. The focus of many nations' development efforts has been to find industries (and jobs) which maximize human intellectual input. Let's look at a simple example. If a nation's economy is "extractive," it earns most of its money selling raw materials (iron ore, wood chips, logs) to other nations who in turn fabricate the materials (autos, paper, houses) using machines and high levels of workers' intelligence. These "other" nations—industrial economies—add considerable value to the raw materials they received (autos on a per pound basis are worth more than the various raw materials which make them up). But as Western, industrial nations learned bitterly from the Middle East oil boycott in the 1970s, their industrial economies could be held hostage by cartels of those nations supplying raw materials.

The search thus began in earnest for a different, less vulnerable method of securing national wealth. How? Consider computer software—the programs that allow one to do word processing or accounting on a personal computer. Very little raw material is used—some plastic and magnetic oxide on the floppy disks worth perhaps a few cents. The real value is brought by the human intelligence implicit in the product—the cleverness of the programmer's code which instructs the personal computer to word process or do accounting. These information products, then, have the highest "value added" by human intelligence. Further, because there is little need for the kind of energy used to make steel or refine oil, most information products are "low energy intensive." Thus, *high value added, low energy intensive* products have become the industrial goals of many national economies. These kinds of products really represent the output of a highly skilled service economy, not one oriented to export of raw materials or heavy industrial products. In short, they make-up information economies.

Is there a pattern or progression that nations go through as they develop into information economies? In a study of employment statistics for the United States accumulated over 120 years, major shifts occurred in the work force (Porat, 1976). The beginning data for the 1860s (see Figure 9.1) show the dominance of agricultural workers—the labor-intensive family farm which included the bulk of settlers in the nation's westward expansion. As the turn-of-the-century approached, cities were absorbing population from the countryside and abroad, incorporating these individuals in the rapid heavy industry growth of that era. This industrial dominance in the workforce per-

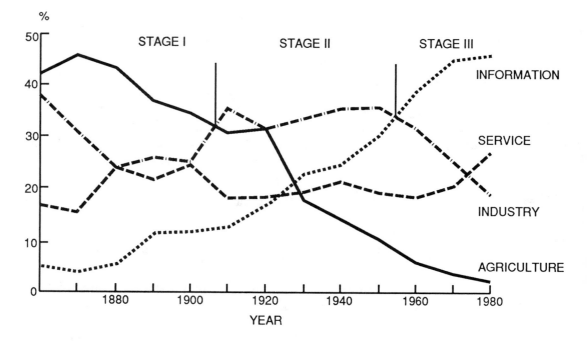

Figure 9.1. Four Sector Aggregation of the U.S. Workforce by Percent from 1860 to 1980.

sisted through World War II, then began a decline as foreign competition and automation at home reduced drastically this sector of the workforce. Finally with the onset of the 1960s, a high growth in service and information jobs is clear. There is, of course much room to argue with Porat's view of what constituted information jobs (these ranged from filing clerks to physicians) but the general trends he illustrates over the years has meet with agreement. Whether by accident or intent, we are increasingly finding our careers in information-intensive work.

The Porat data, however, oversee more than a century of development. What many third world nations hope is that they perhaps, can "leap-frog" some of these stages and thus the time needed to reach the highly profitable information society. India, for example, has admittedly missed the industrial revolution that swept North America and Western Europe at the close of the 19th century. They are making intensive efforts to invest in electronics, computer and other information industries. India has presently the highest production rate for feature films in the world, but largely for domestic audiences. Their technical capability thus has been well-established. What they are searching for are information products that can be exported to the developed world. Other nations—Ireland, Spain, Australia as well as traditionally agrarian states of the U.S. (North Carolina, Georgia, Oklahoma and Puerto Rico, for example)—are attempting similar strategies to reshape their economies without a prior stage of heavy industrialization.

Pre-eminence of the professional and technical classes. If we look back historically, we see shifts in the sort of individual who is pre-eminent, powerful and respected in societies. In the renaissance, powerful monarchies developed based on loyalties amongst those of royal birthright. Noble title often implied great rights of property ownership, and, in very direct way, control over those more humble folk who worked the land. Later, in the 19th century particularly, the industrial revolution created a new basis of wealth and power—the ability to make goods on a mass scale. A new class of power emerged—the manager or entrepreneur. Possessed of financial skills and often an intuitive grasp of politics and organization, these people were able to provide goods and services on a scale never before seen owing to their ability to finance and organize skilled people at higher levels of complexity. Noble birth declined in the power and respect accorded to it. In present times, of course, the highly skilled professional or technician is receiving greater social accord—and wealth. The "yuppie" or young, upwardly mobile professional is more than the lore of social satirists. The high technology industries which have enjoyed rapid growth since the early 1960s needs these individuals. Look at the "Help Wanted" advertisements in the *Wall Street Journal* or *New York Times* to see the kind of workers sought to staff an information economy.

Theoretical knowledge as a source of innovation and policy. Until the industrial revolution, much of the knowledge of the physical world was predictive; that is, people knew *what* would work but not *why*. The builders of medieval cathedrals learned through generations of trial and error the geometry and materials necessary to support the tremendous heights and spaces their buildings enclosed. They did not understand the molecular structure of the stone or the complex physics upon which their formulations were truly dependent. In short, they could predict what would work, but not explain why it would.

In the 18th and 19th century, the natural and physical sciences made tremendous strides. Increasingly, predictive knowledge was replaced by *explanatory* rationales. Once these were confirmed as laws, no longer did long periods of dangerous and expensive trial and error have to occur. The pace of development could proceed more rapidly, at lower cost and with better safety. Knowledge of how and why things performed as they did were increasingly used to develop new products and to analyze their workability before they were actually constructed. Increasingly, then, theoretical knowledge became a source of new products and wealth. Likewise, governments sought to use these same rationales to argue for regulation of pollution, for improved telecommunications and a host of other needs based on theoretical explanations of what forces of nature and man were capable of doing.

Future Orientation. Perhaps this is not uniquely characteristic of the information society. But it certainly is emphasized more vigorously than in the past. With an ability to better explain nature, it becomes possible to build very powerful "what if" models. It is possible, for example, to know within a few percentage points the influence of drought in Sub-Saharan Africa on export sales of U.S. grain. Satellite "remote sensing" of world grain crop conditions combined with models able to estimate crop yields and prices in a competitive market give tremendous advantage to nations possessing the requisite data gathering technology and information processing skills. Ideally, a future orientation gives us an ability to better plan, and to avert major problems before they occur. The essential key to understand is that these future "what if" models depend on the skillful collection and use of data through sophisticated information gathering and processing technologies.

A "smart" intellectual technology. The models just described are examples of an intellectual technology. The industrial revolution of the last century provided many examples of technology that were designed to alleviate physical effort. The sailing craft and the water-powered engines of the 18th century were replaced by the steam engines of the 19th. The brute labor of farmers in harvesting by hand was replaced by mechanized agriculture in the late 19th century. Yet it soon became clear as James Beniger points out in *The Control Revolution* (1986), that the speed and power unleashed by new sources of energy had to be regulated. Industrial accidents caused by exploding boilers could kill and maim dozens. Railway disasters became common-place in the first half of the 19th century. Pressure safety-valves and Thompson governors controlled the problem of run-away steam engines while the telegraph allowed railroads to be safely controlled over long distances (one needed very positive methods to signal converging trains on the same set of rails). What did this control technology provide? Information . . . on steam pressure, on rotations per minute of gears and of the position of trains in a rail network at a given point in time, and "standard" time itself.

Change in the economic and power structure of society. One of the fundamental restrictions challenged by the evolving information society in the past 50 years has been the denial of opportunity to women and minorities. Until World War II the almost exclusive domain of women in the workforce was as secretaries and telephone switchboard operators. While these jobs are often castigated as stereotypically women's work, they nevertheless grew with the need to process and transmit information. Too, they provided some mobility to supervisory and technical jobs within business organizations. Remember that these jobs made ridiculous the need for great physical strength as a qualification for work. The focus of information jobs on one's intelligence and skills, not physical prowess or family connections, began to open the employment door to many previously denied.

Interdependence and vulnerability. Information societies are complex, specialized and interdependent. The ability of the Toyota motorcar plant to work smoothly yet to keep no more than 6 hours worth of production line parts on hand signals tight coordination of suppliers, delivery systems and back-up procedures should something fail. This is called "just in time" inventory management. In the 1970s, the effort needed to produce major computer systems required millions of man-hours of effort from thousands of skilled workers whose products had to dovetail with one another perfectly. Both these examples show the complexity of modern societies. What keeps such massive efforts coordinated and on-track is a delicate, complex managerial and information gathering/processing effort. Think for a moment what chaos the breakdown of a major telephone system could wreak within these large companies. Think, too, about the disruptions caused by natural disaster, insurrection or sabotage. This sort of society is a far cry from one of self-sufficient farmers common over a century ago.

A parallel trend is the integration of information companies. Increasingly, the information companies of today are *vertically* and *horizontally integrated.* Horizontal integration means that a range of products are supplied—what were originally business machine companies like IBM today still manufacture office machines such as computers, but have related businesses such as telecommunications (IBM owns a portion MCI, a major U.S. long distance carrier). As well, it develops and sells software and indicates it wants increasingly to provide information, much as do newspapers, as part of its business. Vertical integration suggests that an organization provides for itself at every stage of manufacture and distribution of services and products. IBM, again, provides components (microchips) used in its computers, provides the software which runs those computers, designs applications to suit various business needs (automated bar code supermarket check-out equipment) and sells them directly through its many sales offices.

So what is the significance of this change? There are several things you may wish to think about. First, a single or a handful of companies controlling the creation and distribution of information could constrain the variety of information easily available or stifle dissent. Secondly, new organizations with differing purposes and pricing might have difficulty competing against large groups. New products and ideas could be stifled. Thirdly, government regulation has relied in part on the easy separation of those creating information (usually not regulated) from those distributing or carrying information (usually regulated). The convergence of these once organizationally separate functions into new groups which cut across these old barriers causes havoc with laws designed to protect the public.

In part, for reasons just discussed, *information and information technologies form a key part of national security.* By disrupting communication pathways and institutions, complex industrial societies can be paralyzed. Further, with complex information technologies working in our behalf, we can extend power and control of others—by manipulating markets and economies, by withholding vital technical information, and so on. Major world governments have strategic information processing bureaus—the Central Intelligence Agency and the National Security Administration are prime examples in the United States federal government.

Dependence on information in leisure and play. In Japan and the United States, consumption of television is a major component of leisure activity. Among school-aged children in these nations it is arguably the largest. Television networks, cable television, personal computers, video games, audio home entertainment, the recording industry, cinema, and so on make an impressively profitable list of information business directed toward our leisure.

Consequences of the Information Society

The initial reaction to our evolving information society, often, is to herald it as an unqualified positive force. After all, the promise of clean, high paying industries, work centered on people's intelligence and inventiveness, the educational promise of widely diffused and inexpensive media and computer technologies seem to have unassailable advantages over dirty and inefficient heavy industries. But many social scientists—particularly planners and economists—harbor fears that many problems of an information society are going unrealized.

Jobs and The Information Society: Probably the greatest claim of the "information society" is its ability to generate clean, smart jobs. This is doubly important as we see traditional jobs in such heavy industries as steel-making and automobiles decline. But do information industries—microchip manufacture, software and so on—really provide us with a solution? Perhaps it is too soon to be sure of long term trends. Porat's chart of the American workforce by sector (see Figure 9.1) suggest high growth of jobs in the information sector. What the chart doesn't show well is, first, a falling off in the number of information jobs in relatively recent times, and, secondly, the skill and salary levels these jobs command (Business Week, 1986).

In research by Jonscher (1983), it is increasingly clear that while growth in number and profitability of information industries remains quite high (upwards of 20 percent in the U.S. in better years), the growth of worker productivity is greater. In short, growth in jobs can be created only when new jobs created outstrip those made redundant by improved productivity. Automation increasingly replaces production line workers in computer plants just as it does in the automobile industry. Even intellectually demanding jobs, such as writing software, are increasingly done by computer for simpler programming tasks. Indeed, the majority of workers in information industries are low wage assembly and clerical workers whose skills are increasingly vulnerable to automation. This is not to deny the creation of high skill, high pay jobs which draw on the very well-educated and inventive person. But such advanced degree holders are in the minority and are not the sort put out of work by the decline in heavy industries.

A second claim is that information industries are "clean." While this is undeniable in the solely intellectual jobs of, say, writing software, manufacture of information hardware—computer chips and electrical components—involves many hazardous chemicals and conditions of work safety which are poorly understood. Water and air contamination, and rises in cancer rates have been noted in areas such as the "Silicon Valley" of California.

Other influences of the information society are less job-oriented and more oriented to the overall quality of living regardless of occupation.

The Educational Potential and Equity: The educational potential of smart communication technologies is tantalizing indeed. Home computer access to distant libraries promise rich informational resources to all unburdened by physical distance. Computer enhanced instruction may offer a sort of sophistication in the classroom barely imagined several decades ago (consider the sort of realism offered by aircraft flight simulators on computers in contrast to dry formulae and still photos offered in physics textbooks). But consider the question again. The equipment, programs and specially trained teachers able to use them come at a price ill-afforded by poorer schools and individuals. If electronic access to libraries and other services hold promise, who receives this advantage? Typically, it is wealthier and "smarter" communities and individuals. One fear, thus, is that information technologies will accelerate a *knowledge gap* dividing those with access to and skills with information technology from those who haven't. While arguably some improvement in the information environment of the disadvantaged will result from wide availability of information technology, those most academically proficient and used to technologies will benefit at a greater rate in the way shown in Figure 9.2. The result is a growing gap in society based in the power of information. Such gaps, it is feared, will create eventually a new sort of class structure based on the power of information.

So far, there is little specific data which convincingly demonstrate the progressive, accelerating nature of this feared knowledge gap linked to the swift introduction of information technologies. It may simply be the case that the smarter and more affluent are

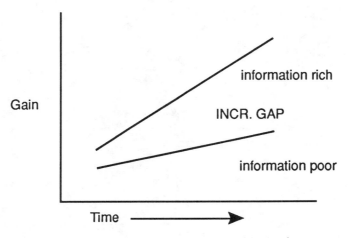

Figure 9.2. The "knowledge gap" Problem of Information Rich Societies.

better able to use information to their advantage at the same level as in the past. In this sense, the information society simply provides an extension of past trends long apparent.

Privacy and Security: Privacy has become one of the most visible problems of information technologies. While it is beyond the scope of this book to go into much detail on this important question, let's touch upon a few central points.

First of all, information technologies characteristically make records of when, how and by whom they are used. Imagine use of an automatic teller machine. Here is a device able to locate you geographically, establish the cash resources you need and the time when you request them. One use may provide little information. Over time, the hour and date when you need cash (11 p.m., Friday night), the place (a venue notorious for prostitution and drugs) and the amount ($300) could suggest to the suspicious mind that your cash requests go to illicit purposes. The bank's computer could, obviously, be

Figure 9.A. From THE WORLD OF QUINO by Joaquin S. Lavado. Copyright © 1986 by Joaquin S. Lavado. Reprinted by permission of Henry Holt and Company, Inc.

programmed to recognize certain patterns such as this and alert authorities to those bank customers fitting the profile. It is only a small step, technologically, to correlate these names with computerized police records (for drug offenses) and health records (drug-related health problems) to further refine a list of suspects.

Other instances are simpler yet. The police department of Seattle, Washington asked the local power company for records of excessive electricity use. With a computer database of electricity use by household over many year's time, sudden large increases could be easily culled out. What the police were looking for was the use of power-greedy halogen plant lights used to grow marijuana indoors. The power company refused the request. Insurance companies routinely analyze their claim records, traffic fine records and driver's license data to isolate high risk individuals to be denied renewals of policies or be denied categorically as new applicants. As you can reason, the dividing line between legitimate use and invasion of privacy may not be fixed or very obvious.

The illustration at the end of the chapter (Figure 9.3) suggests the range of computerized cross-references which can be made about given individuals from a variety of active and passive data gathering means. Passive methods are for example supermarket check-out scanners (*where* and *what* you buy can be associated with *who* you are) to active methods of TV audience measurement through consumer filled-in diaries and logged-in people meters. Each source of information about the individual by itself may be innocent and free of malice, but when cross-referenced with many others, the result can be quite harmful and invasive. To have the convenience of an information society, it seems, we must be prepared to sacrifice some of our privacy. Perhaps more importantly, we must be prepared to develop policies and regulations which curtail harmful uses without sacrificing the benefits of information technology.

Who Owns Information? Another difficult question revolves about property rights and responsibilities—who "owns" information and is liable for its correct performance. Perhaps you're familiar with some of the problems. Consider the copying of computer software. Despite so-called copy protection schemes, copies of expensive software packages can be made often in just a few minutes, denying the author the possibility of a sale. Efforts to find a convenient, enforceable scheme to protect authors has been difficult. In Hollywood, actors and writers have struck production companies over their demands to royalties from videotape sales. Yet once a retail shop buys the videotape, in the U.S. at least, it may be rented many times by the store without additional compensation to the seller (this is the so-called "first use" doctrine). Videotapes, of course, may be illegally copied with little more difficulty than is encountered by software "pirates."

A more subtle problem arises when computer software copies the "look and feel" of a popular word processor or database program, but the actual instructions provided to the computer differ (it's possible to write programs that ask for the same input from users and produce the same outcomes, but achieve these with different internal instructions which the user never sees). Laws protect the actual instructions and in some in-

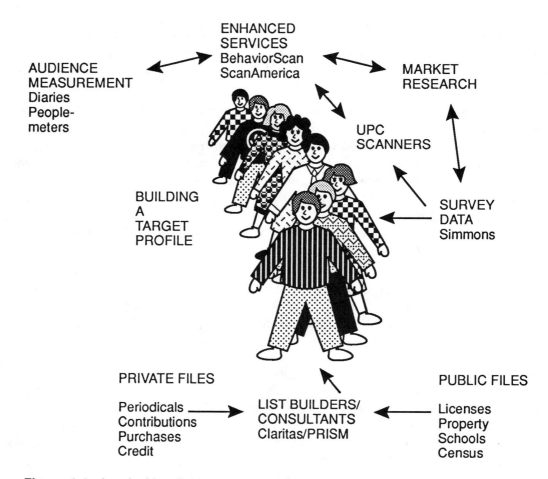

AUDIENCE
MEASUREMENT
Diaries
People-
meters

ENHANCED
SERVICES
BehaviorScan
ScanAmerica

MARKET
RESEARCH

UPC
SCANNERS

BUILDING
A
TARGET
PROFILE

SURVEY
DATA
Simmons

PRIVATE FILES

Periodicals
Contributions
Purchases
Credit

LIST BUILDERS/
CONSULTANTS
Claritas/PRISM

PUBLIC FILES

Licenses
Property
Schools
Census

Figure 9.3. Interlocking Datasets Available on Some U.S. Citizens.

stances the computer screen images produced, but many new companies have succeeded by providing look-alikes/work-alikes of established, popular software at cut-rate prices. Even though the "look and feel" of the established product is almost identical, internally, the new software, arguably, is not infringing. It takes a long time for courts and case law to work out protections to those who have spent years developing an intellectual product, yet not so constrain improvements and new ideas from others.

Let's look at the "property" problem from another angle. There exist powerful programs which aid physicians with medical diagnosis (these are often called "expert systems" or programs which embody the advice of experts on problems which the program helps you define through a question and answer process). Suppose there's an error in the software which results in misdiagnosis and subsequent injury to a patient. Who is responsible? The physician? The software firm who sold the program? Or the "expert" responsible for the advice in the first place? Again, ownership of the information is important to place liability.

Finally, let's look at the traditional academic or public library. Often they are supported by government and allow access without regard to ability to pay. Libraries typically have been "free" or have only charged very modest user fees. However, as information production and distribution becomes more and more a major, profitable industry, governments and others may look to ways to make money from formerly "free" services. In 1986, for example, the Reagan administration attempted to "privatize" the National Technical Information Service, a government library of technical reports of considerable use to business and research organizations. By privatizing, the government would sell this service to private investors who would run the service for profit.

It was argued that the government would make some badly needed income from the sale and save taxpayers the future expense of supporting the NTIS. The costs instead would be carried only by those using this information. Moreover, since the NTIS would be run for profit, it would probably be operated at a greater level of efficiency. The effort was defeated by a combination of federal employees who saw their jobs at stake, but also by professional librarians who felt the public's ability to access vital information easily at low cost was at risk.

But also they feared the introduction of market forces in what had been largely a scholarly enterprise. Libraries often aquire documents based on historical importance, their value to scholars and public education. The value of library acquisitions to profit-making business is also considered, but is not often an overriding consideration. Opponents of privatization argue that it would become the prevailing force in a for-profit library (Stewart, 1990). Business clients would have the money to outspend private citizens and scholars and thus dictate the library's choices. To take this a step further, one could imagine many low demand documents, perhaps of great importance to scholars and the general public, being shunned in favor of what was popular with the most affluent "customers." Meanwhile, relegated to the poorer sectors of the public, free libraries would suffer. There's little sign that this grim progression is taking place. But the high prices paid for information and the coonsequent strains on established libraries have been cause for concern.

Thus it is almost a truism with the information society: the rate at which good policies are developed are often well behind the problems they are intended to prevent. Few inventions are without negative consequences over time. Information products often present difficulties different from the catastrophes we're used to—hurricane damage, railway accidents and chain-reaction expressway smashes. They tend to be more subtle, less visible and requiring technical expertise to understand in terms of negative consequences. Corrective steps are often difficult to agree upon and may have unforeseen negative effects as well. Our effort in this book has been mostly with the effects of established mass media. Because new media have different characteristics, we should consider briefly how they re being studied.

Studying the Effects of New Communications Technologies

What, then, are the major kinds of studies under way now to better understand the effects and consequences of our increasing informationalization. They really divide into several broad types, reflecting the research specialties aimed at traditional communication study. Let's characterize each briefly.

Social and Behavioral Studies: Perhaps most familiar given the focus of this book is a social science perspective, examining the social and psychological consequences of new information media. In many respects, these studies employ many familiar concepts and methods from our examination of the traditional mass media. But while traditional media often are seen as leisure time activities done at home, new technologies typically are examined in the work place as researchers seek to improve the productivity of offices and factories with telecommunications and information technology.

The possibilities of using telephonic and video links for business conferences has been tried both for technical feasibility and its ability to simulate the quality of a face-to-face conference (Phillips, 1983). The savings to large business are obvious—the transport, hotel and time loss costs of assembling people in a central site for the sole purpose of talking with each other seem absurd when modern telecommunications can carry their messages at very low cost in a teleconference. Various mixes of technology have been tried—text-based (as in computerized bulletin boards), audio, and full audio and video transmission of conferences. Since the cost of transmission escalates with higher quality transmissions (full audio, video and color) the research question often has been what level of communication quality is necessary for an effective comfortable meeting. Findings suggest that common sense needs such as showing things or drawings puts a premium on video capabilities, while very routine, short meetings with little need to show things can work effectively with audio only. Further, situations where interaction—that is, back-and-forth discussions among participants—is minimal, the use of low cost text-based systems may suffice.

But this is not the only question raised. Others deal with the affective or emotional content of the meeting and the need to negotiate with others (Christie, 1981). We all know of situations where we feel compelled to talk face-to-face with someone. Our ability to gauge the reactions of others over video, text or audio links is limited compared with being in the same room. Thus politically sensitive situations where we must negotiate often rule out media technologies in the communication path. Teleconferences work well with people familiar with each other transacting structured, routine, and non-emotional business. Further, the easy access of employees to each other, unfettered by physical distance, changes (often by enlarging) the network of coworkers involved in any one individual's tasks. Ideally, this results in better, more efficient expert advice and correspondingly better thought-out decision-making.

Other efforts have been to see what is gained by having employees work at home, linked to their central offices by computer-telephone links (Forester, 1987). Indeed, at Blue Cross Medical Insurance of South Carolina, the routine typing and data entry work are accomplished by at-home workers who are paid for each form completed. In this sort of arrangement, mothers, part-time workers, and handicapped can access the workplace without physically transporting themselves to a downtown office. But they also lose out on company social life, periodic escape from the household and many of the benefits accruing to on-site, regular employees. Trade unions worry that such work styles mimic the abuses of the garment industry "homework" practices of the last century. The efficiency and job satisfaction of the home workers often equals or betters the traditional office worker.

Variations on this theme have involved experimentation with neighborhood work centers where employees of large firms could come to an office close to home and use telecommunications and computer technology to link with downtown offices several days or more a week. In a city like Seattle, Washington, a venue with a large "high tech" work force presently forced to commute on choked freeways, savings in traffic volume alone are figured at over 10 percent. Similar energy, time and stress savings also may be realized (Wash. State Transportation Commission, 1989).

Perhaps the ultimate in telecommuting is the small but growing use of foreign clerical and skilled white collar workers. A large New York bank now uses accountants in Ireland to help with its bookkeeping. Transported by air freight, needed data are brought to a small town in County Mayo where the bank has setup an office. Accounts are processed and the finished records, now in electronic form, are instantly transmitted back to New York by satellite links. These capabilities to cut the effects of distance have a variety of consequence—time and stress savings to be sure, but also the loss of high paying administrative jobs to less costly foreign workers.

The mass media, reporters in particular, have been swift to adopt new technologies—portable computers, satellite video gear and computerized typesetting and composition systems. The net effect has been, seemingly, to allow tighter deadlines (since the technology allows faster production of a finished video or print product once the story content is input. See Neuwirth et al., 1988). Few of the complaints have been echoed about alienation from the social life of the office, but periodic labor actions have revolved around safety hazards of video terminals, the compression of tasks (newspaper editors through their computer terminals now do many tasks formerly done by typesetters, compositors and other graphics arts professionals). Understandably, these people feel the added pressure of these tasks, however automated, and want additional compensation (Weaver, 1983). For the field reporter, the ability to swiftly word process or videotape stories and electronically transmit them to their employers is a decided convenience few involved would willing part with.

Finally, there is the question of public acceptance of new media, at least to a point which makes them commercially feasible. The U.S. record has not been good.

Electronic publishing allows home users with specially equipped television receivers access stories or data on request from a central computer. In a *videotex system*, the home-to-computer link is via telephone—a direct link. In *teletext*, the link is really a one-way broadcast signal offering a wide array of text to show on the home TV screen. A local control box selects and stores for viewing some of this constantly circulating information. In the U.S. neither videotext have been financially successful beyond specialized services aimed at businesses. In reviewing these failures, many users reported they didn't like reading stories from TV screens (it was easier, really, to use a newspaper). Others said the costs were too high, either for the special TV set decoders or for the videotex charges for linking via phone to a remote computer.

The few successful instances of videotex, notably in France, offer not just frames of information to be read, but highly interactive services—two-way communication allowing one to order groceries, pay bills, look up telephone numbers and find out university test scores, to mention a few. The direct user cost in the French *Minitel* system has been kept quite low since the terminal used has replaced the telephone in many French households and is subsidized by the government. Businesses, too, find such systems useful, but only for specific statistical information which changes rapidly (airline schedules, stock market quotes, weather forecasts for aircraft, real estate listings). In short, when new media offer new capabilities such as two-way interaction, the information presented must capitalize on this capability, not just mimic old, static print media.

Economic Studies: The costs of new information technologies must be balanced against their costs. Are they worth it? and for what tasks? Productivity of workers is always a pressing question, since increases in per worker productivity provide the bases for non-inflationary wage increases and prosperity. The office, white collar setting has, until recently, received only a fraction of monies allotted to the heavy industry worker to improve productivity. In an increasingly office-bound service economy in the U.S. and other developed countries, the need to improve the productivity of the office seems clear. Recently, the rise of information technology has made this possible, and the rates of funding improvements have risen with the availability of cheap, efficient information processing equipment.

Other important economic topics concern the relation of modern telecommunications to national development. It is difficult to sustain an advanced economy if telephones, telexes and data links do not work well and are overwhelmed with traffic. Indeed, nations as diverse as Ireland, France, Japan and Singapore have made telecommunications improvement a major national effort for fear of losing foreign markets and a deteriorating internal ability to coordinate complex high tech industry of their own (Bowes & Sullivan, 1988). Consider that the major European aircraft industry, Airbus-Aerospatiale, is shared among England, Germany, France and Italy. Inability to coordinate telephonically the manufacture of something as complex as advanced passenger jet aircraft among these diverse participants is unthinkable.

Computing power and the data bases held by computers also are a major investment which few nations ignore. The United States and Japan followed (at a distance) by England, France and the Federal Republic of Germany are the world's most "informationalized" nations—holding the bulk of world computing and information wealth (Edelstein *et. al.*, 1978). The costs for developing countries to gain the equipment and data to compete can be daunting, particularly when they have to negotiate with the leaders for equipment and information access.

Thus, the economic study is vital in pitting the costs of new technologies against the monies lost by not developing them. Few will risk the latter course as major industrial nations increasingly compete economically on the strength of their telecommunications, computing and information resource capability.

Policy and Legal Studies: If information so strongly affects the national economy, social life and behavior of citizens, the study of policies to regulate information for social or national good is almost sure to follow. In the discussion above, we have raised many issues which ultimately find their way to policy-makers and into law. Take the situation of "intellectual property"—who owns information? The copyright laws in many countries were reasonably adequate to protect printed information. But the ability to rapidly copy, computer alter and reproduce, to create "look and feel"-alike software, for example, rapidly outstripped the protection of existing laws (Office of Technology Assessment, 1985).

The problems of privacy and security demand continual revision of laws. While wiretaps of traditional telephones require court orders in the U.S., police could "wiretap" the broadcast portion of portable cellular telephones until recent legislation made this part of the transmission subject to wiretap laws as well. Some protections come more by threat than legislation. Importation of digital tape recorders into the U.S. from Japan was stalled for several years by recording industry-backed pressure from Congress. Yet other proposals are nipped in the bud by public opinion and outcry. The Australian government's effort to institute a computerized national identity card ("The Australia Card") was dumped quickly in a wave of public and civil libertarian outrage.

The difficulty is to foresee the abuses as well as the promises of information technology. At the heart of the problem are the engineering-inspired "feasibility" studies which so clearly demonstrate efficiency and utility of information technologies but which ignore their possible abuses (see Slack, 1984). The answer, clearly, is a wider range of participation among those vested with evaluating our progress in an information society. Several countries—The United States, France, Japan, and Australia—to name a notable few, have set-up government-funded offices to evaluate new information technologies and to report on their possible consequences and the sort of legislation, if any, the developments warrant.

Technology and Changes in Communication Study

It would be comforting to believe that communication researchers have done all that is necessary to accommodate the burgeoning technologies in their field. While there are many worthy research efforts, there remain a number of problems which reduce our ability to understand new communications and information technologies.

Perhaps foremost is our aged academic division of the communication field into various camps, primarily split between those examining interpersonal communication—from rhetoric to drama—and those taking a mass communications viewpoint, considering the role of journalism, popular culture and media law and policy. But consider this schism against a technology like electronic publishing or videotex. Here is a medium which is at once like a newspaper (text on a screen), like broadcast (delivered on a TV with graphics, color and animation) and interpersonal communication (one interacts with a remote computer somewhat as with another human being). Clearly here is a case which requires a spread of skills to understand better. Other technologies loom posing similar problems with our organizational structure—legal studies split from examination of mass communication effects; international political studies of the multinational corporations who control much of the world's information and computing power.

While links between the academic community and government policy-makers have been set-up in many countries, the typical sort of evaluation made of information technology remains largely one of technical and economic feasibility, not of its social desirability for the mass of population. Clearly these links will have to be sharpened to avoid misuse of information by the powerful and a resistant Luddism toward beneficial information technologies by a suspicious populace. Comparatively few laboratories have been constructed equipped with the latest media technologies and a competent staff to evaluate them. Efforts in Japan, the U.S. and Canada exist a few universities (notably M.I.T.) and venues (such as the *HI-OVIS* experimental town in Japan), but in face of the rate and power of developing technologies, the effort seems small indeed (see, for example, Brand, 1987).

More worrisome yet is the lack of international cooperation. Information and data processing technology do not respect national geopolitical boundaries. Consider briefly the "remote sensing" or spy satellite capable of gathering international information on everything from crops to defense preparedness almost at will. Indeed, strategic value of information technology for commercial competition or national security is such that free exchange of information is increasingly restricted. The American Library Association has officially complained to the U.S. government over the efforts of F.B.I. agents to enlist the cooperation of librarians in reporting individuals requesting certain scientific and technical journals (Schmidt, 1988). For the academic community and open scholarship in communication the dilemma of increasing knowledge hamstrung by corporate or government embargo is chilling indeed.

Finally, the teaching of communication must have a good mix of the practical and the conceptual. It is necessary to know in lay terms what new information technologies can do and, ideally, have "hands-on" experience with them. Yet, more conceptual coursework in policy, social effects, and media economics cannot be ignored if we are to understand the future consequences of those communications-information technologies just on the horizon. In our next and final chapter, we will summarize some of the problems and changes the study of communication must confront.

Key Terms

Control Revolution
Electronic Mail
Extractive Economies
High Value-added
Home Work
Horizontally/Vertically Integrated
Information Economy
Informationalized
Intellectual Property
Knowledge Gap
Leap-frog
Look-and-feel
Low Energy-intensive
Minitel
Passive and Active Surveillance
Pay-per-View
Policy
Privatization
Prodigy
Remote-sensing
Super-station
Telecommuting
Teleconferencing
Teletext
Videotex

Summary

According to many economists and philosophers we have moved from an industrial to a post-industrial, information society. In this system, the industrial focus is upon the creation and distribution of information. Signs of this exchange are especially clear in the abundance of inexpensive information technologies (personal computers, for example), extensive and inexpensive telecommunications and a decline in heavy industrial employment.

Developed economies have moved to services and information industries because they have high value added (they maximize the human intelligence embodied in products), and low energy intensity (requiring little of scarce raw materials of expensive energy).

Daniel Bell enumerated a number of basic characteristics of information societies, including pre-eminence of professionals and technical elites, the value of theoretical knowledge, "smart" technologies, vulnerability of an information society and the importance of information to national security.

Information societies have consequences which can be difficult to predict and may run counter to optimistic views of a better, richer world. Information societies, for example, do not have the need for low and semi-skilled workers as did heavy industries of several decades ago. Knowledge gaps may arise in society as the best educated are able to take advantage of an information-rich environment. By comparison, the educationally poor cannot keep pace and fall progressively behind.

New forms of information gathering and the lowering costs allow more information to be kept on individuals. Protecting privacy is an increasing problem in these circumstances.

The ownership of information is also a difficult matter, since there is rarely anything physical to point to as one's own. "Look and feel" cases test the boundary of what is one person's property. Further, fixing responsibility when software causes damage can also be difficult since the individual responsible is rarely so obvious.

Policies designed to regulate information and new technologies are almost always very dated and unable to deal with changes and new developments as fast as they arise.

Study of new communications technologies arises principally in three areas: (a) social and behavioral studies concerned with such issues as the effectiveness of telecommuting for the worker and employer; (b) economic studies (for example, the cost savings realized with telecommuting); and (c) policy studies which determine if regulation is needed (for example, if trade unions are being disadvantaged in their collective bargaining by at-home, telecommuting workers).

The traditional division of communication study into interpersonal on one hand and mass communication on the other, hampers joint efforts when new media really have characteristics of both mass and interpersonal communication. International cooperation is also essential in economic and policy studies when new communication technologies rarely are neatly contained in their impacts by national borders.

References

Bell, D. (1976). *The Coming of Post Industrial Society: A Venture in Social Forecasting.* New York: Basic Books.

Beniger, J. (1986). *The Control Revolution.* Cambridge: Harvard University Press.

Brand, S. 1987). *The Media Lab: Inventing the Future at MIT.* New York: Viking.

Brezinski, Z. (1970). *Between Two Ages: America's Role in the Technetronic Era.* New York:

Bowes, J. and C. Sullivan (1985). From agriculture to information in Ireland: National development with knowledge-intensive industry. Paper presented to the International Communication Association, Human Communication Technologies Division, Honolulu, Hi.

Christie, B. (1981). *Face to File Communication: A Psychological Approach to Information Systems.* New York: Wiley, p. 171 ff.

Edelstein, A., J. Bowes and S. Harsel (1978). *Information Societies: Comparing the Japanese and American Experiences.* Seattle: University of Washington Press.

Ellul, J. (1964). *The Technological Society.* New York: Vintage.

Forester, T. (1987). *High-Tech Society.* Cambridge: MIT Press, pp. 161–165.

Greenberger, M. (Ed.). *Electronic Publishing Plus: Media for a Technological Future.* White Plains: Knowledge Industry Publications.

Jonscher, C. (1983). Information resources and economic productivity. *Information Economics and Policy,* 1, 19.

Masuda, Y. (1981). *The Information Society as a Post-Industrial Society.* Washington: World Future Society.

Neuwirth, K., C. Lieber, S. Dunwoody and J. Riddle (1988). The effect of "electronic" news sources on selection and editing of news. *Journalism Quarterly,* 85–94.

Office of Technology Assessment (1985). *Intellectual Property Rights in an Age of Electronics.* Washington: U.S. Government Printing Office.

Phillips, A. (1983). Computer conferences: Success or failure. In R. Bostrom (Ed.) *Communication Yearbook 7.* Beverly Hills: Sage, pp. 837–856.

Porat, M. U. (1976). *The Information Economy: Definitions and Measurement.* Washington: Office of Telecommunications, U.S. Department of Commerce, publication 77–12(1).

Schmidt, J. (1988). FBI's library awareness program. A memorandum to academic libraries. Office of Intellectual Freedom, American Library Association, May 18th.

Slack, J. (1984). *Communication Technology and Society.* Norwood: Ablex.

Weaver, D. (1988). *Videotex Journalism.* Hillsdale: Lawrence Erlbaum.

10 Change and New Directions in Communication Research

Introduction

We have spent most of our time (and yours) discussing mass media and their effects from the perspective of social and behavioral sciences with traditional methodologies of survey research, content analysis and experimentation. This perspective, as any other, has its blind spots and shortcomings. Consequently, it is important to consider briefly a growing body of scholarship which takes different conceptual and analytic perspectives on mass communications, attempting in part to redress both the obvious problems of the traditional social sciences and their more subtle drawbacks traced to the culture and values of those doing the research. This short chapter is an effort to address these points and to place this book in a larger context of ongoing scholarly thought in our field.

Problems in Established Social Science Research

In this book, we have kept mainly to research and findings from the social sciences and to a "progressivist" view that mass communication can be useful as a tool to build positive institutions in society and help answer debates over the media's effects. Challenges to the mainstream social research are increasingly common especially as the flaws of "objective" social science become better appreciated. What are the major flaws and challenges?

Long Term Effects: A central complaint is the duration of study given media effects. Take television violence, for example. Few studies, until recently, have followed children through puberty to adulthood to check the lifetime influence of television and violence. In those that have, the results are disturbing. Apparently normal children with high exposure to violent content may show higher violence levels only later in life (see Chapter 8). Much of what we know has only been studied in the short term, and this

211

work frequently shows that there is little or limited influence from the media. But to what extent is the "limited effects" view of mass media due to limited research designs and time frames? Conversely, studies which impute a strong effect based on single exposures to a message (some of the early TV violence research was of this kind), suggest effects which take hold in a very short period. These may fade swiftly as people forget or have their new views challenged by family and friends. We won't know until careful studies of media effects follow people over years of exposure. The money and commitment such work requires is rarely forthcoming in a setting that often values fast answers and high volumes of research productivity.

Context and Situation: Social science methodology puts much value on "external validity" or the generality of a study to cover many similar instances which arise. We seek samples of people and situations which have broad applicability. But media behavior, as should be evident to you by now, is a complex activity which meshes with many others. Subtle influences of home setting, the impact of friends, culture, events immediately preceding and coming after media exposure (viewing TV violence while you're angry at someone, for example)—all can be hard to account for in the quantitative, social science tradition of experimental simplification and control. Some communication researchers, such as Brenda Dervin (1981), are focusing attention on the "situationality" of communication behavior. Dervin adapts many techniques of survey research and quantitative measures to examine the context in which media audiences and the individuals which comprise them are found.

Increasing attention is being paid to qualitative research which can better account for subtleties frequently overlooked in audience research. The influence of television on children, for example, has been studied by participant observers, researchers who live with families so they can experience the context of TV viewing (why the set is turned on and watched, perhaps), how families interact during viewing (what lessons or conversation topics come from the programs viewed), or how access to the TV is used as a reward (Susie can watch another half hour of TV if she brushes her teeth). Some of this research is described in Chapter 8.

Communication as Cause or Effect: But also, some researchers feel communication study has for too long been focused on effects. That is, communication is typically cast as causing something—perhaps attitude shift towards a candidate, product sales, or violent behavior. This is a result of our tradition of practical research aimed at media effects: propaganda, advertising or finding popular program types. Comparatively little is known about situations that create information needs leading to communication. For example, when and in what form do people need informational help in using a new computer program? What in a news story causes people to stop reading and want to ask questions? Likely there are many reasons ranging from ignorance to stress. But the point is that questions such as these have been under-represented in our tradition of media effects research (see, for example, Carter, 1973).

Funding and the Goals of Research Sponsoring Organizations: It doesn't take much money, often, to develop important research ideas. Early research on "opinion leadership" for example, found out much about personal influence through interviews of Ohio farmers living in the same township—work that could be done by volunteers. But take the same idea and apply it to research on a national scale, or to third world nations, and costs escalate rapidly. To demonstrate the utility of good research ideas can ultimately require outlays in the millions of dollars. Who provides the money? Foundations and government look for both utility to the society and its established institutions, and to accepted scientific traditions. They also look to the competence of the researchers and their acceptance in the research community generally. Business often looks for the same qualities as well as practical outcomes of benefit to their activity. Properly, perhaps, radically new ideas must often await a gradual acceptance by a discipline before they achieve sufficient funding.

Some rightfully protest that this gradualism isolates new research, denying it vital support and slowing change. Slack (1986) complains, for example, that "technology assessment" research frequently commissioned by government and industry fails to ask fundamental questions challenging the utility of the technical change itself. Rather, this research too frequently turns the matter around, trying to find ways to get the public to accept a technology or change. Communication research, with its history of persuasion, frequently is the agent. To frame research questions which challenge important industries and government institutions is a risk when prime funding sources are these very organizations. More subtly, perhaps, when researchers employed by these groups are called upon for such research, it is difficult to conceive of "whistle-blowing" or challenging research affecting vested interests.

Challenges to Traditional Research and the Progressivist Tradition

Holistic Research: A major criticism of traditional social sciences and the quantitative techniques they usually employ arise because their methods of observation suit some questions but not others. With the majority of commercial and academic researchers committed to quantification, critics say many important questions "fall between the cracks" of current research emphases. Holistic research seems one such case, a tradition aimed at broad social priorities, ethics and goals. Let's take an important example of what this kind of research attempts to do.

Technology, particularly media technology, has over the past 80 years excited considerable comment from social philosophers. Perhaps one of the most influential commentaries is Jurgen Habermas' paper, "Technology and Science as 'Ideology'' (1971). To Habermas, the main threat to human freedom comes from ideologies which subvert public discussion and debate. These paralyze free participation in government and conceal the true distribution of power and wealth in the society. To shift from this general case to the specifics of the mass media and information industries, one confronts large-scale investment in new information technologies. Critics who suggest that such technologies may serve only a wealthy minority or may help concentrate power in the hands of a few have been dismissed as anti-progress, modern-day Luddites hopelessly trying to forestall the inevitable. To many, such critics seem strange or out-of-place in a prevailing view of technology as somehow value-free or at least free of negative motives. Much of our early education heralds technology and its developers as unmitigated forces for social good. Outsiders trying to enter technological debates have often been dismissed as extremists or cranks who lack the technical expertise to fully appreciate the uses technologies serve.

Let's illustrate this conflict with an example. Major industrial nations are spending great sums of money to upgrade telecommunications to provide services extending well beyond the simple transmission of voice over distance. Computer-to-computer links, high definition television, cellular telephone, optic fiber networks, videotex, and remote-sensing are all new or expanding services. But the investment by taxpayers or telephone company customers may be quite large to bring them about. Who will benefit? Does the average citizen have use for these expanded services? Should all citizens be required to pay? Do these technologies enable their increased power and participation in government, or do they move power and control away, concentrating them in a technological elite? Some of these issues are arising in telephone rate cases where increases to all subscribers may go to underwrite the costs of a comparative few for high tech telecommunications. As Slack suggests, the argument in the public forum often is one of instrumental action—a technical decision of how to *implement* the change, not *whether* the change is advisable. For Habermas, the public's participation in a vital issue is constrained by the language and symbolism of technological reasoning. Such logic rarely considers the need for technology change as much as it does the *best*, most effective technology to bring about a change. The proposed change itself too often goes unexamined when issues are structured by a technological rationalism.

More specific to communication research itself, Daniel Czitrom (1982) looks historically to media inventions and the utopian hopes social critics and scholars held for them. Telegraph, telephone, motion pictures and radio at the time of their introduction were seen as tools to build communities and extend international ties. Amateur radio operators could, for example, communicate instantly with far away countries. Commercial forces soon controlled these powerful inventions, restructuring their use for commercial exploitation. Commercial radio networks came to dominate, while amateur radio remains a hobby for a comparative few. One could easily argue, to the contrary, that commercial entrepreneurs backed their best guess of what would "sell" to the public. And rather than subvert the utopian dreams of a few, through market analysis and skill big business provided what the public was willing to support. Local and long distance telephone, initially a success with business, later took on social uses of keeping in touch with friends and distant relatives. It could be argued that without a practical business use as a marketing "push" that telephones would have developed much more slowly based on more utopian ideas of community cohesiveness. Indeed, Pool (1983) argues that the best predictions of telephone use were based on corporate marketing forecasts, not the ideals of social visionaries. The truth in this debate probably rests somewhere between the extreme views—marketing strategy can determine ultimate adoption and use by society of various media, yet to market communications technologies without knowledge of what the public is willing to accept and pay for is an unlikely sort of corporate blindness.

Czitrom reflects on the recent revival of "holistic" thinking about communication increasingly evident in the research literature. Earlier in this book (Chapter 4), we commented briefly on the thinking of Dewey, Park and others who, soon after the turn of the century, analyzed mass media in global terms of community, inter-connection and culture. With the rising effectiveness of the social sciences in the middle years of the century, communication research became more instrumental, rarely questioning goals and basic social directions. Rather, the effort was to research creation of more cost-effective messages on behalf of big business and government. We became more focused on the means, not the ends or goals. The language and scope of social science seemed comfortable in this range since experimentation, control and statistical methods could deal efficiently with variables like message recall, but not with philosophical issues like the promotion of a consumer culture. Communication scholarship of the 1980s has revived interest in holistic mass communication research as the media industry is buffeted by critics and changing audience goals.

Business Week (4/30/90, p. 70) commented on consumers who are increasingly "Mad, Mad at Madison Avenue." The point is that consumers in unprecedented numbers are resentful of the intrusiveness of commercial messages in their lives. The solution seems not one of altering or fine-tuning commercial messages to be less objectionable, but rather their wholesale reduction. Traditional social sciences may help advertisers find less intrusive vehicles for their messages, but they probably can't suggest basic enough changes in advertising or media financing to satisfy a growing number of critics. Holistic research considers wider questions of social responsibility, ethics and goals.

The important point to remember in the often-heated debates is that research is not conceived in a social vacuum. Prejudices, fads, culture, government and industrial incentives all serve to direct research on certain paths, however altruistic researchers are, and however "objective" scientific methodology claims to be. Challenges to dominant styles of American communication research are not only being heard of from European scholars who have often followed different traditions, but increasingly by new generations of American researchers who are assimilating materials from a wider, more diverse base than their predecessors.

For a rather different and negative view of "the information society" from that frequently presented in the press, for example, several critics in Britain have published "a Luddite analysis" of information technology (Webster and Robins, 1986). Luddism, as some may recall, was a revolt of English factory workers who in 1813 wrecked machinery destined to rob them of their jobs. The gray lining to the silver cloud of present-day information technology is that it may have many unintended and negative effects—not just positive ones. This sort of disagreement is natural and healthy as a field confronts new issues and seeks better answers.

Basic vs. Applied Research: The tradition of mass communication research has been applied—consideration of practical problems and their mass communication solutions. Some research has been more "basic" in nature, aimed at underlying forces which affect communication and its outcomes. Consider research on television violence which studies the frequency and type of violent acts in certain programs. The frequency of rapes, assaults and murders occurring per hour can tell producers or community action groups something about the violence in particular programs, or about the programming of various networks. On the other hand, consider research which looks at the biochemistry of arousal—the physical and psychological changes which occur when violent or sexually explicit content is viewed (see Chapter 8). The intent here is not to provide violence ratings of particular programs; rather, it is to understand basic mechanisms which incite people to violent behavior across a variety of circumstances. Basic research is aimed at *explanation,* finding theories which organize and provide reason for the many responses we see to media.

There is nothing inherently wrong with applied research; it treats specific situations and problems in the present. It is the necessary staple of much of advertising and marketing. But basic research must be given a reasonable share of attention so that we can improve our understanding of communication based on generally applicable principles. Because someone's immediate problems may not be answered by basic research, funding can be very hard to find.

Ethics: We haven't said much about this topic. But its importance in a field where (often) powerful media diffuse persuasive messages to millions cannot be underestimated. Indeed, an academic publication, *The Journal of Mass Media Ethics,* has been established to consider such matters. The ethics of researchers must be carefully considered both in the actual conduct of research, and in the use of findings by others. Studies of 25 years ago which deliberately exposed young children to violent films might not be approved today by university "human subjects review" committees. Could there have been permanent damage to the children's psychological development by the films shown. Unlikely? Probably. But can one be sure? Consider also a possible finding that the dramatic tension caused by violent program content attracts viewers. Producers and networks eager to improve ratings, if not restrained by their ethics, could shamelessly exploit violent themes far beyond what is minimally necessary for good "action-adventure" plots. How about questions of privacy? Consider the newspaper, which, in

216

an attempt at complete coverage, prints the names of rape victims. Credible and complete news accounts have to be reconciled against protection of privacy and victims from further harassment. The research described in this book *can* point to many problems with media (TV violence) but also has its limits in addressing broad social directions and issues.

The moral for you the reader is hopefully obvious. There is much potential for abuse based in even the imperfect research considered in this book. You have a responsibility to inform yourself widely about mass communication choices and issues. Consider reading beyond the material presented here to books and periodicals concerned with journalism and mass communication issues. If you sponsor or do communication research yourself, consider its impact on the individuals you actually study as well as how findings will be used. Is it exploitative? Does it damage a culture—yours or someone else's? Are the people involved in your research treated with dignity and told ultimately of your research intentions and goals? Can its findings constructively contribute to an understanding of human communication in a broad sense, and improve the communication products of your organization in a narrower sense? We hope this book affords you useful information. And we hope you will apply this information wisely and constructively.

Key Terms

arousal
cellular telephones
high definition TV (HDTV)
holistic research
instrumental research
long-term effect
Luddites
optic fiber networks
progressivist
situation, situationality
technological elite
technological rationalism
technology assessment
whistle-blowing

Summary

The limitations of traditional, progressivist social science has attracted attention from a number of critics who see important conclusions being reached based on an incomplete picture.

Holistic research considers long-term goals, values and assumptions in making its assessments of mass communication perhaps better than traditional social science observation and measurement.

Traditional social science is better set to do instrumental research aimed at testing the best technology or message strategy. Critics argue that important questions go unasked with this focus.

Established social science has some methodological and procedural short-comings, including: inadequate consideration of long-term effects, over-emphasis on "normative" or "average" circumstances which deny the range of phenomena and behavior present; untangling cause and effect; and reconciling the goals of funding organizations.

Communication research must balance basic and applied goals. An over-emphasis on applied work robs us of basic, general understandings of how mass communication affects and is affected by society.

Ethics are a growing concern both in mass communication research and the practices of mass media organizations.

References

Carter, R. (1973). Communication as behavior. Paper presented to the annual meeting of the Association for Education in Journalism, Ft. Collins, Co.

Czitrom, Daniel J. (1982). Median and the American Mind: From Morse to McLuhan. Chapel Hill: U. of N. Carolina Press.

Dervin, B. (1981). Changing conceptions of the audience. In W. Paisley and R. Rice (Eds.) Public Communication Campaigns. Beverly Hills: Sage, pp. 71–88.

Habermas, Jurgen (1971). "Technology and Science as 'Ideology'" in *Toward a Rational Society*. London: Heineman.

Pool, Ithiel de Sola (1983). *Forecasting the Telephone: A Retrospective Technology Assessment of Telephone*. Norwood, NJ: Ablex.

Slack, Jennifer D (1983). "Technology Assessment for the Information Society." in Jerry L. Salvaggio (ed) *Telecommunications Issues and Choice for Society*. New York: Longman.

Webster, F. and K. Robins (1986). *Information Technology: A Luddite Analysis*. Norwood: Ablex.

Glossary

AAPOR: is the abbreviation for the American Association for Public Opinion Research. AAPOR, founded in the 1930s, educates and determines standards for good, ethical public opinion measurement practices. Members, which include major international polling organizations, agree to maintain these standards in the work they do.

"Active audience": an assumption of current effects theory, that individuals are not merely passive receivers of mass media messages, but actively seek them out for purposes and motives of their own making.

Advertising: communication efforts that are designed to appeal to consumers and to benefit a sponsor.

Agenda setting: the idea that media can shape public opinion concerning what are the most important issues facing the public through what it chooses to emphasize in its news coverage.

Aggressive Cues: Suggest the presentation of "appropriate situations" for violence. Imagine that an argumentative wife depicted on television was slapped by her husband. By watching such episodes, males could learn that slapping is an appropriate response to argumentative women.

Alpha level: the number of alpha waves per second.

Alpha wave: the most common wave form of the EEG (electroencephalogram); the waves are emitted at 8–12 per second when the individual is at rest.

Assignment Editors: are responsible for assigning reporters and video crews to stories in broadcast news organizations. They frequently determine what events are covered, how they are covered (is there on-location tape?) and by whom.

Attention: the active selection of one component from the field of experience while narrowing the range of objects to which one is responding.

Attitude: an evaluative response toward an object that is based both on familiarity with the object (salience) and comparisons with others objects (pertinence).

(Audience) segment: a particular group within a mass audience which is defined in terms of characteristics held in common—e.g., age, sex, income, personality type, lifestyle, etc.

Bandwagon effect: a hypothesized effect of publishing the results of political polls in which voters are expected to change their votes to favor the candidate leading in the polls.

Beta level: the number of beta waves per second.

Beta wave: an EEG pattern that is shallower and faster than the alpha wave and indicative of active attention.

Brain waves: spontaneous fluccuations in the electrical activity of the brain.

Candidate image: the individual's "mental picture" of a candidate, consisting of those qualities and issue positions the individual considers relevant.

Causal Direction: refers to a common problem in analyzing events which correlate. Violent youth may watch violent television programs—the two go together. But what is the cause? Violent youth may seek violent programs. Violent programs may nurture violent youth. Or the two could be linked by a third cause in common.

Cellular telephones: are the successor to radio-telephones used in automobiles. Blanketing an area with multiple transmitters, each covering a small area or cell, 2-way communication can be maintained more reliably and to a greater number of mobile telephones.

Characterization: an image construction process in which the individual associates qualities of a candidate (e.g., "experience") with their implications (e.g., "experience" is a *strength* for this particular office).

Chicago School: was the name given to the scholarly activity of Dewey, Park and others in the social sciences at the University of Chicago in the period of about 1910–30. Their scholarship emphasized that social science could have positive effects on the development of society. Mass media were important agents in the progressive, positive development. Consequently, much attention was given to newspapers—the dominant mass media of the period—and their role in the life of cities.

Cognition (cognitive process): the process by which the individual constructs knowledge of the external environment; for example, transforming a message into meaningful information.

Cognitive strategy: actively thinking about something through a series of inter-related steps. For example, decision-making is a cognitive strategy for making a choice by making a series of comparisons between the same set of alternatives.

Collective Behavior: is a sociological term referring to group or organizational activity.

Communication effects: the outcomes of any communication process; includes primary and secondary effects.

Communication: the process by which individuals or groups can share a common idea of something.

Communications: the skills, techniques and technologies that are employed in behalf of the effort to communicate.

Community Press: refers to local, often small town newspapers. In many cities, "zoned" editions of large daily newspapers include a section covering a community within its circulation area. Independent, suburban papers and free "shoppers" compete in this category as well. News is directed toward community events, issues and personalities.

Comprehension: the meaning of a message to the person who receives it based on both the content of the message and the receiver's cognitive interpretation.

Concept-orientation: a pattern of family communication in which parents stress the sharing and discussion of ideas; one of two dimensions of family behavior on which the Family Communication Pattern (FCP) model is based.

Concept: a way of thinking or making sense of experience by using abstract ideas that organize experience into meaningful categories.

Concrete operational stage: a stage of cognitive development (beyond preoperational) in which the child can mentally manipulate the objects of perception.

Consensual: a family communication pattern in which parents stress *both* family harmony (socio-orientation) and the sharing and discussion of ideas (concept-orientation).

Content analysis: a tool for the objective, systematic analysis of message content. Usually, a system of categories is built for classifying content units (e.g., words, phrases, filmed episodes, etc.), rules created for coding these units into categories, and tests designed to verify the objectivity of the coding procedures.

Control group: those participants in an experiment who are not exposed to the experimental treatment, and thereby serve as a baseline for determining experimental effects.

Control Revolution: A necessary companion of the industrial revolution of the 19th century, communication and information control systems where required to regulate and synchronize the scale and forces unleashed in the machine age. Telegraph, signalling systems for railways, inventory controls, time-keeping for workers are examples of this communication and control overhead. It is a thesis advanced by James Beniger who wrote a book by this title (see Chapter 9).

Conversion: a change in preference or behavioral intention; for example, in an election campaign, changing one's voting intention from one candidate to another.

Coorientation: an exchange of ideas between two parties in which there is an effort to arrive at a mutual understanding in which each party accurately perceives the ideas of the other.

Correlation: refers to Lasswell's idea that the press can bring together diverse events, and show their relationship or pattern. The now-famous Watergate investigation by The Washington Post linked a number of small events together to show a picture of political corruption.

Crystallization: the process of arriving at a preference or decision; for example, changing one's mind from being undecided to being decided, from having no preference to having a preference.

Cultivation: refers to a long-term learning model where violent media content provide examples of an unsafe and chaotic world. Over time, individuals with high TV exposure and few alternative paths for information, come to exaggerate the implications of both fictional and news violence.

Cultural Imperialism: refers to the pressure on traditional ways of life in third world countries paced by media-portrayed culture largely from Hollywood studios. Western popular music may drive out native music, for example.

Developmental model: a model which distinguishes "stages" based on differences in children's cognitive abilities (see "pre-operational" and "concrete operational").

Diffusion: the spread of a message from its source throughout a population; plotting the numbers of persons who have heard about a news event over time yields a **diffusion curve,** which gives an indication of the *"rate"* of diffusion.

Early voting returns: because of the difference in time zones between Eastern and Western U.S. the polls in the west are still open after results in Eastern states are broadcast; these are "early returns," since a Western voter might hear about them before going to vote.

Electronic Mail: Use of computer networks to deliver messages almost instantaneously to network users. Most university computer networks have some kind of electronic mail function. *Bitnet,* a cooperative electronic mail system, links universities world-wide.

Empathic Ability: or social foresight (in Dewey's terms) is the idea of seeing oneself or others in different, future circumstances. In so doing, one can change, moving toward these goals according to a "best way" determined by social science.

Evaluation: a cognitive process of arriving at a choice by comparing two or more alternatives; for example, a voter might compare the pros and cons of both candidates.

Experiment: generally speaking, experiments are any form of controlled observation. "Control" involves such procedures as random assignment of subjects to experimental groups and careful manipulation of experimental conditions.

Experimental group: those participants in an experiment who are exposed to the experimental treatment.

Exposure: processing a message without focused attention; e.g., a viewer might be exposed to a tv commercial without attending to its meaning.

External validity: the extent to which the findings of an experiment are (thought to be) generalizable beyond the controlled setting of the experiment.

Extractive Economies: Nations whose earnings depend largely on the value of their raw materials. Work is dominated by the mining or harvesting of these resources and their transport to developed nations for manufacturing.

Face-to-face: another term for interpersonal communication. Occasionally "word of mouth" is used to imply the same thing.

Family Communication Pattern (FCP): A conceptual model which distinguishes four types of family communication (laissez-faire, protective, pluralist and consensual) based on relative emphasis on social harmony and sharing of ideas.

Feedback: refers to audience comment and reaction to media content. Feedback can take many forms, but most commonly it consists of audience ratings for broadcasting and letters to the editor or readership research for the print media.

First-hand information: information that is derived from direct observation of an object or event; for example, seeing a football game as opposed to reading about it.

Frequency: the number of spots in an advertising schedule seen by the typical viewer.

Gatekeeping: refers to the selection of content from a supply which greatly exceeds the space or time available to present it in the media. Wire services, for example, provide a tremendous quantity of content which must be vigorously sifted by editors.

Gross rating points: the total percentage of the audience exposed to a series of ads making up an advertising schedule. For example, if the ratings for three ads are 40, 80 and 60, the gross rating points for the schedule is 180.

Hard News: is a slang expression for such topics as politics, civic, national and international events, crime, natural disasters—the serious or important news.

High Definition TV (HDTV): is a new form of television promising a considerably sharper and wider picture, and high quality stereophonic sound.

High involvement model: an idealized conception of advertising communication in which a rational consumer makes decisions (assumed to be important) by working through a linear hierarchy of steps beginning with "awareness" and ending with "purchase."

High Value-added: Value-added refers to the worth added to raw materials by each subsequent stage of manufacture and distribution through human activity as products are created. Products which capitalize largely on human intelligence, such as computer software and professional services, are said to be high value-added. Products which are little modified from raw material form are low value-added. Extractive economies are typically based on low value-added industries.

Holistic Research: consider broad social issues and goals, particularly cultural, political and life quality considerations of new technologies and the industries they sustain.

Home Work: In the present, home work refers to office work done from afar through telecommunications and computer technology. These electronic pathways link the remote worker to the central workplace. This practice is sometimes referred to as *telecommuting.*

Horizontally Integrated: Ownership or control of related businesses. Warner Communication, Inc., not only produces films, but owns cable systems over which they are shown, videocassette companies which sell the VCR tapes, etc.

Industrial Revolution: began in the English Midlands at the close of the 18th century. The invention of steam engines, railways, iron and steel-making, mass production and great advances in applied science, changed economies of North America and Europe from being based in agriculture and land to ones based in capital and manufacturing.

Information Society: This term, attributed to the Japanese scholar Masuda, refers to a shift in social and economic priorities to information-based industries and activities. Japan and the United States can be said to have many characteristics of societies of this kind: industries based on information technologies, use of information widely in leisure, a large service sector based in the processing and distribution of information, etc.

Informationalized: A term popular in the "information societies" literature which speaks to levels of information available or circulating in a nation. Figures such as the annual production of newspapers and books, the number and power of computers in operation, the telecommunications (broadcast, telephone, etc.) capacity are examples of the kind of data used to calculate levels of informationalization.

Informed choice: a choice between candidates in which the voter knows what he/she wanted to find out about the candidates (as opposed to what the candidates wanted voters to know).

Instrumental Research: considers more the narrow choices or path to achieve an outcome. Social science frequently helps in such choosing, for example, as between alternate persuasive message strategies.

Intellectual Property: The legal term for (typically) ownership of content such as contained in books, films, computer software, etc. However, many newer forms of "intellectual property" do not fit well the laws such as copyright designed to protect developers of traditional products of this kind.

Interactive media: media which allow members of the audience to both send and receive messages; e.g., a two-way interactive cable system.

Interpersonal projection: assuming or inferring that the opinion of another person or group is similar to your own.

Involvement hypothesis: the hypothesis that the effect of an advertising message depends upon the receiver's level of involvement with a choice.

Involvement: the extent to which an object is cognitively relevant in a given situation. For example, an individual's involvement with a political campaign would be high if the campaign is viewed as having outcomes that would impact the amount of taxes to be paid. If the campaign is not viewed as having any significant outcomes, involvement is (defined as) low.

Justification of Violence: may increase its influence by encouraging imitation and identification with the aggressor.

Knowledge gap: a difference in knowledge between those of low and high socio-economic status (SES). As mentioned in Chapter 9, the "gap" is said to arise as those schooled in effective use of information use become increasingly productive in an information rich environment. The gap arises in comparison to those who lack such skills and access. They may marginally benefit from information richness about them, but at a much lower rate.

Laissez-faire: a family communication pattern in which parents do not attempt to enforce either social harmony or discussion of ideas.

Law of Minimal Consequence: the proposition that early voting returns can have only minimal impact on voter turnout because so few people are vulnerable to influence.

Lead Sentence: is the first sentence in a news story. It is designed to attract the reader's interest and (often) suggest the perspective or point-of-view being taken by the writer. In print media, the lead contains much of the basic factual content— the main personality involved, the events, etc. In broadcast, a "soft" lead is used to attract the readers interest and link it to previous stories aired in the newscast. Basic factual content follows in the next few sentences. This more gradual approach allows the viewer to better grasp the content because it is only spoken once. The newspaper reader can, of course, re-read at will.

Leap-frog: A plan where third world countries decide to concentrate development efforts on electronics and high technology, professional service and software. In doing so, they are trying to move directly from an agricultural to a high tech post-industrial economy without having to pass through a stage of heavy industrial development. India, for example, is trying this approach.

Limited (minimal) effects: J. Klapper's 1960 summary of communication effects research, which proposed that the effects of mass communication are largely confined to the reinforcement of peoples' existing intentions.

Linear Flow Models: represent human communication as a series of almost mechanistic steps where information is transmitted from sender to receiver. These have often been based on the Shannon-Weaver model of communications, conceived to analyze long-distance telephony. This model, modified to human behavior and institutions, as by Berlo (1960), describes a message *source, encoding* of the message, its *transmission* through a channel (mass media, for example), its *decoding* and ultimate *use* by a receiver. Conditions of noise and feedback may affect the quality of the message and its likelihood of misinterpretation.

Long-term Effect: refers to the kind of influence media might have over years and decades of exposure, not just the few days or weeks often considered in many studies.

Low Energy-Intensive: Refers to industries that require little energy or costly raw materials to make their products.

Low involvement model: a model of advertising communication which assumes that many consumer decisions are not important, and that consumer choice does not follow a linear hierarchy of steps.

Luddites: were coal miners of the 19th century who smashed the technologies destined to rob them of their jobs. In today's parlance, the term refers to those who resist and/or fear new technology

"Magic bullet theory": the idea that communication effects are unlimited because messages can be designed to trigger the psychological needs of the receiver.

Market segmentation study: a study designed to identify distinctive groups of consumers so that advertising appeals can be tailored to each group.

Mass communication: the process by which large groups of individuals can share or produce a common idea. For example, the process by which the citizens of a community would share their ideas about a community problem and synthesize a solution that would reflect the ideas shared. (Note: in this definition mass communication is definitely not equated with mass media.)

Mass communications: the skills, techniques and technologies employed on behalf of the effort to achieve mass communication (Note: in this definition, mass media are included as one way in which the skills, techniques and technologies used to achieve mass communication might be organized.)

Meaning: the cognitive interpretation of sensory input (e.g., words, pictures, events, etc.). Meaning is held to be an interaction between the content of sensory input and the conceptual structure that is used to interpret it.

Media reliance: the idea that individuals depend on a single medium as their sole (or primary) source of information for certain topics; for example, the idea that television is the sole source of political news for some (or most) Americans.

Mediated: is a basic characteristic of mass media in that a technology (a broadcast transmitter, for example) is used to convey content from source to audience.

Mediating condition: a condition that modifies the difference that some other condition makes; e.g., the effect that a message has may depend upon the receiver's level of education—little or no effect if education is high, substantial effect if education is low (education is the "mediating condition").

Memory: the ability to "see" events that are no longer directly accessible in the environment.

Message appeal: the sender's strategy for obtaining a communication effect as reflected in the content of the message. For example, a "fear appeal" strategy will be accompanied by content designed to arouse the receiver's anxiety.

Minimal effects: see "limited effects" model.

Minitel: is a videotex system constructed by the *DGT,* the French telephone system. About 5 million people are said to use the system which was installed free of charge to many households during the 1980s to bring telephone users an electronic form of the telephone directory. Many other services followed, now said to number nearly 10,000.

Model: an abstract map of the relationships between major elements of a communication process.

Newshole: is a slang expression for the amount of space or time given to editorial content that remains to be filled. As deadline time approaches, the newshole is progressively filled with content, stories.

Nielsen rating: an estimate of television audience size based on the number of television sets that are tuned to a particular channel.

Not-so-limited effects: the current (or "modern") view of mass communication, which provides for effects above and beyond reinforcement of existing intentions.

Opinion leader: a person who acts as a bridge between mass media and persons who are not in the audience for certain messages; for example, a debate viewer who is asked his opinion on last night's debate by someone who did not watch. (According to the two-step flow hypothesis, such persons are in a position to be influential.)

Optic Fiber Networks: refers to the use of glass filaments and laser light to carry and switch (route) information The capacity, speed, noise resistance, durability and frequently cost of optic fibers are quite superior to traditional metallic wire and electrical transmission.

Para-social interaction: the idea that members of a mass communication audience can relate to media personalities on a (somewhat) interpersonal basis.

Paradigm change: a fundamental change in theory, and consequently in the questions which a scientific field addresses.

Paradigm: the accepted view or consensus within a scientific field concerning the theory which guides research and the questions judged to be most important.

Partisan: a person who supports a particular political party (e.g., Democrat or Republican) and tends to vote for the party's candidates.

Passive and Active Surveillance: Passive methods look at artifacts or records generated for another purpose, such as cash machine transactions and supermarket receipts. Both data sets can tell much about a person's life apart from amounts spent in a given transaction. Patterns of use and consumption are important. In active methods, the purpose behind the data collection is clear. Those using "people meters," for example, know they are recording their TV program choices for audience ratings.

Pay-per-View: A system of cable television where users pay a fee for each program watched. This is different from the prevailing U.S. system where programs are seen for a flat monthly fee.

Payne Fund Studies: were carried out in the early 1930s to assess the influence of movies on U.S. youth.

Perceptual set: a readiness to perceive an object or event in a certain way.

Personal Media: are typically simple or individual technologies serving a mass media-like purpose. Cassette recorders, fax machines and primitive duplicating machines all have been used for grassroots mass media.

Persuasion paradigm: the approach to communication effects in which effects are viewed from the point of view of the sender and seen as being under the sender's control.

Pertinence: a relationship discriminated between two objects by comparing them on a particular attribute; for example, "Ken is stronger than Jim."

Pluralistic: family communication pattern in which parents stress the active discussion of ideas, and children are free to disagree with parents' opinions.

Political malaise ("videomalaise"): a complex of political "symptoms" in which the individual becomes disinterested in politics, feels powerless to influence political outcomes, and is generally distrustful of government.

Political socialization: the process by which adolescents become informed participants in the political system. (Both mass media and family communication patterns are thought to play an important role.)

Preoperational stage: an early stage of cognitive development in which the child responds primarily to the immediately perceived environment.

Primacy: In a series of messages, the first one to which the audience is exposed has "primacy." For example, the first of two speakers.

Primary effects: those effects most closely associated with the communication process—e.g., gaining the receiver's attention, comprehension of the message, as opposed to more remote effects such as attitude or behavior change.

Privatization, privatizing: The process of converting government agencies to be run as a private business on a for-profit basis.

Prodigy: Is a videotex system being promoted in the U.S. by Sears and IBM (1989–90). It offers service to home computer users for a modest flat fee per month.

Programmed: refers to the sequencing or placement of content for (typically) broadcast transmission.

Progressivist: refers to a view that science leads incrementally to a better understood world and improved life standard. It is an optimistic view that by using scientific methods many problems will be solved.

Protective: family communication pattern in which parents stress social harmony through acceptance of and agreement with parental values.

Public information: messages which contain an element of reform and are intended to bring about change which is beneficial to the receiver (without a monetary benefit to the sender).

Publics: audience segments which are defined in terms of their relationship to a communication situation (rather than in terms of their demographic characteristics).

Quota sampling: a non-random sample selected to represent certain characteristics of a population. For example, a quota sample might be designed to select equal numbers of males and females within a defined set of age groups.

Random sample: a sample drawn from a population in a manner which gives every member of the population an equal chance of being drawn.

Reach: the percentage of a target audience that is exposed to at least one spot in an advertising schedule.

Reaction time: the amount of time that it takes an individual to respond to a random stimulus while attending to some other stimulus, such as a televised message.

Readability formula: a formula based on characteristics of a written message (such as word and sentence length), which can be used to predict its level of difficulty for readers.

Recency: a message which is received second (or last) in a series of messages is said to have ''recency.'' For example, the second of two speakers.

Reinforcement: a communication effect in which the receiver's pre-existing intention is strengthened (rather than changed). For example, a voter who already has a preference may become more certain of his/her intention after viewing a televised debate. In Klapper's view of media violence, anti-social behavior is merely strengthened a bit by exposure, it is not created.

Remote-sensing: Special satellite-based cameras are able to detect many earth-bound activities such as troop movements and crop yields. These data may be used strategically or for benign purposes. It is, perhaps, a polite term for ''spy satellite''.

Robert Park: was a sociologist at the University of Chicago who, during the early 1900s, studied the press for its role in creating a sense of community in large, rapidly growing cities of the U.S.

Rumor: a message that has become distorted in the process of being exchanged several times through interpersonal channels.

Rural Media Forums: are groups assembled to listen or read limited mass media. In rural India, a single community television set may serve several hundred viewers. In this way, scarce media technologies are stretched to serve a large number. A local agent or *cadre* helps organize the groups and report on their activity.

Salience: an evaluative response to an object that is conditioned by experience or familiarity. For example, ''Seattle's a part of me; I've lived here all my life.''

Schema: a prototypic pattern by which information is organized in long-term memory.

Scientific Agriculture: refers to the application of scientific method to determine the most efficient agricultural practices. Land grant colleges for applied arts and sciences were established to be centers of this research. Many are major state universities today, such as the Universities of Illinois, Wisconsin and Minnesota. Communication of this new knowledge to farmers was and is a major concern. Communication schools were established, often under such headings as ''agricultural journalism'' or agricultural extension'', to develop techniques of conveying and assessing this effort.

Scientific Public Opinion: refers to the use of statistically sound sampling and analysis methods so that public opinion findings based on samples could be generalized to a population with a known risk. Other techniques evolved dealing with the intricacies of question-asking in ways which minimized unintentional biases.

Second-hand information: information about an object or event that is a product of symbolic representation. For example, listening to the football game on the radio as opposed to being there.

Secondary effects: those effects of communication that are not closely associated with the process itself, such as attitude or behavior change. Communication is a necessary but not a sufficient condition for such effects—i.e., they do not occur in the absence of primary effects, but the occurrence of primary effects is no guarantee of secondary effects.

Selective exposure: exposure to information that is supportive of one's existing attitudes and/or behavior, and avoidance of non-supportive information.

Selective filter: (In Broadbent's information processing model) the process by which incoming sensory data are screened to determine which data will receive attention. According to Broadbent, most information received by the sense organs is not processed at the cognitive level.

Self report: a description of behavior that is heavily dependent on a respondent's ability to reconstruct and interpret his/her own behavior.

Sensory image: a mental reconstruction of an external object that is (assumed to be) derived from sensory input. For example, the idea that we never actually see external objects, only an ''image'' of the object projected on the retina.

Sensory Modes: refers to the human senses activated by a particular mass medium. Radio obviously is only auditory, while television has both vision and sound as it modes.

Singularity principle: the principle that attention is limited to one thing at a time. For example, we might appear to watch television and carry on a conversation simultaneously, but we only focus our attention on one of these activities at once. This means that each instant that we focus on the television screen we will miss part of the conversation, and vice versa.

Situation, Situationality: refers to consideration of circumstances surrounding an individual involved in communication. The terms speak to a re-orientation of investigative concern from media effects on the audience, to the audiences needs and the communication best able to serve them.

Situational theory: a predictive theory that explains communication behavior in terms of the individual's cognitive relationships to the situation being communicated about.

Slant: (as in reporting, writing) refers to a perspective or point of view used in a story. An earthquake, for example, could be reported in terms of the lives interrupted by the catastrophe or, alternately, in terms of the rebuilding costs.

Slanting: the phenomenon that reconstruction of any event necessarily distorts the original event to conform to the expectations of the observer.

Sleeper effect: an effect of communication that does not appear immediately after exposure, but only after a sufficient period of time has elapsed.

Social Engineering: refers to the use of social sciences to find a best way method of managing society. This point-of-view had great favor in the first half of this century as social scientists tried to make social systems efficient and orderly in the same manner the applied physical sciences had brought efficiency to manufacturing and industry.

Social utility: the observation that certain mass communication content (e.g., sports, weather) appears to play a role in the maintenance of social relationships.

Socio-orientation: a pattern of family communication in which parents stress getting along and sharing parental values. One of two dimensions of communication behavior used to define family communication patterns (FCP).

Socioeconomic status (SES): the social status of a group as defined by such characteristics as income, education level, and type of job. For example, persons earning $20,000 at clerical jobs and having high school educations would be lower SES than persons with college degrees earning more money in professional or managerial occupations.

Soft News: is a slang expression for entertainment content: humorous stories, consumer news, advice to the lovelorn, society news and so on.

Space-binding: refers to media which, according to Innis, are easily transportable. They tend to extend government, strengthen secular institutions.

Spiral of silence: the proposition that individuals are sensitive to the climate of public opinion, and that if they sense that their own opinion is in the minority they will be less willing to express their view publicly.

Stereotyping: the cognitive act of simplifying one's perception of an object or person to include a consistent set of identifying attributes. Usually such perceptions are "fixed" and "polarized," i.e., they do not vary from one situation to another and they assign an extreme amount of the attribute.

Stopping principle: the principle that a shift in focus of attention must be preceded by a stop. This principle implies that messages must be processed in meaningful units punctuated by stops between adjacent units.

Subliminal message: a message that the individual is not consciously aware of either because exposure is too brief to allow attention, or because it is "embedded" within a larger message.

Subliminal perception: a (poorly understood) process by which behavior is affected by stimuli (e.g., messages) the individual does not consciously perceive.

Subliminal: a stimulus that is below the *limen*—i.e., below the level of conscious awareness for most individuals most of the time.

Super-station: A television station which distributes its signals over a wide area by satellite and cable television. WTBS (Atlanta) was the first such station in the United States. Its audience through cable and satellite retransmission is much greater than its local Atlanta audience who receive WTBS directly over-the-air.

Surveillance: refers to the role of the media as a look-out or sentry. For example, by regularly examining the performance of government institutions it can warn of their problems.

Survey: a method for *estimating* the characteristics of a population by observing a sample of persons (or other entities) selected from the population.

Take-off: is a term used by Daniel Lerner to describe a point of national development where a critical level of education and urbanization was present to sustain prolonged economic and industrial development with mass media assistance.

Technological Elite: are highly educated specialists who understand and can use complex technologies or knowledge tools: engineers, computer scientists, economists, etc. With this ability, they attain a heightened level of financial and, often, political power.

Technology Assessment (or T.A.): is a process of evaluating the costs versus benefits of a technology to solve some problem. T.A. has often been criticized for the narrowness often used, self-servingly, in defining the extent of a problem and the negative results of using certain technologies.

Telecommuting: Use of *home work* technologies to obviate the need to commute to a central workplace.

Teleconferencing: Use of audio-video and telecommunications technologies to link distant offices and people together in an electronic conference. This saves enormously in transportation, time and hotel costs. However, it cannot substitute effectively for all types of meetings.

Teletext: A system of coding in text and graphics in standard broadcast TV signals. Users with decoders on their TV sets can extract and display these signals. In one popular application, teletext is used to caption programs for the deaf. In the United Kingdom, teletext (Ceefax, Oracle) is popular for weather, headline news, sports and weather. A hand control allows users to select basic categories of information from the variety on offer. There is, however, no true two-way connection between user and sender as with *videotex.*

Theory: a proposition (or related set of propositions) that serves as an explanation for expected relationships among concepts.

Time-binding: media, according to Innis, are durable and will survive for perhaps centuries. They stabilize cultures, but typically can't be transported easily. For example, stone monuments are difficult to carry long distances. These media favor traditional religious authority.

Two-step flow hypothesis: the hypothesis that mass communication messages reach certain members of the audience through interpersonal exchanges with "opinion leaders." (Opinion leaders are hypothesized to be more informed as a result of direct exposure to mass media.)

UNESCO: is a United Nations agency responsible for education and cultural development.

Universal Education: refers to significant social reforms of the mid-19th century in North America and Europe: providing basic literacy, moral and computational instruction to all citizens.

Unlimited effects: the idea that members of the mass communication audience were socially isolated and pychologically defenseless, thereby allowing for powerful communication effects limited only by the skill of the communicator.

Uses & Gratifications: effects of communication that are controlled largely by the receiver and connected to purposes and motives of the receiver.

Validity: the property of a measuring instrument which actually measures what it intends to measure. For example, a survey questionnaire might be designed to measure the number of articles read in the newspaper the previous day. The validity of this measure will depend on respondent's ability to recall accurately what they read and to refrain from reporting items they did not read but feel they should have.

Valuation: a process of arriving at a choice in which the alternatives are evaluated singly rather than in relationship to one another. For example, a voter might arrive at a choice by following only one candidate at a time.

Value-free Evaluation: attempts to use the control techniques of scientific methods to minimize cultural and personal biases in posing and answering communication research questions. Beyond specific techniques, it is suggests an attitude of neutrality and detachment by the researcher.

Vertically Integrated: Ownership or control of industries which bring a product from its development through its manufacture and sale. Bell telephone was, prior to its break-up by the U.S. government, a vertically integrated organization. It produced electronic components, developed and built its own equipment, distributed it, sold it and serviced it.

Vicarious Participation: involves strong identification with a role played by an actor. In doing so, one experiences many of the emotions the actor is portraying.

Videotex: A system for electronic publishing which uses telephone lines to link a home terminal or computer to distant computer data bases and information networks. Text and simple graphics can be easily requested and sent through these systems. Their primary advantage is that users can carry out individual transactions with remote services, such as banking and catalog shopping.

Voter turnout: the proportion of registered voters who actually vote in a given election.

Voter volatility: the extent to which voters remain undecided and make up their minds late in the election campaign.

Whistle-blowing: is a slang term for alerting the public or responsible regulators to major problems, ethical faults or criminal activity in some socially important organization. These individuals often risk persecution for calling into question the practices of powerful organizations.

Whorf-Sapir hypothesis: the view that language incorporates pre-conceptions of the external environment and thereby biases perception. For example, the division of the color spectrum into categories that conform to our color vocabulary is thought to influence perception of color.

Subject Index

237

238

239

rural media forums, 97

saccades, 45
salience, 114–115
schema, 48–50, 52
scientific agriculture, 5–6
scientific public opinion, 7
second-hand information, 33–34, 36
secondary effects, 107–113, 130–131
selective exposure, 40–42, 119, 140, 143–144,
    154, 165–166
selective filter 43–44
selective perception, 153, 154–155
semantic differential, 38
semantic space, 37
sensory image, 35–36
sensory modes, 86
serial transmission, 48–49
settlers, 90
singularity principle, 42–44
situation, situationality, 212
situational theory, 142–143
slant, 93
slanting, 66
sleeper effect, 54
social engineering, 6
social utility, 67, 68, 72
socio-orientation, 68, 69–70
socioeconomic status (SES), 144–145
soft news, 90
space-binding, 88
spiral of silence, 70–72
spy satellite, 206
stereotyping, 106, 155
stopping principle, 44–45
subliminal, 137
subliminal message, 136–138
subliminal perception, 137–138
super-station, 189
supportive information, 41
surveillance, 95
surveillance need, 110

survey, 15–17
synchronicity, 145

take-off, 91
technological elite, 213–214
technological rationalism, 214
technology assessment, problems, 213
telecommuting, 203
teleconferencing, 202
teletext, 204
theater test, 130–132
theory, 19–20, 25–26, 110, 111, 113, 142–143
time, 88
time spent with media, 175, 178
time-binding, 88
two-step flow process, 73–75, 144
typology, 23–24

UNESCO, 94
UNESCO and gatekeeping of news, 94
universal education, 6
unlimited effects, 114–118, 136
urbanization, 90
uses and gratifications, 108–110, 145

validity, 109
valuation, 168
veiled source, 35
verifiability, 13–14
videomalaise (see political malaise)
videotex, 86, 97, 204
voter turnout, 159, 160
voter volatility, 165

War of the Worlds, 86, 115–116
whistle-blowing, 213
Whorf-Sapir hypothesis, 47–48
wire services and gatekeeping, 92

Author Index

ACA-0799